NORTH AMERICAN

LOCOMOTIVE PRODUCTION

1968-1989

COMPILED AND WRITTEN BY

JAMES T. BRADLEY

PUBLISHED BY BRADLEY ENTERPRISES

IRVING, TEXAS

ACKNOWLEDGMENTS

In compiling the roster information for this book, many sources were relied upon. Other than my own first hand information, the following books, magazines and periodicals were used in researching the vast amount of information required to produce this book.

Diesel Locomotive Rosters by C.W.McDonald
Amtrak Car & Locomotive Spotter by Wayner Publications
The Second Diesel Spotters Guide by J.A.Pinkepank
Trackside Guide Canadian Motive Power and Equipment
by Bytown Railway Society, Inc.
American Shortline Railway Guide by E.A.Lewis
Union Pacific Motive Power Review 1968-77
by Motive Power Services
Santa Fe Motive Power by J.McMillan
Burlington Northern 1977-80 Annual
by Motive Power Services
The Official Railway Equipment Register
by R.E.R.Publishing Corp.
Southern Pacific Review 1980 by J.A.Strapac
Rock Island Diesel Locomotives 1930-1980 by L.A.Marre
Union Pacific 1977-1980 by G.R.Cockle
Passenger Train Journal Magazine, by Interurban Press
Pacific Rail News Magazine by Interurban Press
CTC Board Magazine by Hyrail Productions
Trains Magazine by Kalmbach Publishing
Railfan & Railroad Magazine by Carstens Publishing
Special thanks to Don Dover of Extra 2200 South Magazine
by Railfax

All Photography is my own, or my one and only railfan son, James David Bradley. Any other contibutors, names will be duly noted in the photo credit line.

ISBN 0-9624633-0-2

Printed and bound in the United States of America

FORWARD

This book deals with all locomotives produced in the United States and Canada, over fifty tons, in the time period Jan. 1, 1968 thru mid 1989. Excluding export locomotives, other than Canada and Mexico.

The style of reference used in this book traces each locomotive, or as in most cases, a number of locomotives ordered at one time, to there present owners or untimely demise. Where as, most books of this nature, list locomotives, using there present owner and number, we have listed them from there original production numbers.

Some locomotive orders which overlap Jan 1, 1968, will be shown from the original production date. Many of the large class 1 roads have sold or rebuilt locomotives of certain types, usually fifteen years old or older, and where this has occurred, these orders have been broken down into more easily understood numbers. In some instances where large classes of locomotives have been sold or rebuilt, reference is made only to what class they have been moved to, rather than individual numbers, especially when the numbering has been mixed.

Although, some of these records may not be complete, this book is not designed to give a complete history of each locomotive, but where space permits and the information was available, I have included as much as possiable. The Book is designed as a reference tool, with pictures as a visual guide. The first three chapters are arranged by owner and number. The fourth chapter is the same material as the first three, but, arranged by builder and production date. The production run will be shown at the top of each catagory of locomotive. The total number of units built in the period 1968 thru mid 1989, per locomotive type, appears in the locomotive index, page 220. The pictures will correspond to the information on that page, generally the line of information just above or below.

In using this book, if looking up a locomotive by its road number, and it is not shown under that company. Refer to chapter 4, and look under the type of locomotive, as the locomotive may have been traded or purchased 2nd hand. Also, chapter 4 will have more detailed histories. Remember, all locomotives are cataloged by there original road number.

This book was conceived when, in trying to look up builders dates to label locomotive slides, many of which you see in this book, many hours were being spent rummaging thru various rosters and books. So, why couldn't all this information be in just one book. Well now, it is!

James T. Bradley
Irving, Texas

Pictures front cover;
Top left, WP GE U23B, Top right, MKT EMD GP40.
Bottom left, CP GMD SD40-2, Bottom right, UP GMD SD60M

Rear Cover;
Top left, BN GE B30-7A(B), Top right, MKT EMD GP38-2
Bottom left, CRR EMD SD45-2, Bottom right, UP EMD SD45

CONTENTS

COMMON CARRIER RAILROADS 1968-1989

QTY.	BLDR.	MODEL	DELV.NO.	BLDR.DATE	NOTES
AC-ALGOMA CENTRAL RAILWAY					
3	GMD	SD40	180-182	71/10	
6	GMD	SD40-2	183-188	73/08-73/10	
3	GMD	SD40-2	190-192	73/08	
6	GMD	GP38-2	200-205	81/04	
ADN-ASHLEY DREW & NORTHERN RAILWAY CO.					
1	EMD	SW1500	150	70/05	
ALQS-ALIQUIPPA & SOUTHERN RAILROAD CO.					
2	EMD	SW1001	1000-1001	73/02	
1	EMD	SW1001	1002	75/03	SOLD TO RIVER TERM. 109
ALS-ALTON & SOUTHERN RAILWAY CO					
6	EMD	SW1500	1500-1505	69/05	
6	EMD	SW1500	1506-1511	70/02	
6	EMD	SW1500	1512-1517	71/05	
1	EMD	MP15DC	1522	80/11	
AMTK-AMTRAK (NATIONAL RAILROAD PASSENGER CORP.)					
2	BBD	LRC(B)	38-39	80/02,80/06	LEASED ONLY, RET'D BBD 1982
30	EMD	F40PH	200-229	76/03-76/04	202 WRK/REBLT W/AC T.MOTORS
25	EMD	F40PHR	230-254	77/07-77/10	246 WRK/SCR.
15	EMD	F40PHR	255-269	77/11-78/01	
10	EMD	F40PH	270-279	77/11-78/01	
14	EMD	F40PHR	280-293	78/03-78/07	
6	EMD	F40PHR	294-299	79/06-79/07	
10	EMD	F40PH	300-309	79/04-79/06	
12	EMD	F40PHR	310-321	79/07-79/08	
7	EMD	F40PHR	322-328	79/09-79/10	
3	EMD	F40PHR	329-331	80/08	
15	EMD	F40PH	332-346	80/08-80/11	
13	EMD	F40PH	347-359	80/11-80/12	
1	EMD	F40PHR	360	80/12	
30	EMD	F40PHR	361-390	81/04-81/08	
10	EMD	F40PHR	391-400	85/08	
9	EMD	F40PHR	401-409	87/11-88/01	
2	EMD	F69PH-AC	450-451	89/04	HAVE AC TRACTION MOTORS
11	EMD	SDP40F	500-510	73/06	TRADED TO EMD
1	EMD	SDP40F	511	73/06	TO ATSF SDP40FU 5251
14	EMD	SDP40F	512-525	73/06-73/07	TRADED TO EMD
1	EMD	SDP40F	526	73/07	TO ATSF SDP40FU 5255
13	EMD	SDP40F	527-539	73/07	TRADED TO EMD
40	EMD	SDP40F	540-579	74/03-74/05	T/I TO EMD, 569 TO EMD 134
35	EMD	SDP40F	580-614	74/05-74/06	T/I TO EMD, 609 TO EMD 169
1	EMD	SDP40F	615	74/06	TO ATSF SDP40FU 5252
5	EMD	SDP40F	617-621	74/06-74/07	TRADED TO EMD

NOTE: F40PHR, is a locomotive built with some SDP40F trade-in components.

AMTK-AMTRAK
718, GE, P30CH
BLT. 75/12
CHICAGO, IL. 80/06

QTY.	BLDR.	MODEL	DELV.NO.	BLDR.DATE	NOTES
1	EMD	SDP40F	622	74/07	TO ATSF SDP40FU 5257
5	EMD	SDP40F	623-627	74/07	TRADED TO EMD
2	EMD	SDP40F	628-629	74/07	ATSF SDP40FU 5258,5262
1	EMD	SDP40F	630	74/07	ATSF SDP40FU 5253
1	EMD	SDP40F	631	74/07	TRADED TO EMD
1	EMD	SDP40F	632	74/07	ATSF SDP40FU 5264
1	EMD	SDP40F	633	74/07	TRADED TO EMD"
2	EMD	SDP40F	634-635	74/07	ATSF SDP40FU 5261,5254
2	EMD	SDP40F	636-637	74/07	TRADED TO EMD
2	EMD	SDP40F	638-639	74/07	ATSF SDP40FU 5260,5263
1	EMD	SDP40F	640	74/07	ATSF SDP40FU 5256
2	EMD	SDP40F	641-642	74/07	TRADED TO EMD
2	EMD	SDP40F	643-644	74/08	ATSF SDP40FU 5250,5266
1	EMD	SDP40F	645	74/08	ATSF SDP40FU 5267
3	EMD	SDP40F	646-648	74/08	TRADED TO EMD
1	EMD	SDP40F	649	74/08	ATSF SDP40FU 5265
25	GE	P30CH	700-724	75/08-76/01	SOME NOW OFF ROSTER
30	EMD	AEM7	900-929	79/11-81/08	BUDD/ASEA,900,03,04 WRK
17	EMD	AEM7	930-946	81/09-82/07	BUDD/ASEA, 911 WRK.
7	EMD	AEM7	947-953	88/	ASEA COMPONENTS
2	GE	E60CP	950-951	74/10	RE# 620,957.957 RE# 604
5	GE	E60CP	952-956	74/10-75/11	RE# 610,611,608,612,601
1	GE	E60CP	957	75/11	RE# 951, LATER RE# 609
7	GE	E60CP	958-964	75/11-76/10	958-963 TO NJT, SAME #
11	GE	E60CH	965-975	75/11-76/01	967,971-973 /NJT,SAME# 966,968 NAVAJO MINE RR
12	BUDD	SPV2000	988-999	80/04-80/07	OWNED BY CONN.DOT.

AN-APALACHICOLA NORTHERN RAILROAD CO.

4	EMD	SW1500	712-715	69/05
4	EMD	SW1500	716-719	70/08-70/09
3	EMD	GP15T(AC)	720-722	83/04

QTY.	BLDR.	MODEL	DELV.NO.	BLDR.DATE	NOTES

ANR-ANGELINA & NECHES RIVER RAILROAD CO.

QTY.	BLDR.	MODEL	DELV.NO.	BLDR.DATE	NOTES
1	EMD	SW1500	1500	72/11	
1	EMD	GP38-2	2000	80/08	

AR-ABERDEEN & ROCKFISH RAILROAD CO.

QTY.	BLDR.	MODEL	DELV.NO.	BLDR.DATE	NOTES
1	EMD	GP38	400	68/06	

ARR-ALASKA RAILROAD CORP.

QTY.	BLDR.	MODEL	DELV.NO.	BLDR.DATE	NOTES
4	EMD	GP49	2801-2804	83/08-83/09	
5	EMD	GP49	2805-2809	85/05	
6	EMD	GP40-2	3000-3005	75/04	3000 RE# 3006
5	EMD	GP40-2	3007-3011	76/05	
4	EMD	GP40-2	3012-3015	78/09	

ASAB-ATLANTA & ST ANDREWS BAY, # 507, EMD, GP39
BLT. 70/07
PANAMA CITY, FL. 84/10

ASAB-ATLANTA & SAINT ANDREWS BAY RAILWAY CO.

QTY.	BLDR.	MODEL	DELV.NO.	BLDR.DATE	NOTES
1	EMD	GP39	507	70/07	
2	EMD	GP38-2	508-509	73/05	
1	EMD	GP38-2	510	75/06	

AT-AUTO-TRAIN CORP.

QTY.	BLDR.	MODEL	DELV.NO.	BLDR.DATE	NOTES
5	GE	U36B	4000-4004	71/11	4001,4004 WRK/SCR 73/03
5	GE	U36B	4005-4009	72/12	REST SCR. BY E/85
3	GE	U36B	4010-4012	74/05	SCR. BY E/85

QTY.	BLDR.	MODEL	DELV.NO.	BLDR.DATE	NOTES

ATSF-ATCHISON TOPEKA & SANTA FE RAILWAY CO.

QTY.	BLDR.	MODEL	DELV.NO.	BLDR.DATE	REMFG.MOD. NEW NO's
20	EMD	F45	1900-1919	68/06	F45u 5900-5919, re# 5950-5969
20	EMD	F45	1920-1939	68/06-68/07	F45u 5920-5939, re# 5970-5989
23	EMD	GP38	3500-3522	70/06	GP38u 2300-2322
1	EMD	GP38	3523	70/06	WRK & SCR.73/04
5	EMD	GP38	3524-3528	70/06	GP38u 2324-2328
19	EMD	GP38	3529-3547	70/08	GP38u 2329-2347
1	EMD	GP38	3548	70/08	GP38u 2348, SCR 87/03
1	EMD	GP38	3549	70/08	GP38u 2349
2	EMD	GP38	3550-3551	70/09	GP38u 2350,2351
1	EMD	GP38	3552	70/09	SCR 73/04
8	EMD	GP38	3553-3560	70/09	GP38u 2353-2360
17	EMD	GP39-2	3600-3616	74/08	
10	EMD	GP39-2	3617-3626	75/01	RE# 3400 CLASS MIXED NO.s
13	EMD	GP39-2	3627-3639	75/02	RE# 3400 CLASS MIXED NO.s
8	EMD	GP39-2	3640-3647	75/03	RE# 3400 CLASS MIXED NO.s
1	EMD	GP39-2	3648	75/03	WRK & SCR 84/10
3	EMD	GP39-2	3649-3651	75/03	RE# 3400 CLASS MIXED NO.s
14	EMD	GP39-2	3652-3665	75/04	RE# 3400 CLASS MIXED NO.s
1	EMD	GP39-2	3666	75/04	RE# 3426, WRK & SCR. 86/07
2	EMD	GP39-2	3667-3668	75/04	RE# 3400 CLASS MIXED NO's
14	EMD	GP39-2	3669-3682	77/11	3672 WRK/SCR 84/10
13	EMD	GP39-2	3683-3695	79/06	3692 WRK/SCR 83/11
10	EMD	GP39-2	3696-3705	80/04	
1	EMD	GP40X	3800	78/06	(RCT)
1	EMD	GP40X	3801	78/06	(RCR)
8	EMD	GP40X	3802-3809	78/04-78/05	

ATSF-SANTA FE
3804, EMD, GP40X
BLT. 78/04
CHICAGO, IL. 78/06

ATSF-ATCHISON TOPEKA & SANTA FE RAILWAY CO. cont'd

QTY.	BLDR.	MODEL	DELV.NO.	BLDR.DATE	NOTES
					REMFG.MOD. NEW NO's
7	EMD	GP50	3810-3822	81/01-81/02	(RCT) EVEN NO.
7	EMD	GP50	3811-3823	81/01-81/02	(RCR) ODD NO.
16	EMD	GP50	3824-3839	81/03-81/04	
15	EMD	GP50	3840-3854	85/04	
12	EMD	SD39	4000-4011	69/05	REBLT & RE# 1556-1567
20	GMD	GP60	4000-4019	88/05-88/06	(2nd)
20	GMD	GP60	4020-4039	89/06-89/07	(2nd)
8	EMD	SD39	4012-4019	69/05-69/06	(RCT), REBLT,RE# 1568-1575
8	EMD	SD40-2	5020-5027	77/11	EVEN RCT,ODD RCR,5024 RET.
30	EMD	SD40-2	5028-5057	77/10-77/11	5028,5034 WRK/RET.
13	EMD	SD40-2	5058-5070	79/04-79/05	
38	EMD	SD40-2	5071-5108	79/09-79/10	
8	EMD	SD40-2	5109-5123	79/11	(RCR) ODD NO.
8	EMD	SD40-2	5110-5124	79/10	(RCT) EVEN NO.5015 WRK/SCR
8	EMD	SD40-2	5125-5139	80/11-80/12	(RCR ODD#) 5037 SCR 78/03
8	EMD	SD40-2	5126-5140	80/11	(RCT) EVEN NO.
29	EMD	SD40-2	5141-5169	80/09-80/10	
23	EMD	SD40-2	5170-5192	81/10-81/12	
14	EMD	SD40-2	5200-5213	78/10	5208 WRK/RET 86/08
2	EMD	SD45	5590-5591	69/04	SD45U 5386,5388
2	EMD	SD45	5592-5593	69/04	SD45U 5403,5383
2	EMD	SD45	5594-5595	69/04	SD45U 5400,5397
2	EMD	SD45	5596-5597	69/04	SD45U 5402,5394
2	EMD	SD45	5598-5599	69/05	SD45U 5384,5399
2	EMD	SD45	5600-5601	69/05	SD45U 5382,5385
2	EMD	SD45	5602-5603	69/05	SD45U 5389,5395
2	EMD	SD45	5604-5605	69/05	SD45U 5396,5401
2	EMD	SD45	5606-5607	69/05	SD45U 5393,5392
2	EMD	SD45	5608-5609	69/05	SD45U 5391,5381
1	EMD	SD45	5610	69/05	WRK & SCRAPPED 78/03
2	EMD	SD45	5611-5612	69/05	SD45U 5390,5387
2	EMD	SD45	5613-5614	69/05	SD45U 5404,5398
2	EMD	SD45	5615-5616	70/06	SD45U 5379,5372
2	EMD	SD45	5617-5618	70/06	SD45U 5380,5371
2	EMD	SD45	5619-5620	70/06	SD45U 5377,5374
2	EMD	SD45	5621-5622	70/06	SD45U 5373,5375
2	EMD	SD45	5623-5624	70/06	SD45U 5378,5376
1	EMD	SD45-2	5625	72/05	REENG.W/CAT.ENG.RE# 5855
1	EMD	SD45-2	5626	72/05	SD45-2B 5513
6	EMD	SD45-2	5627-5632	72/05	SD45-2u,5800,7200 CLASS
1	EMD	SD45-2	5633	72/05	SD45-2B 5515
10	EMD	SD45-2	5634-5643	72/05	SD45-2u,5800,7200 CLASS
1	EMD	SD45-2	5644	72/05	WRK & SCR. 77/06
6	EMD	SD45-2	5645-5650	72/05	SD45-2u,5800,7200 CLASS
1	EMD	SD45-2	5651	72/05	SD45-2B 5510(2nd)
6	EMD	SD45-2	5652-5657	72/05	SD45-2u,5800,7200 CLASS
1	EMD	SD45-2	5658	72/05	WRK & SCR. 77/11
3	EMD	SD45-2	5659-5661	72/05	SD45-2u,5800,7200 CLASS
4	EMD	SD45-2	5662-5665	73/05	SD45-2u,5800,7200 CLASS
1	EMD	SD45-2	5666	73/05	SD45-2u,7205,WRK,RE#5805
9	EMD	SD45-2	5667-5675	73/06	SD45-2u,5800,7200 CLASS

ATSF-ATCHISON TOPEKA & SANTA FE RAILWAY CO. con't

ATSF-SANTA FE
6353, GE, B23-7
BLT. 78/04
CHICAGO, IL. 78/06

QTY.	BLDR.	MODEL	DELV.NO.	BLDR.DATE	NOTES REMFG.TO: RE# TO:
1	EMD	SD45-2	5676	73/06	SD45-2B 5511(2nd)
7	EMD	SD45-2	5677-5683	73/06	SD45-2u,5800,7200 CLASS
1	EMD	SD45-2	5684	73/06	SD45-2B 5516
2	EMD	SD45-2	5685-5686	73/06	SD45-2u, 7211,7212
1	EMD	SD45-2	5687	73/05	WRK & SCR. 80/08
12	EMD	SD45-2	5688-5699	73/05	SD45-2u,5800,7200 CLASS
2	EMD	SD45-2	5700-5701	73/05	SD45-2B 5517,5514
1	EMD	SD45-2	5702	73/05	SD45-2u 5842
1	EMD	SD45-2	5703	73/05	SD45-2B 5512(2nd)
1	EMD	SD45-2	5704	73/05	SD45-2u 5834
8	EMD	SD45-2	5705-5714	74/05	5706 WRK & SCR. 80/08
32	GE	U23B	6300-6331	70/06-70/10	ALL TRADED OR SCR.
1	GE	U23B	6332	70/12	SFB30 7200 IN M/87
16	GE	U23B	6333-6348	70/12-71/02	6341 T/I GE 83,RETAINED AS TEST BED, #26-1, REST T/I TO GE BY L/88
14	GE	B23-7	6350-6363	78/04-78/05	MOST UPGRADED 3000hp,7200's
26	GE	B23-7	6364-6389	79/04-79/06	MOST UPGRADED 3000hp,7200's
15	GE	B23-7	6390-6404	80/04	
14	GE	B23-7	6405-6418	84/04-84/05	DELV. IN 84/12
1	GE	B39-8	7400	84/01	TEST PROTOTYPE (RCT)
1	GE	B39-8	7401	84/12	PROTOTYPE TEST UNIT
1	GE	B39-8	7402	84/09	PROTOTYPE TEST UNIT
20	GE	DASH840B	7410-7429	88/06	
20	GE	DASH840B	7430-7449	89/04	
16	GE	B36-7	7484-7499	80/10-80/11	7484,86 (RCT) 7485,87(RCR)
20	GE	U23C	7500-7519	69/05-69/07	RET'D TO LESSOR 84/12,SCR.
10	GE	C30-7	8010-8019	77/12	
38	GE	C30-7	8020-8057	78/03-78/06	
6	GE	C30-7	8058-8063	78/10	

ATSF-ATCHISON TOPEKA & SANTA FE RAILWAY CO. cont'd

QTY.	BLDR.	MODEL	DELV.NO.	BLDR.DATE	NOTES
35	GE	C30-7	8064-8098	79/04-79/05	
24	GE	C30-7	8099-8122	80/05-80/06	
30	GE	C30-7	8123-8152	81/05-81/07	8138-8152 EVEN (RCT)
14	GE	C30-7	8153-8166	82/12	8133-8151 ODD (RCR)
25	GE	U33C	8500-8524	69/06-69/08	RET'D TO LESSOR 84/12,SCR.
6	GE	U36C	8700-8705	72/05-72/06	SFC30 9500 SERIES
1	GE	U36C	8706	72/06	WRK & SCR. 81/01
15	GE	U36C	8707-8721	72/06-73/03	SFC30 9500 SERIES
1	GE	U36C	8722	73/03	WRK & SCR. 77/11
13	GE	U36C	8723-8735	73/03-73/04,	SFC30 9500 SERIES
27	GE	U36C	8736-8762	74/05-74/07	
1	GE	U36C	8763	74/11	WRK & SCR. 78/03
36	GE	U36C	8764-8799	74/11-75/02	SFC30 9500 SERIES

AWP-ATLANTA & WEST POINT
729, EMD, GP40
BLT. 69/01
DOLTON,IL. NEW I/T,69/02

AWP-ATLANTA & WEST POINT RAILROAD CO.

QTY.	BLDR.	MODEL	DELV.NO.	BLDR.DATE	NOTES
1	EMD	GP40	727	68/07	TO SBD-CSXT 6647
2	EMD	GP40	728-729	69/01	TO SBD-CSXT 6648-6649
3	EMD	GP40	730-732	70/05	TO SBD-CSXT 6650-6652
1	EMD	GP40-2	733	74/11	SBD 6645,RE# SBD-CSXT 6391
2	EMD	GP38-2	6007-6008	79/04	FL-SBD TO CSXT 2658,2659

BAP-BUTTE ANACONDA & PACIFIC RAILWAY

QTY.	BLDR.	MODEL	DELV.NO.	BLDR.DATE	NOTES
1	EMD	GP38-2	108	77/01	SOLD TO ARR 2001
1	EMD	GP38-2	109	78/11	SOLD TO ARR 2002

BCH-BRITISH COLUMBIA HYDRO
& POWER AUTHORITY
# 911, GMD, SW900m
BLT. 69/03
NEW WESTMINSTER, BC. 73/06

QTY.	BLDR.	MODEL	DELV.NO.	BLDR.DATE	NOTES
BCH-BRITISH COLUMBIA HYDRO & POWER AUTHORITY					
3	EMD	MP15DC	151-153	75/11	
1	EMD	SD38AC	381	71/10	
2	EMD	SD38-2	382-383	72/12	
1	EMD	SD38-2	384	74/08	
1	GMD	SW900M	911	69/03	
BCOL-BRITISH COLUMBIA RAILWAY CO.					
8	MLW	M420W	640-647	73/09-73/10	
8	MLW	M420B	681-688	75/06-75/07	(RCR)
6	MLW	M630	717-722	72/12	
8	MLW	M630W	723-730	73/10-73/11	
12	GMD	SD40-2	751-762	80/09	751-756(RCT) 755, SCR.
5	GMD	SD40-2	763-767	85/07	767 (RCT) 760 WRK/SCR/86
7	GMD	GF6C	6001-6007	83/11-84/07	ASEA COMPONENTS
BLE-BESSEMER & LAKE ERIE RAILROAD CO.					
6	EMD	SD38AC	864-869	71/07	864 OFF ROSTER
9	EMD	SD38-2	870-878	73/03-73/05	871,874,OFF ROSTER 875 SCR. 86/10
1	EMD	SD38-2	879	74/02	
2	EMD	SD38-2	890-891	75/04	891 TRANSFERED TO EJE 86/05
1	EMD	SD38-2	892	76/03	892 TRANSFERED TO DMIR 86/05

QTY.	BLDR.	MODEL	DELV.NO.	BLDR.DATE	NOTES
BM-BOSTON & MAINE CORPORATION					
12	EMD	GP38-2	201-212	73/12	212 RE# 200, 206 RET.84 REST TO KCS 4012-4023,88/07
18	EMD	GP40-2	300-317	77/12	
BMLP-BLACK MESA & LAKE POWELL					
1	GE	E60C	6000	72/12	RE# 6003, SHIPPED 73/04
2	GE	E60C	6001-6002	72/12	
3	GE	E60C	6004-6006	76/09-76/10	
BN-BURLINGTON NORTHERN RAILROAD CO.					
15	EMD	SW1500	310-324	73/01	
15	EMD	SW1000	375-389	72/01-72/02	
5	EMD	SW1000	390-394	72/10	
8	EMD	SW1000	427-434	71/01-71/02	
15	EMD	SW1000	435-449	70/11-71/01	ORD.CB&Q, 442 REBLT"B UNIT"
7	EMD	SD45	868-874	71/10	CS OWNED, RE# 6570-6576,RET
18	EMD	SD40-2	900-917	72/03-72/05	CS OWNED, RE# 6348-6365
8	EMD	SD40-2	918-925	74/02	CS OWNED, RE# 6366-6373
2	EMD	SD40-2	930-931	77/05	CS OWNED, RE# 7800-7801
5	EMD	SD40-2	932-936	77/05	CS OWNED, RE# 7802-7806
13	EMD	SD40-2	937-949	77/06	CS OWNED, RE# 7807-7819
10	EMD	SD40-2	950-959	74/11	CS OWNED, RE# 7820-7829
2	EMD	SD40-2	960-961	77/06	CS OWNED, RE# 7830-7831
1	EMD	SD40-2	980	74/02	CS OWNED, RE# 6850
1	EMD	SD40-2	996	74/02	CS OWNED, RE# 6950

BN-BURLINGTON NORTHERN
427, EMD, SW1000
BLT. 71/01
VANCOUVER, WA. 78/10

BN-BURLINGTON NORTHERN RR CO. cont'd

QTY.	BLDR.	MODEL	DELV.NO.	BLDR.DATE	NOTES
6	EMD	GP38	2072-2077	70/02	ORDERED BY SP&S
10	EMD	GP38-2	2078-2087	72/05	
22	EMD	GP38-2	2088-2109	74/11	
5	EMD	GP38-2	2150-2154	80/06	OWNED BY FW&D
40	EMD	GP39-2	2700-2739	81/03-81/04	
10	EMD	GP50	3100-3109	80/12	3100 DELV. IN SLSF PAINT
48	EMD	GP50	3110-3157	85/06-85/11	
5	EMD	GP50	3158-3162	85/11	5 MAN CREW CAB
53	GE	B30-7A(B)	4000-4052	82/06-82/09	4051 WRK & SCR.
67	GE	B30-7A(B)	4053-4119	83/08-83/10	
1	GE	C30-7	5000	79/09	
7	GE	C30-7	5001-5007	79/06	
39	GE	C30-7	5008-5046	79/09-79/10	
29	GE	C30-7	5047-5075	80/02-80/03	
36	GE	C30-7	5076-5111	80/03-80/05	
15	GE	C30-7	5112-5126	80/06-80/07	
15	GE	C30-7	5127-5141	81/02-81/05	5136 WRK & SCR
6	GE	U30C	5300-5305	72/01	RE# 5800-5805,MOST RET.L87
6	GE	U30C	5300-5305	75/05	(2nd)
14	GE	U30C	5306-5319	72/01-72/02	ALL RET. ONLY 5306,18 LEFT
5	GE	U30C	5320-5324	72/03-72/04	ALL RET, 5323, 5324 SCR.
1	GE	U30C	5325	72/04	RET. WAS RE# 1776, RWB
9	GE	U30C	5326-5334	72/04-72/05	ALL RET. 5327-5329 SCR.
18	GE	U30C	5335-5352	72/11-72/12	5336 TO B-UNIT, SCR.86/02
12	GE	U30C	5353-5364	75/05	(2nd) 5363 WRK/SCR.79/12
12	GE	U30C	5353-5364	72/12	RE#5900-5911,5902,5906,SCR
30	GE	U30C	5365-5394	74/08-74/11	5366,68,89,93 RET.BY E/87
3	GE	B32-8	5497-5499	84/01	PROTOTYPE TEST UNITS
1	GE	C30-7	5500	76/09	
9	GE	C30-7	5501-5509	76/12	
20	GE	C30-7	5510-5529	77/04-77/07	
15	GE	C30-7	5530-5544	77/11-77/12	
22	GE	C30-7	5545-5566	78/09-78/10	
15	GE	C30-7	5567-5581	79/02	
18	GE	C30-7	5582-5599	79/05-79/06	
4	GE	U33C	5725-5728	71/02	ORDERED BY CB&Q, SCR.M/86
6	GE	U33C	5729-5734	71/02-71/03	ALL SCR. M/86
29	GE	U33C	5735-5763	71/07-71/09	ALL SCR.M/86,5752 TO SQUAW CREEK, CONSOLIDATED COAL
8	GE	U30C	5806-5813	73/07	
10	GE	U30C	5814-5823	73/11-73/12	5814 WRK & SCR. L/86
10	GE	U30C	5824-5833	74/04-74/05	5830 RET.86/05, 5832 87/05 RET'D LESSOR 89/04, 5825, 5828, 5830 TO LSI
6	GE	U30C	5834-5839	75/06	
7	GE	U30C	5912-5918	73/07	5913,5914 SCR.
10	GE	U30C	5919-5928	73/11-73/12	
10	GE	U30C	5929-5938	74/04-74/05	RET'D LESSOR 89/04, 5929, 5931,5932,5934,5937 TO LSI
6	GE	U30C	5939-5944	75/06	
1	EMD	SD40	6300	71/10	WRK & SCR. 87/05
1	EMD	SD40	6301	71/10	TO MRL 201
1	EMD	SD40	6302	71/10	TO SD40B 7600,TO SOO 6450
3	EMD	SD40	6303-6305	71/10	6305 RET. 86/05

BN-BURLINGTON NORTHERN RAILROAD CO. cont'd

BN-BURLINGTON NORTHERN
7122, EMD, SD40-2
BLT. 79/01
SPOKANE, WA. 79/01

QTY.	BLDR.	MODEL	DELV.NO.	BLDR.DATE	NOTES
3	EMD	SD40	6306-6308	71/10	TO MRL
4	EMD	SD40	6309-6312	71/10-71/11	6310,6312 TO MRL,6311 SCR.
5	EMD	SD40	6313-6317	71/11	6315-6317 TO MRL,6314 RET.
7	EMD	SD40	6318-6324	71/11	6320,6322,6324 TO MRL
1	EMD	SD40-2	6325	72/01	TEMP.RE# 1976, THEN 1876
9	EMD	SD40-2	6326-6334	72/01-72/02	6330 RE-ENG. W/CAT IN 87
2	EMD	SD40-2	6335-6336	72/02	RE# 6912-6913
1	EMD	SD40-2	6337	72/02	RE# 6914,TO SD40-2B 7501
2	EMD	SD40-2	6338-6339	72/02	RE# 6915-6916
12	EMD	SD40-2	6340-6351	73/03	RE# 6800-6811, 6800 SCR.
1	EMD	SD40-2	6352	73/03	RE# 6812,TO SD40-2B 7502
11	EMD	SD40-2	6353-6363	73/03-73/04	RE# 6813-6823
12	EMD	SD40-2	6364-6375	73/03-73/04	RE# 6900-6911
10	EMD	SD40-2	6376-6385	74/04	6376 SCR,6377 TO MRL 250
20	EMD	SD45	6472-6491	70/07-70/08	ORD/NP, RET'D LESSOR 85
6	EMD	SD45	6492-6497	70/08	ORD/CB&Q, ALL RET.BY M/86
45	EMD	SD45	6498-6542	71/05-71/08	ALL RET. BY M/86
25	EMD	SD45	6543-6567	71/11-71/12	ALL RET. BY M/86
12	EMD	F45	6614-6625	70/07-70/09	ORDERED BY GN,ALL RET.M/86
20	EMD	F45	6626-6645	71/04-71/05	6640,44 TO NYSW,ALL RET.86 6635,6642 TO NRE 6641 TO DOYLE McCORMACK,87
8	EMD	SD40-2	6700-6707	74/12	
35	EMD	SD40-2	6708-6742	76/02-76/03	6714 SCR.
10	EMD	SD40-2	6743-6752	76/03	

BN-BURLINGTON NORTHERN RAILROAD CO. cont'd

QTY.	BLDR.	MODEL	DELV NO.	BLDR.DATE	NOTES
20	EMD	SD40-2	6753-6772	76/11	6760,6765,6767 SCR.
8	EMD	SD40-2	6773-6780	77/05	
5	EMD	SD40-2	6781-6785	77/11	
5	EMD	SD40-2	6786-6790	77/12	
9	EMD	SD40-2	6791-6799	77/11	
13	EMD	SD40-2	6824-6836	73/11-73/12	6827 RET.80/06
12	EMD	SD40-2	6917-6928	73/11-73/12	6922 SCR. 6924 SCR.86/05
29	EMD	SD40-2	7000-7028	77/11-77/12	7019 SCR.
20	EMD	SD40-2	7029-7048	78/02-78/03	
5	EMD	SD40-2	7049-7053	78/03-78/04	
9	EMD	SD40-2	7054-7062	78/06	
12	EMD	SD40-2	7063-7074	78/07	
51	EMD	SD40-2	7075-7125	78/10-78/12	
35	EMD	SD40-2	7126-7160	79/01-79/02	
6	EMD	SD40-2	7161-7166	79/04	
39	GMD	SD40-2	7167-7205	79/08-79/09	
30	GMD	SD40-2	7206-7235	80/05-80/07	7221 TO SD40-2B 7500
56	EMD	SD40-2	7236-7291	80/01-80/04	7241 SCR.
24	EMD	SD40-2	7832-7855	78/07-78/08	C&S OWNED
13	EMD	SD40-2	7856-7868	78/09-78/10	C&S OWNED
20	EMD	SD40-2	7869-7888	79/03-79/04	C&S OWNED
35	EMD	SD40-2	7889-7923	79/04-79/07	C&S OWNED, 7899,7907 SCR.
17	EMD	SD40-2	7924-7940	80/03-80/05	C&S OWNED
10	EMD	SD40-2	8000-8009	77/06	
20	EMD	SD40-2	8010-8029	78/03	
1	EMD	SD40-2	8030	79/07	
43	EMD	SD40-2	8031-8073	79/09-79/12	8043 SCR.
16	GMD	SD40-2	8074-8089	79/08-79/09	
92	EMD	SD40-2	8090-8181	80/05-80/07	
3	EMD	SD60	8300-8302	85/11	PROTOTYPES, RET'D EMD 87/12

BN-BURLINGTON NORTHERN
8081, GMD, SD40-2
BLT. 79/09
IRVING, TX. 81/09

BO-BALTIMORE & OHIO
4812, EMD, GP38
BLT. 70/09
RIVERDALE, IL. 83/10

BO-BALTIMORE & OHIO RAILROAD CO.

QTY.	BLDR.	MODEL	DELV NO.	BLDR.DATE	NOTES
1	EMD	GP40-2	GM50	72/09	RE# 4164, TO CSXT 6063
1	EMD	GP40-2	1977	72/09	1977 (2nd)TO CSXT 6392
40	EMD	GP40	3700-3739	69/02-69/04	TO GATX IN 85, 3701 SCR.86 3703,3710 REBLT MK TO GP39H-2, MARC 73,74. 3708,18,27,20 TO CMI 8801-8804 /88. 3700,04,13,14,16, 22,23,25,28,39,REBLT TO GP40G FOR BN #3075-3084
25	EMD	GP40	3740-3764	70/12-71/02	CS TO CSXT 6516-6540
13	EMD	GP40	3765-3777	71/02-71/03	3773 RET.CSXT 6541-6552
2	EMD	GP40	3778-3779	71/03	CS TO CSXT 6553,6554
55	EMD	GP40	4000-4054	71/08-71/10	(2nd)CS TO CSXT 6575-6629
10	EMD	GP40	4055-4064	71/10-71/11	(2nd)CS TO CSXT 6630-6639
63	EMD	GP40-2	4100-4162	72/08-72/10	(2nd)4105 RET.CSXT 6001-62
62	EMD	GP40-2	4185-4246	75/04-75/06	CS TO CSXT 6084-6145
10	EMD	GP40-2	4247-4256	77/02	CS TO CSXT 6146-6155
21	EMD	GP40-2	4287-4307	78/01-78/02	CS TO CSXT 6186-6206 6186,6187,REBLT/RE# 6425,6426
4	EMD	GP40-2	4308-4311	78/03	CS TO CSXT 6207-6210
30	EMD	GP40-2	4322-4351	79/02-79/03	CS TO CSXT 6221-6250
26	EMD	GP40-2	4422-4447	81/05-81/06	CS TO CSXT 6320-6345
20	EMD	GP38	4800-4819	70/08-70/12	CS TO CSXT 2100-2119,4810 TO NRL
4	EMD	SD40	7497-7500	69/04	TO M-K 84/07,TO WFAX 1-3, 7500 LEASED TO MKT,THEN SOO
20	EMD	SD40-2	7600-7619	77/01-77/02	7603 RET.TO CSXT 8242-8261
20	EMD	SD50	8576-8595	84/07-84/08	CS TO CSXT SAME #

QTY.	BLDR.	MODEL	DELV.NO.	BLDR.DATE	NOTES

BRC-BELT RAILWAY CO. OF CHICAGO

QTY.	BLDR.	MODEL	DELV.NO.	BLDR.DATE	NOTES
6	EMD	GP38-2	490-495	72/08	
2	EMD	SW1500	531-532	68/03	
2	EMD	MP15DC	533-534	75/06	534 DELV. RED/WHITE/BLUE
2	EMD	MP15DC	535-536	80/02	

BS-BIRMINGHAM SOUTHERN RAILROAD CO.

QTY.	BLDR.	MODEL	DELV.NO.	BLDR.DATE	NOTES
2	EMD	SW1000	12-13	69/01	RE# 212-213
1	EMD	SW1000	14	69/10	SCR. 73
1	EMD	SW1000	15	71/01	SCR. 73
2	EMD	SW1000	16-17	71/10	SCR. 73
2	EMD	SW1001	18-19	73/05	RE# 218-219 IN 73/10
5	EMD	SW1001	220-224	74/01	
1	EMD	SW1001	225	74/10	
2	EMD	MP15DC	260-261	76/08	

BXN-BAUXITE & NORTHERN
16, EMD, MP15DC
BLT. 74/11
BAUXITE, AR. 86/10

BXN-BAUXITE & NORTHERN RAILWAY CO.

QTY.	BLDR.	MODEL	DELV.NO.	BLDR.DATE	NOTES
2	EMD	MP15DC	15-16	74/11	

CBQ-CHICAGO BURLINGTON & QUINCY RAILROAD CO.

QTY.	BLDR.	MODEL	DELV.NO.	BLDR.DATE	NOTES
5	GE	U30B	150-154	68/01	2nd,TO BN 5480-5484,SCR.86
9	GE	U23C	460-468	69/04	BN 5200-5208, SCR. 84/11
15	EMD	SD45	516-530	69/01	BN 6457-6471, MOST TO CNW
20	EMD	GP40	620-639	68/02	BN 3020-3039, SOME REBLT.MK L/88
9	EMD	SD40	879-887	68/04	C&S/BN 6339-6347 SOME RET.
4	GE	U30C	890-893	68/06-68/07	C&S/BN 5396-5399 SCR.87/03

QTY.	BLDR.	MODEL	DELV.NO.	BLDR.DATE	NOTES

CCR-CORINTH & COUNCE RAILROAD CO.

QTY.	BLDR.	MODEL	DELV.NO.	BLDR.DATE	NOTES
1	EMD	SW1001	1003	74/10	
1	EMD	SW1001	1004	80/01	
1	EMD	SW1001	1005	81/05	

CHP-FERROCARRIL de CHIHUAHUA AL PACIFICO, S.A. de C.V.

QTY.	BLDR.	MODEL	DELV.NO.	BLDR.DATE	NOTES
10	EMD	GP38-2	900-909	79/02-79/03	(2nd) TO NDM 9428-9437
2	EMD	GP38-2	910-911	80/04	TO NDM 9438,9439,HI-NOSE STEAM GEN.
8	EMD	GP40	1000-1007	71/06	TO NDM 8410-8417
9	EMD	GP40-2	1008-1016	75/06	TO NDM 7000-7008 (2nd)
6	EMD	GP40-2	1017-1022	76/01	TO NDM 7009-7014,(2nd), 1019-22 HAVE HI-NOSE STEAM GEN. EQUIPPED
7	EMD	GP40-2	1023-1029	81/07	TO NDM 7015-7021 (2nd)
7	EMD	GP40-2	1030-1036	82/03	TO NDM 7022-7028 (2nd)

CHZ-COAHUIL & ZACATECAS RAILWAY (MEXICO)

QTY.	BLDR.	MODEL	DELV.NO.	BLDR.DATE	NOTES
1	EMD	GA18	800	68/02	

CI-CAMBRIA & INDIANA RAILROAD CO.

QTY.	BLDR.	MODEL	DELV.NO.	BLDR.DATE	NOTES
2	EMD	SW1500	15-16	68/06	
2	EMD	MP15DC	19-20	75/08	

CIM-CHICAGO & ILL. MIDLAND
70, EMD, SD38-2
BLT. 74/05
GALESBURG, IL. 80/11

CIM-CHICAGO & ILLINOIS MIDLAND RAILWAY CO.

QTY.	BLDR.	MODEL	DELV.NO.	BLDR.DATE	NOTES
6	EMD	SD38-2	70-75	74/05	

QTY.	BLDR.	MODEL	DELV.NO.	BLDR.DATE	NOTES

CLC-COLUMBIA & COWLITZ RAILWAY CO.

QTY.	BLDR.	MODEL	DELV.NO.	BLDR.DATE	NOTES
1	ALCO	C415	701	68/11	

CMER-CURTIS, MILBURN & EASTERN RAILROAD CO.

QTY.	BLDR.	MODEL	DELV.NO.	BLDR.DATE	NOTES
1	EMD	GP38-2	810	81/01	LATER LETTERED FOR CW,
3	EMD	GP38-2	817-819	81/01	(CHEHALIS WESTERN)

CN-CANADIAN NATIONAL
5022, GMD, SD40
BLT. 68/02
DULUTH, MN. 80/06

CN-CANADIAN NATIONAL RAILWAYS

QTY.	BLDR.	MODEL	DELV.NO.	BLDR.DATE	NOTES
19	GMD	HBU-4	260-278	78/10-78/11	HUMP BOOSTER SLUG
4	GMD	HBU-4	279-282	80/03	HUMP BOOSTER SLUG
12	GMD	YBU-4	451-462	80/07	YARD BOOSTER SLUG
42	MLW	C630	2002-2043	67/12-68/06	
4	BBD	HR616W	2100-2103	82/02-82/08	LEASED 83/02, BBD FOR DEMOS
16	BBD	HR616W	2104-2119	82/02-82/08	
20	MLW	M636	2300-2319	70/04-70/09	(2300-04,11,12,18,21,30,
20	MLW	M636	2320-2339	71/01-71/03	31, TO CARTIER MINING)
30	MLW	M420W	2500-2529	73/05-73/10	2511,2526 SCR.RE#3500-3529
30	MLW	M420W	2530-2559	74/03-74/07	2535,2552 SCR.RE#3530-3559
20	MLW	M420W	2560-2579	76/10-77/02	RE# 3560-3579 IN 1986
10	BBD	HR412W	2580-2589	81/09-81/11	
68	GMD	SD40	5008-5075	67/11-68/12	5011,5018 SCR. 5062 IN 86
50	GMD	SD40	5076-5125	69/02-69/12	5103 SCR.87/03, 5104 IN 86
50	GMD	SD40	5126-5175	69/12-71/04	5140,5151 SCR.
65	GMD	SD40	5176-5240	71/04-71/12	
21	GMD	SD40-2W	5241-5261	75/05-75/06	5253 SCR.
17	GMD	SD40-2W	5262-5278	75/06-75/07	
15	GMD	SD40-2W	5279-5293	76/01	

CN-CANADIAN NATIONAL RAILWAYS, cont'd

CN-CANADIAN NATIONAL
5360, GMD, SD40-2W
BLT. 80/12
REGINA, SK. 83/10

QTY.	BLDR.	MODEL	DELV.NO.	BLDR.DATE	NOTES
20	GMD	SD40-2W	5294-5313	78/07-78/10	5299-5313 OWNED ONT.HYDRO
10	GMD	SD40-2W	5314-5323	79/12	
30	GMD	SD40-2W	5324-5353	80/04-80/05	
10	GMD	SD40-2W	5354-5363	80/12	
25	GMD	SD50F	5400-5424	85/04-85/08	
15	GMD	SD50F	5425-5439	85/08-86/02	
20	GMD	SD50F	5440-5459	87/02-87/07	
37	GMD	GP38-2	5500-5536	72/11-73/02	RE# 4700-4736
20	GMD	SD60F	5504-5523	89/02-89/03	
23	GMD	GP38-2	5537-5559	73/02-73/03	RE# 221-224, 200-220 EVEN #'s ONLY, 201-215 ODD #'s ONLY
1	GMD	GP38-2W	5560	73/06	
50	GMD	GP38-2W	5561-5610	73/10-74/01	5586 86/03,5601,5604 SCR.
25	GMD	SD50F	9000-9024	88/10-88/12	
91	GMD	GP40-2LW	9400-9490	74/03-74/09	9435 SCR.87/03, 9487 SCR.
40	GMD	GP40-2LW	9491-9530	74/09-74/11	
65	GMD	GP40-2LW	9531-9595	75/02-75/05	
37	GMD	GP40-2LW	9596-9632	75/07-75/09	
35	GMD	GP40-2LW	9633-9667	76/03-76/05	
4	GMD	SD60F	9900-9903	85/08-85/10	PROTOTYPE TEST UNITS

CNJ-CENTRAL RAILROAD CO. of NEW JERSEY

13	EMD	GP40P	3671-3683	68/10	TO NJT 4100-4112

CNW-CHICAGO & NORTH WESTERN
4626, EMD, GP38-2
BLT. 79/12
BEVERLY, IA. 80/10

QTY.	BLDR.	MODEL	DELV.NO.	BLDR.DATE	NOTES
CNW-CHICAGO & NORTH WESTERN TRANSPORTATION CO.					
7	GE	U30C	930-936	68/01-68/02	934 TO NJT U34CH 4183,78/10 REST TO NDM SAME #, ALL RET. BY L/88, EXCEPT 932
41	EMD	SD45	937-977	69/01-69/02	942-945,953,960-963 RET.86
2	GE	SL136	1198-1199	78/10	TO BN 1100-1101,82/11, THEN 1101 TO SEPX 1101
5	EMD	MP15DC	1302-1306	75/02	
10	EMD	MP15DC	1307-1316	75/03	
25	EMD	GP15-1	4400-4424	76/06-76/07	
26	EMD	GP38-2	4600-4625	79/11-79/12	ORIG. ORDERED BY RI
9	EMD	GP38-2	4626-4634	79/12	ORIG. ORDERED BY RI
50	EMD	GP50	5050-5099	80/05-80/09	5051 WRK/SCR L/86
10	EMD	SD38-2	6650-6659	75/01	
10	EMD	SD40-2	6801-6810	73/08	
5	EMD	SD40-2	6811-6815	73/12	
50	EMD	SD40-2	6816-6865	74/02-74/04	
25	EMD	SD40-2	6866-6890	74/09	6870 WRK, TO NRE
35	EMD	SD40-2	6891-6925	75/01-75/02	
10	EMD	SD40-2	6926-6935	76/11	
35	EMD	SD50	7000-7034	85/11-85/12	
55	EMD	SD60	8001-8055	86/08-86/10	
CO-CHESEAPEAKE & OHIO RAILWAY CO.					
25	EMD	GP15T(AC)	1500-1524	82/10-82/11	CS TO CSXT SAME #
15	GE	U23B	2300-2314	69/09	(TO CSXT 3200,03-05,09-11
15	GE	U23B	2315-2329	69/10	3218,21-25,29,REST SCR.86)
9	GE	U30C	3304-3312	68/05-68/06	TO CS,ALL RET.83/08,SCR.84
15	EMD	GP40	3780-3794	71/12	TO CS/CSXT 6555-6569

CO-CHESEAPEAKE & OHIO RAILWAY CO. cont'd

QTY.	BLDR.	MODEL	DELV.NO.	BLDR.DATE	NOTES
20	EMD	GP39	3900-3919	69/05-69/07	TO CS/CSXT 4280-4299
6	EMD	GP40	4065-4070	71/05	TO CS/CSXT 6640-6645
18	EMD	GP40	4071-4089	71/05-71/08	TO CS/CSXT 6826-6844
10	EMD	GP40	4090-4099	71/12	TO CS/CSXT 6845-6854
20	EMD	GP40-2	4165-4184	72/11	4170 RET.TO CS/CSXT 6064-6083
20	EMD	GP40-2	4262-4281	78/01	4275 RET.TO CS/CSXT 6161-80,RE# 6400-19
5	EMD	GP40-2	4282-4286	78/02-78/03	CS TO CSXT 6181-6185, RE# 6420-6424
20	EMD	GP40-2	4372-4391	80/01	CS TO CSXT 6270-6289
30	EMD	GP40-2	4392-4421	80/02-80/03	CS TO CSXT 6290-6319
6	EMD	GP38	4820-4829	70/07-70/08	TO CS/CSXT 2120-2125
1	EMD	GP38	4826	70/08	TO CS, WRK/RET TO NRE
3	EMD	GP38	4827-4829	70/08	TO CS/CSXT 2127-2129
6	EMD	SD40	7501-7506	69/04	TO CS/CSXT 8360-8365
20	EMD	SD40	7507-7526	70/06-70/07	CS/CSXT 8366-8385,7518 RET
10	EMD	SD40	7527-7536	71/03	TO CS/CSXT 8386-8395
10	GE	U30B	8200-8209	71/12	TO CS/CSXT 5328-5337
13	GE	U30B	8210-8222	72/11-72/12	CS TO CSXT 5338-5350
10	GE	U30B	8225-8234	74/12	CS TO CSXT 5351-5362
10	GE	B30-7	8235-8244	78/05	CS/CSXT 5517-26,17,18 RET.
10	GE	B30-7	8245-8254	79/01-79/02	CS/CSXT 5527-36,34,35 RET.
10	GE	B30-7	8255-8264	79/06	CS TO CSXT 5537-5546
14	GE	B30-7	8265-8278	80/01	CS TO CSXT 5547-5560
20	GE	B30-7	8279-8298	81/03-81/05	CS TO CSXT 5561-5580
23	EMD	SD50	8553-8575	84/01-84/02	CS TO CSXT SAME #
20	EMD	SD50	8624-8643	85/10-85/11	CS TO CSXT SAME #

CP-CANADIAN PACIFIC RAILWAY (CP RAIL)

QTY.	BLDR.	MODEL	DELV.NO.	BLDR.DATE	NOTES
6	GMD	GP38AC	3000-3005	70/05	
15	GMD	GP38AC	3006-3020	71/02-71/03	
20	GMD	GP38-2	3021-3040	83/03-83/06	
45	GMD	GP38-2	3041-3085	85/10-86/01	
50	GMD	GP38-2	3086-3135	86/02-86/06	
8	MLW	C630	4500-4507	68/07-68/10	4506 WRK/SCR.
5	MLW	M630	4508-4512	69/11-70/01	
4	MLW	M630	4513-4516	70/01	RE# 4558-4561 IN 1971
8	MLW	M630	4550-4557	69/09-70/02	4552 SCR.
4	MLW	M630	4570-4573	69/10-70/03	
8	MLW	M630	4574-4581	69/10-70/03	RE# 4562-4569 IN 1971
44	MLW	M636	4700-4743	69/11-70/12	
1	MLW	M640	4744	71/02	4000HP, ONLY ONE BUILT
1	GMD	SD40-2	5560(2nd)	81/03	BUILT W/WRK COMPONENTS
24	GMD	SD40-2	5565-5588	72/02-72/03	1st 5583,84,86,88 SCR.
1	GMD	SD40-2	5583(2nd)	85/01	BUILT W/WRK COMPONENTS
1	GMD	SD40-2	5584(2nd)	83/09	BUILT W/WRK COMPONENTS
40	GMD	SD40-2	5589-5628	72/05-72/07	5598 SCR. BY 79
30	EMD	SD40-2	5629-5658	72/11-72/12	5634 SCR. BY 79
16	GMD	SD40-2	5659-5674	73/04-73/06	
43	GMD	SD40-2	5675-5717	74/12-75/02	1st 5693 SCR.
1	GMD	SD40-2	5693(2nd)	83/09	BUILT W/WRK COMPONENTS
40	GMD	SD40-2	5718-5757	75/09-75/11	
20	GMD	SD40-2	5758-5777	76/01-76/02	

CP-CANADIAN PACIFIC RAILWAY (CP RAIL), cont'd

CP-CANADIAN PACIFIC
5864, GMD, SD40-2
BLT. 78/07
KAMLOOPS, BC. 78/12

QTY.	BLDR.	MODEL	DELV.NO.	BLDR.DATE	NOTES
1	GMD	SD40-2	5778	78/02	
11	GMD	SD40-2	5779-5789	78/02-78/07	OWNED BY ONT. HYDRO
10	GMD	SD40-2	5790-5799	78/11-78/12	
6	GMD	SD40-2	5800-5805	74/12	(RCT)
10	GMD	SD40-2	5806-5815	74/01-74/02	(RCT)
20	GMD	SD40-2	5816-5835	74/02-74/03	(RCT)
1	GMD	SD40-2	5836	74/12	(RCT)
23	GMD	SD40-2	5837-5859	77/10-78/02	
5	GMD	SD40-2	5860-5864	78/07	OWNED BY ONT. HYDRO
15	GMD	SD40-2	5865-5879	84/09-84/10	(RCT)
15	GMD	SD40-2	5900-5914	78/12-79/01	
35	GMD	SD40-2	5915-5949	79/10-79/11	
75	GMD	SD40-2	5950-6024	80/10-81/03	6008 WRK/RET 86/05
30	GMD	SD40-2	6025-6054	82/12-83/08	
15	GMD	SD40-2	6055-6069	84/11-85/01	
25	GMD	SD40-2F	9000-9024	88/10-88/12	

CR-CONSOLIDATED RAIL CORP. (CONRAIL)

100	EMD	GP15-1	1600-1699	79/07-79/12	
40	GE	B23-7	1900-1939	78/04-78/06	1903-1909 TO MNCR 801-807
27	GE	B23-7	1940-1966	78/07-78/09	
25	GE	B23-7	1967-1991	79/03-79/05	
32	GE	B23-7	1992-2023	79/06-79/09	
10	GE	U23B	2789-2798	77/05-77/06	
17	GE	B23-7	2800-2816	77/09-77/11	
4	GE	U36B	2971-2974	76/09	AT 4013-16,BUT NEVER DELV
33	EMD	GP40-2	3280-3312	77/04-77/05	
33	EMD	GP40-2	3313-3345	78/05-78/06	3317,3319 SCR.

CR-CONSOLIDATED RAIL CORP.(CONRAIL) con't

QTY.	BLDR.	MODEL	DELV.NO.	BLDR.DATE	NOTES
40	EMD	GP40-2	3346-3385	79/03-79/05	
18	EMD	GP40-2	3386-3403	80/01-80/02	3394 WRK/SCR 88/01
49	GE	B36-7	5000-5048	83/10-83/12	5017 WRK/SCR 88, 5045 SCR
11	GE	B36-7	5049-5059	83/12	
30	GE	DASH840B	5060-5089	88/04-88/05	
22	GE	C39-8	6000-6021	86/06-86/08	
25	GE	DASH840C	6025-6049	89/03-89/04	
46	EMD	SD40-2	6358-6403	77/06-77/08	
37	EMD	SD40-2	6404-6440	77/08-77/09	
42	EMD	SD40-2	6441-6482	78/09-78/11	
42	EMD	SD40-2	6483-6524	79/07-79/10	
50	GE	C30-7A	6550-6599	84/05-84/06	
10	GE	C30-7	6600-6609	77/11	
10	GE	C32-8	6610-6619	84/09	
25	GE	C36-7	6620-6644	85/06	
40	EMD	SD50	6700-6739	83/10-83/12	
40	EMD	SD50	6740-6779	84/04-84/06	
25	EMD	SD50	6780-6804	85/04-85/05	

CR-CONRAIL
6817, EMD, SD50
BLT. 86/01
BINGHAMTON, NY. 87/06

30	EMD	SD50	6805-6834	86/01-86/02	
25	EMD	SD60	6845-6869	89/06-89/07	
18	EMD	GP38-2	8163-8180	77/06	
21	EMD	GP38-2	8181-8201	78/05-78/06	
22	EMD	GP38-2	8202-8223	78/07-78/08	
32	EMD	GP38-2	8224-8255	78/09	
26	EMD	GP38-2	8256-8281	79/05-79/06	

QTY.	BLDR.	MODEL	DELV.NO.	BLDR.DATE	NOTES

CRR-CLINCHFIELD RAILROAD CO.

QTY.	BLDR.	MODEL	DELV.NO.	BLDR.DATE	NOTES
1	EMD	SD40	3008	68/09	TO FL 8283, TO SBD/CSXT 8342
6	EMD	SD40	3009-3014	69/01-69/02	FL 8284-8289, TO SBD/CSXT 8343-8348
5	EMD	SD40	3015-3019	71/06-71/07	FL 8290-8294, TO SBD/CSXT 8349-8353
5	EMD	SD40	3020-3024	71/06	FL 8295-8299, TO SBD/CSXT 8354-8358
7	GE	U36C	3600-3606	71/10-71/11	TO SCL 2125-2131, TO SBD/CSXT 7300-7306
10	EMD	SD45-2	3607-3716	72/11	FL 3607-3616, TO SBD/CSXT 8965-8974

CRR-CLINCHFIELD RR. CO.
3617, EMD, SD45-2
BLT. 74/02
DOLTON,IL.NEW I/T, 74/03

QTY.	BLDR.	MODEL	DELV.NO.	BLDR.DATE	NOTES
8	EMD	SD45-2	3617-3624	74/02	TO FL 3617-24, TO SBD/CSXT 8975-8982
5	EMD	GP38-2	6000-6004	78/06	NEW FL, TO SBD/CSXT 2651-2655
2	EMD	GP38-2	6005-6006	79/04	NEW FL, TO SBD/CSXT 2656-2657
1	EMD	GP38-2	6045	79/08	NEW FL, TO WofA, TO SBD/CSXT 2696
3	EMD	SD40-2	8127-8129	80/08	NEW FL, TO SBD/CSXT 8127-8129
1	EMD	SD40-2	8131	81/09	NEW FL, TO SBD/CSXT 8131
1	EMD	SD40-2	8132	81/09	NEW FL, TO SBD/CSXT 8132

CSL-CHICAGO SHORT LINE RAILWAY CO.

QTY.	BLDR.	MODEL	DELV.NO.	BLDR.DATE	NOTES
2	EMD	SW1001	28-29	74/09	
1	EMD	SW1500	30	68/09	
1	EMD	SW1500	31	71/07	

CSS-CHICAGO, SOUTH SHORE & SOUTH BEND RAILROAD

QTY.	BLDR.	MODEL	DELV.NO.	BLDR.DATE	NOTES
10	EMD	GP38-2	2000-2009	81/01	

CUVA-CUYAHOGA VALLEY RAILWAY CO.

QTY.	BLDR.	MODEL	DELV.NO.	BLDR.DATE	NOTES
1	EMD	SW1001	1051	73/02	

QTY.	BLDR.	MODEL	DELV.NO.	BLDR.DATE	NOTES

CW-COLORADO & WYOMING RAILWAY CO.

2	EMD	GP38-2	2001-2002	73/11	

DH-DELAWARE & HUDSON RAILWAY CO.

8	GE	U23B	301-308	68/08	RE# 2301-08,TO MEC 280-287 ALL BUT 285,288 SCR.88/02
6	GE	U23B	309-314	68/09	RE#2309-14,TO MEC 288-293
1	GE	U23B	315	68/09	SCRAPPED 1971
1	GE	U23B	316	68/09	RE#2316,TO MEC 294,THEN SOLD TO PERU COPPER CO. IN 1986
6	GE	U30C	707-712	68/01	TO NDEM SAME # 12/78, RET.M/80's
3	GE	U33C	754-756	70/09	ALL RET. BY E/88
3	GE	U33C	757-759	70/11	758,759 RE# 658,659,RET E/88
3	GE	U33C	760-762	70/12	761,762 RE# 661,662,RET E/88
20	EMD	GP39-2	7601-7620	76/03-76/04	TO BM 350-369 MIXED NO's RET'D TO DH L/88,7316 RET 88

DMIR-DULUTH, MISSABE & IRON RANGE RAILWAY CO.

8	EMD	SD38AC	201-208	71/06	
5	EMD	SD38-2	209-213	75/03	210 TO BLE 86/05, SAME #

DRGW-RIO GRANDE
3101, EMD, GP40-2
BLT. 72/04
DENVER, CO. 77/10

DRGW-DENVER, RIO GRANDE & WESTERN RAILROAD CO.

3	EMD	SW1000	147-149	68/04	
5	EMD	GP40	3081-3085	69/10	
8	EMD	GP40	3086-3093	71/11	
12	EMD	GP40-2	3094-3105	72/04	
10	EMD	GP40-2	3106-3115	72/12	

DRGW-DENVER, RIO GRANDE & WESTERN RAILROAD CO. cont'd

QTY.	BLDR.	MODEL	DELV.NO.	BLDR.DATE	NOTES
12	EMD	GP40-2	3116-3127	74/09	
1	EMD	GP40-2	3128	74/11	
2	EMD	GP40-2	3129-3130	83/03	
12	EMD	SD45	5325-5336	68/03-68/05	
4	EMD	SD45	5337-5340	68/03	
15	EMD	SD40T-2	5341-5355	74/10	
18	EMD	SD40T-2	5356-5373	75/07-75/08	
12	EMD	SD40T-2	5374-5385	77/01	
12	EMD	SD40T-2	5386-5397	78/08	
16	EMD	SD40T-2	5398-5413	80/03	
17	EMD	SD50	5501-5517	84/08-84/09	BUILT TO CSX SPECS

DS-DURHAM & SOUTHERN RAILWAY CO.

4	EMD	GP38-2	2000-2003	72/12	TO SBD 556-559, TO CSXT 2556-2559

DTI-DETROIT,TOLEDO &
IRONTON RR.CO.
219, EMD, GP38AC
BLT. 71/07
BLUE ISLAND, IL. 83/10

DTI-DETROIT, TOLEDO & IRONTON RAILROAD CO.

2	EMD	GP38	205-206	69/09	TO GTW 6205-6206
8	EMD	GP38	207-214	70/05-70/05	TO GTW 6207-6214
6	EMD	GP38AC	215-220	71/07	TO GTW 6215-6220
7	EMD	GP38-2	221-227	75/07	TO GTW 6221-6228
3	EMD	SD38	250-252	69/07-69/08	TO GTW 6250-6252
2	EMD	SD38AC	253-254	71/07	TO GTW 6253-6254
6	EMD	GP40	400-405	68/06	TO GTW 6400-6405
8	EMD	GP40-2	406-413	72/10	TO GTW 6406-6413
8	EMD	GP40-2	414-421	73/10	TO GTW 6414-6421
4	EMD	GP40-2	422-425	79/11	TO GTW 6422-6425
1	EMD	GP38-2	1776	75/07	R/W/B, RE#228,TO GTW 6228

QTY.	BLDR.	MODEL	DELV.NO.	BLDR.DATE	NOTES

DVR-DEVCO RAILWAY, CAPE BRETON DEVELOPMENT CORP.

QTY.	BLDR.	MODEL	DELV.NO.	BLDR.DATE	NOTES
4	GMD	GP38-2	216-219	79/05-79/06	
4	GMD	GP38-2	220-223	81/03	
4	GMD	GP38-2	224-227	82/06	
1	GMD	GP38-2	228	83/07	

EEC-EAST ERIE COMMERCIAL RAILROAD

QTY.	BLDR.	MODEL	DELV.NO.	BLDR.DATE	NOTES
2	GE	SL85	21-22	80/03	

EJE-ELGIN,JOLIET & EASTERN
650, EMD, SD38
BLT. 70/01
CHICAGO HEIGHTS, IL. 72/01

EJE-ELGIN, JOLIET & EASTERN RAILWAY CO.

QTY.	BLDR.	MODEL	DELV.NO.	BLDR.DATE	NOTES
2	EMD	SW1001	444,445	71/08	
6	EMD	SD38	650-655	70/01-70/02	
4	EMD	SD38-2	656-659	74/01	
5	EMD	SD38-2	660-664	75/01	
4	EMD	SD38-2	665-668	75/11	668 PAINTED R/W/B IN 76
4	EMD	GP38-2	700-703	72/12	(2nd) SOLD TO BS 700-703
1	EMD	GP38-2	704	73/10	(2nd) SOLD TO BS 704

EL-ERIE LACKAWANNA RAILWAY CO.

QTY.	BLDR.	MODEL	DELV.NO.	BLDR.DATE	NOTES
3	GE	U33C	3301-3303	68/07	TO DH 751-753, TO CR 6564-6566,RE# 6869-6871 RET. 86
3	GE	U33C	3304-3306	68/07	TO CR 6567-6569, RE# 6872-6874, ALL RET.TO NW IN 84 T/I GE 85
9	GE	U33C	3307-3315	69/08	(3600 hp),TO CR 6570-6578 RE# 6875-6883, RET.87/12
13	GE	U36C	3316-3328	72/11	TO CR 6587-6599, RE# 6884-6896, RET 87/12

EL-ERIE LACKAWANNA RAILWAY CO. cont'd

QTY.	BLDR.	MODEL	DELV.NO.	BLDR.DATE	NOTES
23	GE	U34CH	3351-3373	70/10-71/05	TO CR SAME#,TO NJT 4151-73
9	GE	U34CH	3374-3382	72/12-73/01	TO CR SAME#,TO NJT 4174-82
14	EMD	SD45	3621-3634	68/05	TO CR 6086-6099, RET.BY 86
2	EMD	SDP45	3635-3636	69/05	TO CR 6667,6668,TO NW SAME#
1	EMD	SDP45	3637	69/05	WRK,TO NW SLUG 9920,RE#9950
16	EMD	SDP45	3638-3653	69/05-69/06	TO CR 6669-6684,TO NW SAME#
15	EMD	SDP45	3654-3668	70/07-70/08	TO CR 6685-6699,TO VMV 86
13	EMD	SD45-2	3669-3681	72/10	TO CR 6654-6666

FCP-FERROCARRIL del PACIFICO (MEXICO)

QTY.	BLDR.	MODEL	DELV.NO.	BLDR.DATE	NOTES
4	GE	U30C	401-404	69/10-69/12	401 SCR. TO BE RE# NDM 7901-7903
4	GE	U30C	405-408	71/03	405,407 SCR. TO BE NDM 7904,7906
10	GE	U36C	409-418	75/02-75/03	410 RET. TO BE RE# NDM 8988-8996
4	GE	C36-7	419-422	79/07	TO BE RE# NDM 9653-9656
11	GE	C36-7	423-433	79/10	433 RET.82, TO BE NDM 9657-9666
22	GE	C30-7	434-455	81/06-81/08	449 RET. TO BE RE# NDM 9667-9687
4	GE	C30-7	456-459	86/05	NDEM OWNED,TO BE NDM 11149-11152
15	MLW	M420TR	522-536	75/07-75/09	526-528 WRK/SCR.TO NDM 7600-7611
10	GE	U23B	537-546	75/08-75/09	TO BE RE# NDM 9182-9191
16	MLW	M424W	560-575	80/07-81/07	560,63,66,68 RET.T/NDM 9556-9567
4	ALCO	C628	607-610	68/12	607 RET. TO BE RE# NDM 8335-8337
8	MLW	M636	651-658	72/06	654 RET.82 TO BE NDM 8000-8006(2nd)
8	MLW	M636	659-666	73/11-73/12	660 RET. TO BE RE# NDM 8007-8013(2nd)

FEC-FLORIDA EAST COAST RAILWAY CO.

QTY.	BLDR.	MODEL	DELV.NO.	BLDR.DATE	NOTES
10	EMD	GP40	401-410	71/01-71/03	402 WRK/SCR. 79/07
5	EMD	GP40-2	411-415	72/11	
3	EMD	GP40-2	416-418	74/10	
5	EMD	GP40-2	419-423	79/10	423 WRK/REBLT TO 437,87/12
1	EMD	GP40-2	424	80/01	
5	EMD	GP40-2	425-429	80/08	
2	EMD	GP40-2	430-431	84/12	
1	EMD	GP40-2	432	85/12	
2	EMD	GP40-2	433-434	86/12	LAST GP40-2's BUILT
4	EMD	GP38-2	501-504	77/11	
6	EMD	GP38-2	505-510	78/04	
1	EMD	GP38-2	511	78/04	

FUS-FERROCARRILES UNIDOS del SURESTE (MEXICO)

QTY.	BLDR.	MODEL	DELV.NO.	BLDR.DATE	NOTES
2	EMD	GP38	512-513	71/06	TO BE RE# NDM 8255,8256
3	EMD	GP38-2	514-516	72/08	514 RET.TO BE RE# NDM 9415,9416
5	EMD	GP38-2	517-521	75/07	TO BE RE# NDM 9417-9421
3	GE	B23-7	522-524	79/12	ASSEMBLED IN BRAZIL,522,524 RET. 523 TO BE RE# NDM 9181
3	MLW	M424W	525-527	81/08	TO BE RE# NDM 9553-9555
3	EMD	GP38-2	528-530	81/08	TO BE RE# NDM 9422-9424
3	EMD	GP38-2	531-533	82/03	TO BE RE# NDM 9425-9427
4	EMD	SD40-2	601-604	72/09	TO BE RE# NDM 13005-13008

GA-GEORGIA RR.
753, EMD, GP40
BLT. 68/07
DOLTON,IL.NEW I/T,68/08

QTY.	BLDR.	MODEL	DELV.NO.	BLDR.DATE	NOTES
GA-GEORGIA RAILROAD					
2	EMD	GP40	753-754	68/07	TO SBD/CSXT 6655,6656
2	EMD	GP40-2	755-756	72/12	TO SBD 6643,6644, TO CSXT 6389,6390
2	EMD	GP38-2	6009-6010	79/04	FL TO SBD/CSXT 2660-2661
GBW-GREEN BAY & WESTERN RAILROAD CO.					
1	ALCO	C430	315	68/02	STORED UNSERVICEABLE
GMO-GULF, MOBILE & OHIO RAILROAD CO.					
20	EMD	GP38	701-720	69/08	TO ICG 9520-9539
12	EMD	GP38AC	721-732	71/03-71/04	TO ICG 9540-9551
1	EMD	GP38AC	733	71/12	TO ICG 9552
15	EMD	GP38-2	740-754	72/04-72/08	TO ICG 9560-9574
GN-GREAT NORTHERN RAILWAY CO.					
9	EMD	SD45	418-426	68/07	TO BN 6448-6456, TO CNW
6	EMD	F45	427-432	69/05-69/06	TO BN 6600-6605, ALL SCR.
3	EMD	F45	433-435	69/08	TO BN 6606-08,TO UTAH S/#
4	EMD	F45	436-439	69/08	TO BN 6609-6612, ALL SCR.
1	EMD	F45	440	69/08	TO BN 6613, TO UTAH SAME#
9	GE	U33C	2530-2538	68/05-68/06	TO BN 5700-5708, ALL SCR.84
6	GE	U33C	2539-2544	69/04	TO BN 5709-5714, ALL SCR.84
GNA-GRAYSONIA, NASHVILLE & ASHDOWN RAILROAD CO.					
1	EMD	MP15DC	80	80/09	

QTY.	BLDR.	MODEL	DELV.NO.	BLDR.DATE	NOTES

GNWR-GENESEE & WYOMING RAILROAD CO.

2	EMD	MP15DC	45,46	80/10,80/11	

GRR-GEORGETOWN RAILROAD CO.

1	EMD	MP15DC	1011	78/12	
1	EMD	MP15DC	1012	80/11	
1	EMD	MP15DC	1013	81/05	WRK/85,SOLD NRE,NOW REBLT

GTRA-GOLDEN TRIANGLE RAILROAD

1	EMD	MP15AC	G1	80/09	OWNED BY WEYERHAUSER CORP.

GTW-GRAND TRUNK WESTERN
5922, EMD, SD40
BLT. 70/08
SOUTH HOLLAND, IL. 74/10

GTW-GRAND TRUNK WESTERN RAILROAD CO.

12	EMD	GP38AC	5800-5811	71/11	5808 TRANSFERED TO CV 88/12
20	EMD	GP38-2	5812-5831	78/12	
5	EMD	GP38-2	5832-5836	80/01	
12	EMD	SD40	5900-5911	69/08-69/10	5904-5911 ASSIGNED DWP
9	EMD	SD40	5912-5920	70/01	
9	EMD	SD40	5921-5929	70/08-70/09	

GWF-GALVESTON WHARVES

2	EMD	SW1001	301-302	75/10	
1	EMD	SW1001	303	77/12	
2	EMD	SW1001	304-305	80/07	

QTY.	BLDR.	MODEL	DELV.NO.	BLDR.DATE	NOTES

HBT-HOUSTON, BELT & TERMINAL RAILWAY CO.

QTY.	BLDR.	MODEL	DELV.NO.	BLDR.DATE	NOTES
3	EMD	SW1000	40-42	68/01	40 RET. SOLD TO NRE
3	EMD	SW1500	50-52	69/12	
3	EMD	SW1500	53-55	71/05-71/10	
5	EMD	MP15DC	60-64	79/10	

IC-ILLINOIS CENTRAL
6005, EMD, SD40
BLT. 68/01
MARKHAM, IL. 72/03

IC-ILLINOIS CENTRAL RAILROAD CO.

QTY.	BLDR.	MODEL	DELV.NO.	BLDR.DATE	NOTES
6	ALCO	C636	1100-1105	68/05	TO PNC 80/01
10	EMD	GP40	3060-3069	69/08	
1	EMD	GP40	3070	70/02	REBLT RE# 3077 IN 1974
1	EMD	GP40	3071	70/02	REBLT RE# 3070(2nd)
3	EMD	GP40	3072-3074	70/02	RETURNED TO LESSOR L/85,THEN HL
10	GE	U33C	5050-5059	68/04-68/05	5055 SCR 69/09,REST SCR.84
6	EMD	SD40	6000-6005	68/01	
13	EMD	SD40A	6006-6018	69/08-69/09	6012 REBLT RE# 6024
5	EMD	SD40A	6019-6023	70/01	TO HL, L/86, RE# 5019-5023
10	EMD	GP38AC	9500-9509	70/02	TO MKT 325-334
1	EMD	GP38AC	9510	70/02	RETIRED
9	EMD	GP38AC	9511-9519	70/02	TO MKT 335,337-343,9512 TO CMNW 2048 87/04

ICG-ILLINOIS CENTRAL GULF RAILROAD CO.

QTY.	BLDR.	MODEL	DELV.NO.	BLDR.DATE	NOTES
4	EMD	SD40-2	6030-6033	75/12	
40	EMD	GP38-2	9600-9639	74/11-74/12	

IHB-INDIANA HARBOR BELT RAILROAD CO.

QTY.	BLDR.	MODEL	DELV.NO.	BLDR.DATE	NOTES
6	EMD	SW1500	9216-9221	68/06-68/07	9219-21 SLUG MASTER UNITS
5	EMD	SW1500	9223-9227	70/06	RESOLD PC ON DELV.9226 SCR.

QTY	BLDR	MODEL	DELV.NO.	BLDR.DATE	NOTES

ITC-ILLINOIS TERMINAL RAILROAD CO.

QTY	BLDR	MODEL	DELV.NO.	BLDR.DATE	NOTES
6	EMD	SW1500	1509-1515	70/02	TO NW 2290-2296,2294 TO SAN 2295 TO MRS 257, 88/01
4	EMD	GP38-2	2001-2004	77/05	TO NW 4160-4163
3	EMD	SD39	2301-2303	69/05	TO NW 2961-63,BM 690-692
3	EMD	SD39	2304-2306	69/05	TO NW 2964-2966,2964 T/ATSF SLUG 140(2nd),REST T/MK 84, 2965 SCR. 2966 TO MEC 693

IU-INDIANAPOLIS UNION RAILWAY CO.

QTY	BLDR	MODEL	DELV.NO.	BLDR.DATE	NOTES
1	EMD	SW1500	26	68/10	
3	EMD	SW1500	30-32	72/12	

KCNW-KELLEY'S CREEK & NORTHWESTERN RAILROAD CO.

QTY	BLDR	MODEL	DELV.NO.	BLDR.DATE	NOTES
1	EMD	MP15DC	1	76/12	
1	EMD	MP15DC	2	80/09	

KCS-KANSAS CITY SOUTHERN
677, EMD, SD40-2
BLT. 78/03
SHREVEPORT, LA. 81/08

KCS-KANSAS CITY SOUTHERN RAILWAY CO.

QTY	BLDR	MODEL	DELV.NO.	BLDR.DATE	NOTES
4	EMD	SD40	614-617	68/08	
2	EMD	SD40	618-621	68/08	(RCT), 620,621 (RCR)
4	EMD	SD40	622-625	70/06	TO HL, TO SOO 6400-6403
1	EMD	SD40	626-627	70/06	TO HL, TO SOO 6404,6405
4	EMD	SD40	628-633	71/03	632,633 HAVE RCT
2	EMD	SD40	634-635	71/03	(RCR)
1	EMD	SD40	636	71/03	
10	EMD	SD40-2	637-646	72/01	
6	EMD	SD40-2	647-652	72/11	
2	EMD	SD40-2	653-654	72/11	(RCT)

KCS-KANSAS CITY SOUTHERN RAILWAY CO, cont'd

QTY.	BLDR.	MODEL	DELV.NO.	BLDR.DATE	NOTES
2	EMD	SD40-2	655-656	72/11	(RCR)
4	EMD	SD40-2	657-660	74/01	
3	EMD	SD40-2	661-663	74/01	(RCT)
3	EMD	SD40-2	664-666	74/01	(RCR)
8	EMD	SD40-2	667-674	76/08	673,674 HAVE RCT
2	EMD	SD40-2	675-676	76/08	(RCR)
3	EMD	SD40-2	677-679	78/03	(RCT)
3	EMD	SD40-2	680-682	78/03	(RCR)
2	EMD	SD40-2	683-684	78/06	(RCT)
2	EMD	SD40-2	685-686	78/06	(RCR)
2	EMD	SD40-2	687-688	80/06	(RCT)
4	EMD	SD40-2	689-692	80/06	689,690 HAVE RCR
2	EMD	SD40X	700-701	79/09	(RCT)
2	EMD	SD40X	702-703	79/09	(RCR)
10	EMD	SD50	704-713	81/05-81/06	
2	EMD	GP40-2	796-797	81/02	SLUG MASTER EQUIPPED
2	EMD	GP40-2	798-799	79/08	SLUG MASTER EQUIPPED
14	EMD	SW1500	1504-1517	68/08	RE# 4324-4337
6	EMD	SW1500	1518-1523	71/04	RE# 4338-4343
8	EMD	SW1500	1524-1531	71/04-71/05	RE# 4344-4351
10	EMD	SW1500	1532-1541	72/01	RE# 4352-4361
10	EMD	GP38-2	4000-4009	74/01	
2	EMD	GP38-2	4010-4011	78/06	
4	EMD	MP15DC	4363-4366	75/08	

KIT-KENTUCKY & INDIANA TERMINAL RAILROAD

2	EMD	SW1500	70-71	68/02	TO SOU SAME #
5	EMD	SW1500	72-76	71/03	TO SOU SAME #
3	EMD	SW1500	77-79	72/09	TO SOU SAME #
2	EMD	SW1500	80-81	73/10	TO SOU SAME #
2	EMD	SW1500	82-83	74/01	TO SOU SAME#,82 LAST BUILT

KNOR-KLAMATH NORTHERN RAILWAY CO.

1	GE	SL125	207	82/12	

LEF-LAKE ERIE, FRANKLIN & CLARION RAILROAD CO.

1	EMD	SW1500	23	71/08	TO WEIRTON STEEL, WV.
1	EMD	SW1500	24	72/11	TO WEIRTON STEEL, WV.
1	EMD	MP15DC	25	76/08	
1	EMD	MP15DC	26	77/10	
1	EMD	MP15DC	27	78/12	
1	EMD	MP15DC	28	79/11	

LI-LONG ISLAND RR.CO.
100, EMD, SW1001
BLT. 77/03
NEW YORK, NY. 87/09
PHOTO: JAMES D. BRADLEY

QTY	BLDR	MODEL	DELV.NO.	BLDR.DATE	NOTES

LI-LONG ISLAND RAILROAD CO.

QTY	BLDR	MODEL	DELV.NO.	BLDR.DATE	NOTES
8	EMD	SW1001	100-107	77/03	
23	EMD	MP15AC	150-172	77/03-77/04	
8	ALCO	C420	222-229	68/08	
22	EMD	GP38-2	250-271	76/01-76/02	252 DELV. R/W/B
6	EMD	GP38-2	272-277	77/03	

LN-LOUISVILLE & NASHVILLE RAILROAD CO.

QTY	BLDR	MODEL	DELV.NO.	BLDR.DATE	NOTES
5	EMD	SD40	1229-1233	69/04	TO SBD/CSXT 8305-8309
5	EMD	SD40	1234-1238	70/04	TO SBD/CSXT 8310-8314
10	EMD	SD40	1239-1248	70/08-70/09	TO SBD/CSXT 8315-8324
10	EMD	SD40	1249-1258	71/05	TO SBD/CSXT 8325-8334
2	EMD	SD40-2	1259-1260	74/03	TO SBD/CSXT 8163-8164
18	EMD	SD40-2	1261-1278	74/03	TO CSXT 8165-81,1270 SCR.
30	GE	U30C	1470-1499	72/06-72/08	1499 D/"XR" SCHEME,SCR/77 TO SBD/CSXT 7200-7228
14	GE	U30C	1534-1547	69/03-69/04	TO CSXT 7229-41,1542 SCR.
15	GE	U30C	1548-1562	69/10-70/03	TO SBD/CSXT 7242-7256
20	GE	U30C	1563-1582	71/06-71/07	TO SBD/CSXT 7257-7276
10	GE	U23B	2708-2717	73/01-73/04	TO SBD/CSXT 3238-3247
1	GE	U23B	2718	73/01-73/04	WRK/SCR. 77/11
9	GE	U23B	2719-2727	73/01-73/04	TO SBD/CSXT 3248-3256
25	GE	U23B	2728-2752	73/06-73/09	TO SBD/CSXT 3257-3281
18	GE	U23B	2753-2770	74/02-74/04	TO SBD/CSXT 3282-3299
1	GE	U23B	2771	74/04	WRK/SCR. 80/05
1	GE	U23B	2772	74/04	TO SBD/CSXT 3300
3	GE	U23B	2800-2802	74/12	TO SBD/CSXT 3301-3303
1	GE	U23B	2803	74/12	WRK/SCR.78/07
14	GE	U23B	2804-2817	74/12-75/02	TO SBD/CSXT 3305-3318
1	GE	U23B	2818	75/02	RE# 2803(2nd),CSXT 3304

LN-LOUISVILLE & NASHVILLE RAILROAD CO. cont'd

QTY	BLDR	MODEL	DELV.NO.	BLDR.DATE	NOTES
6	GE	U23B	2819-2824	75/02-75/03	TO SBD/CSXT 3319-3324
30	EMD	SD40-2	3554-3583	74/10-74/11	TO SBD/CSXT 8182-8211
22	EMD	SD40-2	3584-3605	77/09	FL TO SBD/CSXT 8212-8233
4	EMD	SD40-2	3606-3609	77/10	(RCT)FL/SBD/CSX 8234-8237
4	EMD	SD40-2	3610-3613	77/10	(RCR)FL/SBD/CSX 8238-8241
20	EMD	GP38AC	4000-4019	70/06-70/07	TO SBD 6221-6240,TO CSXT 2131-49,6221 WRK/SCR 86/02
10	EMD	GP38AC	4020-4029	71/05	TO SBD 6241-6250,TO CSXT 2150-2159
20	EMD	GP38AC	4030-4049	71/05-71/06	TO SBD 6251-6270,TO CSXT 2160-2179
10	EMD	GP38-2	4050-4059	72/01	TO CSXT 2560-2569
10	EMD	GP38-2	4060-4069	72/04	TO CSXT 2570-2579
20	EMD	GP38-2	4070-4089	72/09-72/10	TO CSXT 2580-2599
5	EMD	GP38-2	4090-4094	72/10	TO CSXT 2600-2604
1	EMD	GP38-2	4095	72/10	WRK/SCR. 80/01
4	EMD	GP38-2	4096-4099	72/10	TO CSXT 2605-2608
2	EMD	GP38-2	4100-4101	73/02	CSXT 2609, 4101 SCR.80/05
13	EMD	GP38-2	4102-4114	73/02-73/03	CSXT 2610-2622, 4108 SCR.
10	EMD	GP38-2	4115-4124	73/03	TO CSXT 2623-2632
20	EMD	GP38-2	4125-4144	73/08-73/09	CSXT 2633-2652, 4137 SCR.
10	EMD	MP15AC	4225-4234	78/03	DELV.FL.TO CSXT 1130-1139
5	EMD	SD38-2	4500-4504	75/01	TO SBD/CSXT 2450-2454
10	EMD	SW1500	5000-5009	70/04	TO SBD/CSXT 1100-1109
10	EMD	SW1500	5010-5019	71/11	TO SBD/CSXT 1110-1119
10	EMD	SW1500	5020-5029	72/11	TO SBD/CSXT 1120-1129
10	EMD	MP15DC	5030-5039	75/01	TO SBD/CSXT 1140-1149
8	GE	B23-7	5115-5122	78/02	FL.TO SBD/CSXT 3115-3122
1	GE	B23-7	5123	78/02	WRK/SCR. 82/01
6	GE	B23-7	5124-5129	78/02	FL TO SBD/CSXT 3123-3128

LN-LOUISVILLE & NASHVILLE
5117, GE, B23-7
BLT. 78/02
DOLTON, IL. 78/06

LN-LOUISVILLE & NASHVILLE RAILROAD CO. cont'd

QTY	BLDR	MODEL	DELV.NO.	BLDR.DATE	NOTES
20	EMD	GP38-2	6011-6030	79/02-79/04	FL.TO SBD/CSXT 2662-2681
14	EMD	GP38-2	6031-6044	79/07-79/08	FL.TO SBD/CSXT 2682-2695
17	EMD	GP40-2	6600-6616	80/03-80/04	FL.TO SBD/CSXT 6366-6382
					6370 REBLT & RE# 6413
16	GE	C30-7	7000-7015	79/02-79/03	FL.TO SBD/CSXT SAME#
20	GE	C30-7	7032-7051	79/09	FL.TO CSXT 7032-7044(2nd)
8	GE	C30-7	7062-7069	80/08	FL.TO SBD/CSXT SAME#
34	EMD	SD40-2	8000-8033	79/03-79/04	FL.TO SBD/CSXT SAME#
6	EMD	SD40-2	8034-8039	79/08	FL.TO SBD/CSXT SAME#
20	EMD	SD40-2	8067-8086	79/10-79/11	FL.TO SBD/CSXT SAME#
21	EMD	SD40-2	8095-8115	80/05-80/06	FL.TO SBD/CSXT SAME#
11	EMD	SD40-2	8116-8126	80/08	FL.TO SBD/CSXT SAME#
30	EMD	SD40-2	8133-8162	81/09-81/10	FL.TO CRR/SBD/CSXT SAME#

LPN-LONGVIEW, PORTLAND & NORTHERN RAILWAY CO.

QTY	BLDR	MODEL	DELV.NO.	BLDR.DATE	NOTES
1	EMD	SW1500	130	69/12	

LSI-LAKE SUPERIOR &
ISHPEMING RAILROAD CO.
2301, GE, U23C
BLT. 68/03
CHICAGO,IL.NEW I/T,68/04

LSI-LAKE SUPERIOR & ISHPEMING RAILROAD CO.

QTY	BLDR	MODEL	DELV.NO.	BLDR.DATE	NOTES
2	GE	U23C	2300-2301	68/03	
1	GE	U23C	2302	69/09	
2	GE	U23C	2303-2304	70/09	

LT-LAKE TERMINAL RAILROAD CO.

QTY	BLDR	MODEL	DELV.NO.	BLDR.DATE	NOTES
1	EMD	SW1001	1021	68/09	

CR-CONRAIL (LEHIGH VALLEY)
7657, ex LV 311
EMD, GP38AC, BLT. 71/12
FT. WORTH, TX. 89/03

QTY	BLDR	MODEL	DELV.NO.	BLDR.DATE	NOTES
LV-LEHIGH VALLEY RAILROAD					
4	EMD	GP38AC	310-313	71/12	TO CR 7656-7659
8	EMD	GP38-2	314-321	72/03	TO DH 7314-7321
4	EMD	GP38-2	322-325	72/08	TO DH 7322-7325
12	GE	U23B	501-512	74/12	TO CR 2777-2788
MCRR-MONONGAHELA CONNECTING RAILROAD CO.					
1	ALCO	T6	400	68/07	TO MKC IN 1982
1	EMD	SW1001	420	70/02	
2	EMD	SW1001	421-422	74/04,74/03	
1	EMD	SW1001	423	75/03	
2	EMD	SW1001	424-425	76/03	DELV. R/W/B
1	ALCO	C415	701	68/07	OFF ROSTER
MCSA-MOSCOW, CAMDEN & SAN AUGUSTINE RAILROAD					
1	GE	SL110	548	78/10	TO CHAMPION INTERNATIONAL
MEC-MAINE CENTRAL RAILROAD CO.					
10	GE	U18B	400-409	75/05-75/06	
MGA-MONONGAHELA RAILWAY CO.					
5	EMD	GP38	2000-2004	69/06	

MILW-MILWAUKEE ROAD
4001, EMD, SD45
BLT. 68/01
BENSONVILLE, IL. 74/03

QTY.	BLDR.	MODEL	DELV.NO.	BLDR.DATE	NOTES	
MILW-CHICAGO, MILWAUKEE, ST PAUL & PACIFIC RAILROAD CO.						
5	EMD	FP45	1-5	68/12	ALL SCR.	
10	EMD	SD40-2	21-30	73/07	TO SOO 6306-6314	
11	EMD	SD40-2	171-181	73/07	TO SOO 6300's,	
28	EMD	SD40-2	182-209	74/05-74/06	TO SOO 6300's	
6	EMD	GP38-2	350-355	73/05	TO SOO 4500-4505	
10	EMD	GP38-2	356-365	74/08	TO SOO 4506-4515	
32	EMD	MP15AC	434-465	76/01-76/02	TO SOO 1500-1531	
32	EMD	MP15AC	466-497	75/09	TO SOO 1532-1563	
5	EMD	SDL39	581-585	69/03	581 SCR. 582-584 TO WCL	
5	EMD	SDL39	586-590	72/11	587,589 TO WCL	
10	EMD	GP40	2047-2056	68/01	RET'D TO LESSOR 84,2053 SCR 2050 RBLT.TO MARC 75,GP39H-2	
4	EMD	GP40	2057-2060	68/12	TO SOO 4231-4234	
5	EMD	GP40	2061-2065	68/12	T/SOO 4235-39,4236,38,39 NRE	
2	EMD	GP40	2066-2067	68/12	TO SOO 4660,4240	
15	EMD	SD40-2	3000-3014	72/07-72/08	RE# 130-144	To NDM via MK & VMV, 87-88
1	EMD	SD40-2	3015	72/07-72/08	RE# 145,SCR	reblt to SD40-2 standards,
25	EMD	SD40-2	3016-3040	72/07-72/08	RE# 146-170	re# 13009-13048 mixed #'s.
6	EMD	SD45	4000-4005	68/01-68/02	RE# 6-11, ALL SCR.	
4	EMD	SD45	4006-4009	68/12	RE# 12-15, ALL SCR.	
5	GE	U23B	4800-4804	73/06	RE# 5000-5004(2nd),ALL RET.	
8	GE	U30C	5651-5658	74/08	ALL STORED,OFF ROSTER	
5	GE	U30B	6005-6009	68/01	RE# 5605-5609,ALL RET.BY 83	
4	GE	U33C	8000-8003	68/01-68/02	RE# 5700-5703,ALL RET.BY 83	
4	GE	U36C	8500-8503	72/06	RE# 5800-5803,ALL RET.BY 84	

MKT-MISSOURI-KANSAS-TEXAS
352, GE, U23B
BLT. 73/05
PARSONS, KS. 81/06

QTY.	BLDR.	MODEL	DELV.NO.	BLDR.DATE	NOTES
MKT-MISSOURI-KANSAS-TEXAS RAILROAD CO.					
4	EMD	SW1500	52-55	68/08-68/09	TO UP 1324-1327
4	EMD	MP15AC	56-59	80/09	TO UP 1393-1396
17	EMD	GP40	194-210	68/08-68/10	NOT TO BE RETAINED BY UP
20	EMD	GP40	211-230	69/11	222 WRK,REBLT SLUG 501,TO UP S-33, 217,221.233 RET.89/03 REST TO BE UP 581-599
4	EMD	GP38	300-303	69/12	TO UP 1975-1978
10	EMD	GP38-2	304-313	72/12	TO UP 2335-2344
4	EMD	GP38-2	314-317	74/08	TO UP 2345-2348
4	EMD	GP38-2	318-321	76/06	TO UP 2060-2063
3	GE	U23B	350-352	73/05	TRADED EMD 84, SCR.
20	EMD	GP39-2	360-379	84/03-84/06	TO UP 2359-78,GP49 CARBODIES
7	EMD	SD40-2	600-606	78/08	TO UP 3809-3815
4	EMD	SD40-2	607-610	78/10	TO UP 3816-3819
2	EMD	SD40-2	611-612	79/09	TO UP 3820,3821
1	EMD	SD40-2	613	79/09	WRK/REBLT,RE# 637,TO UP 3844
5	EMD	SD40-2	614-618	79/09	TO UP 3822-3826
10	EMD	SD40-2	619-628	80/07	628 SCR.83,REST UP 3827-3835
8	EMD	SD40-2	629-636	81/09	TO UP 3836-3843
MNS-MINNEAPOLIS, NORTHFIELD & SOUTHERN RAILWAY					
2	EMD	SD39	40-41	68/09	TO SOO 6240,6241
MON-MONON RAILROAD					
8	GE	U23B	601-608	70/03-70/04	LN 2700-07,CSXT 3230-3237

MP-MISSOURI PACIFIC
674, GE, U23B
BLT. 73/01
CHICAGO,IL.NEW I/T,73/02

QTY	BLDR	MODEL	DELV.NO.	BLDR.DATE	NOTES
MP-MISSOURI PACIFIC RAILROAD CO.					
7	GE	U23B	668-674	73/01	RE# 2250-2256,RE# 4500-4506,TO UP 534-540, RET'D TO LESSOR 88/12, ALL EXCEPT 537 TO CENTRAL MICHIGAN RR.(CMI)
14	EMD	SD40	720-733	68/01-68/02	RE#3020-3033,UP 4020-4033,3025 RET.88
20	EMD	SD40	734-753	69/02	RE#3034-3053,RET'D LESSOR,see p.121
16	EMD	SD40	754-769	70/01	RE#3054-3069,UP 4054-69,3055,58,RET.88
20	EMD	SD40	770-789	71/03-71/04	RE#3070-3089, RET'D TO LESSOR,see p.122
5	EMD	SD40-2	790-794	73/08	RE#3090-3094,UP 4090-4094
20	EMD	SD40-2	795-814	73/08-73/09	RE#3095-3114,UP 4095-4114
24	EMD	SD40-2	816-839	73/12-74/01	TP SUB-LTR,RE#3115-3138,TO UP 4115-4138
45	EMD	GP38-2	858-902	72/01-72/02	RE#2009-2053, RET'D LESSOR, SOME TO GTW
6	EMD	GP38-2	903-908	72/09	RE#2054-2059,UP 2380-2385
4	EMD	GP38-2	909-912	72/10	RE#2060-2063,UP SAME #
10	EMD	GP38-2	913-922	72/10	RE#2064-2073,UP SAME #
10	EMD	GP38-2	923-932	73/01	RE#2074-2083,UP SAME #,RET'D TO LESSOR
27	EMD	GP38-2	933-959	73/02-73/06	RE#2084-2110,UP SAME #,RET'D TO LESSOR 2074-2110 NOW LEASED BACK.
6	GE	U30C	960-965	68/03-68/04	RE# 1-6, 3300-05,2965-70
4	GE	U30C	966-969	69/05-69/06	RE# 7-10,3306-09,2971-74
4	GE	U30C	970-973	70/06	RE# 11-14,3310-13,2975-78
5	GE	U30C	974-978	71/08-71/09	RE# 15-19,3314-18,2979-83
5	GE	U30C	979-983	72/02	RE# 20-24,3319-23,2984-88
5	GE	U30C	984-988	73/06	RE# 25-29,3324-28,2989-93 ALL TO UP SAME#,SOME SCR.
20	EMD	MP15DC	1356-1375	82/01	TO UP SAME #
17	EMD	MP15DC	1376-1392	82/10-82/11	TO UP SAME #
4	EMD	SW1500	1518-1521	72/12	RE# UP 1318-21,1318,19 TO CRL 18,19/88
5	EMD	MP15DC	1530-1534	74/02	RE# UP 1330-1334
5	EMD	MP15DC	1535-1539	74/09	RE# UP 1335-1339
5	EMD	MP15DC	1540-1544	74/09	RE# UP 1340-1344

MP-MISSOURI PACIFIC RAILROAD CO. cont'd

QTY	BLDR	MODEL	DELV.NO.	BLDR.DATE	NOTES
10	EMD	MP15DC	1545-1554	75/02	RE# UP 1345-1354
15	EMD	GP15-1	1555-1569	76/06-76/07	TO UP SAME #
5	EMD	GP15-1	1570-1574	76/07	SUB-LTR C&EI,TO UP SAME#
15	EMD	GP15-1	1575-1589	76/12	TO UP SAME #
25	EMD	GP15-1	1590-1614	77/07	TO UP SAME #
30	EMD	GP15-1	1615-1644	79/09-79/11	TO UP SAME #
20	EMD	GP15-1	1645-1664	81/08	TO UP SAME #
40	EMD	GP15-1	1665-1704	82/02-82/03	TO UP SAME #
10	EMD	GP15-1	1705-1714	82/03	TO UP SAME #
30	EMD	GP15-1(AC)	1715-1744	82/11-82/12	TO UP SAME #
10	EMD	GP38-2	2111-2120	74/09	TO UP SAME #
12	EMD	GP38-2	2121-2132	75/01	TO UP SAME #
5	EMD	GP38-2	2133-2137	76/07-76/08	TO UP SAME #
20	EMD	GP38-2	2138-2157	77/10-77/11	TO UP SAME #
40	EMD	GP38-2	2158-2197	80/01-80/02	TO UP SAME #
40	EMD	GP38-2	2198-2237	80/07-80/08	TO UP SAME #
11	GE	U23B	2257-2267	74/10-74/11	RE#4507-4517/UP 541-551
3	GE	U23B	2268-2270	75/03	RE#4518-4520,ALL RET.87
1	GE	U23B	2271	75/03	WRK/SCR 78/10
2	GE	U23B	2272-2273	75/03	RE#4521-4522/UP 555-556
5	GE	U23B	2274-2278	76/06	RE#4523-4527/UP 557-561
10	GE	U23B	2279-2288	77/01-77/02	RE#4528-4537/UP 562-571
10	GE	B23-7	2287-2298	78/01	RE#4600-4609/UP 100-109
30	EMD	GP38-2	2290-2319	81/02-81/03	(2nd)TO UP SAME #
20	GE	B23-7	2299-2318	78/10-78/11	RE#4610-4629/UP 110-129
20	GE	B23-7	2319-2338	79/12	RE#4630-4649/UP 130-159
15	EMD	GP38-2	2320-2334	81/07-81/08	(2nd)TO UP SAME #
11	EMD	SD40-2	3139-3149	74/02	TO UP 4139-4149
14	EMD	SD40-2	3150-3163	74/02	SUB-LTR C&EI,UP 4150-4163
38	EMD	SD40-2	3164-3201	75/02-75/03	TO UP 4164-4201

MP-MISSOURI PACIFIC
3201, EMD, SD40-2
BLT. 75/03
DOLTON, IL. NEW, 75/03

MP-MISSOURI PACIFIC RAILROAD CO. cont'd

QTY.	BLDR.	MODEL	DELV.NO.	BLDR.DATE	NOTES
14	EMD	SD40-2	3202-3215	75/08	TO UP 4202-4215
20	EMD	SD40-2	3216-3235	78/09	(2nd)TO UP 4216-4235
20	EMD	SD40-2	3216-3235	76/07-76/09	RE#6000-6019,UP 3900-3935
16	EMD	SD40-2	3236-3251	78/09	TO UP 4236-4251
14	EMD	SD40-2	3252-3265	78/08	TO UP 4252-4265
26	EMD	SD40-2	3266-3291	79/05-79/06	TO UP 4266-4291
10	EMD	SD40-2	3292-3301	79/07	(2nd)TO UP 4292-4301
10	EMD	SD40-2	3302-3311	79/12	(2nd)TO UP 4302-4311
10	EMD	SD40-2	3312-3321	80/04	(2nd)TO UP 4312-4321
6	GE	U30C	3329-3334	74/02	TP SUB-LTR,RE# 2994-2999, TO UP SAME#, T/I GE L87

MP-MISSOURI PACIFIC
3502, EMD, GP50
BLT. 80/11
FT. WORTH, TX. 88/08

QTY.	BLDR.	MODEL	DELV.NO.	BLDR.DATE	NOTES
10	EMD	GP50	3500-3509	80/11	TO UP 50-59, RE# 960-969
16	EMD	GP50	3510-3525	81/01	TO UP 60-75, RE# 970-985
4	EMD	GP50	3526-3529	81/01	TO UP 76-79, RE# 986-989
10	GE	B23-7	4650-4659	80/04	TO UP 150-159
10	GE	B23-7	4660-4669	80/06	TO UP 160-169
15	GE	B23-7	4670-4684	81/04-81/05	TO UP 170-184
35	GE	B30-7A	4800-4834	81/11-82/01	TO UP 200-234
14	GE	B30-7A	4835-4848	82/01-82/02	TO UP 235-248
6	GE	B30-7A	4849-4854	82/02	TO UP 249-254
60	EMD	SD50	5000-5059	84/11-84/12	TO UP SAME #, 3600HP.
34	EMD	SD40-2	6020-6053	79/06	TO UP 3920-3953
20	EMD	SD40-2	6054-6073	80/04	TO UP 3954-3973
60	GE	C36-7	9000-9059	85/09-85/11	UP SAME#, 9025 W/SCR 87/11

MCR-McCLOUD RIVER RAILROAD CO.

QTY.	BLDR.	MODEL	DELV.NO.	BLDR.DATE	NOTES
3	EMD	SD38	36-38	69/04	
1	EMD	SD38-2	39	74/08	

QTY.BLDR.MODEL DELV.NO. BLDR.DATE NOTES

MRS-MANUFACTURERS RAILWAY CO.

QTY.	BLDR.	MODEL	DELV.NO.	BLDR.DATE	NOTES
2	EMD	MP15DC	251-252	75/08	
1	EMD	MP15DC	254	83/01	

MSE-MISSISSIPPI EXPORT RAILROAD CO.

QTY.	BLDR.	MODEL	DELV.NO.	BLDR.DATE	NOTES
1	EMD	SW1500	64	73/08	
1	EMD	GP38-2	65	75/09	
1	EMD	GP38-2	66	79/04	

MTFR-MINNESOTA TRANSFER
304, EMD, SW1500
BLT. 69/04
MINNEAPOLIS, MN. 78/06

MTFR-MINNESOTA TRANSFER RAILWAY CO.

QTY.	BLDR.	MODEL	DELV.NO.	BLDR.DATE	NOTES
1	EMD	SW1500	302	68/03	
2	EMD	SW1500	303-304	69/04	
2	EMD	SW1500	305-306	70/05	305 TO MTW 83, 83/10

NAR-NORTHERN ALBERTA RAILWAYS CO.

QTY.	BLDR.	MODEL	DELV.NO.	BLDR.DATE	NOTES
4	GMD	SD38-2	401-404	75/12	TO CN 5700-5703,RE# 4850-4853

NDEM-NATIONAL RAILWAYS OF MEXICO (FERROCARRILES NATIONALES de MEXICO)

QTY.	BLDR.	MODEL	DELV.NO.	BLDR.DATE	NOTES
1	GE	110T	N/A	68/01	
39	GE	E60C	EA001-039	82/09-83/12	
1	GE	C30-7	6700	78/12	(2nd)
9	GE	C30-7	6701-6709	79/09	(2nd), 6704 WRK/RET.
50	GE	C30-7	6710-6759	79/10-79/12	6716,6737,6750,6759 WRK/RET.
25	GE	C30-7	6760-6784	79/12-80/01	6763,6779 WRK/RET.
15	GE	C30-7	6785-6799	80/07	
22	ALCO	C628	8310-8331	68/02-68/03	8312,8316 RET.MOST REBLT.TO C630

NDEM-NATIONAL RAILWAYS OF MEXICO (FERROCARRILES NATIONALES de MEXICO), cont,d

QTY.	BLDR.	MODEL	DELV.NO.	BLDR.DATE	NOTES
3	EMD	SD40	8500-8502	68/03	
19	EMD	SD40	8503-8521	68/05	8513 WRK/SCR. 71/07
10	EMD	SDP40	8522-8531	68/05	
4	EMD	SDP40	8532-8535	70/05	
40	EMD	SD40	8536-8575	71/11	8545,8558 RET.
10	GMD	SD40	8576-8585	72/01	
20	MLW	M630	8600-8619	72/06-72/08	8602,8612,8615,8619 RET.

NDEM-NATIONAL RY of MEXICO
\# 8702, EMD, SD40-2
BLT. 72/09
LA GRANGE, IL. NEW, 72/09

10	EMD	SD40-2	8700-8709	72/09	
6	EMD	SD40-2	8710-8715	72/12	
40	EMD	SD40-2	8716-8755	73/10-73/12	8723,8748 RET.
12	EMD	SD40-2	8756-8767	75/12	8762 WRK/RET.
10	EMD	SD40-2	8768-8777	80/02	
21	EMD	SD40-2	8778-8798	80/08-80/09	8792 WRK/RET.
60	EMD	SW1504	8800-8859	73/05-73/08	
38	GE	U36C	8900-8937	73/07-73/11	8906,8912,8918,8919 RET. 8920 SCR.74/01 8921,8923-8925,8930-8932,8935,8936 RET.
20	GE	U36CG	8938-8957	74/04-74/05	8946,8947 RET, 8949 WRK/RET. 8953 RET.
29	GE	U36C	8958-8986	74/01-74/03	8970,8971,8974,8979,8983 RET.
45	GE	U18B	9000-9044	74/01-74/10	9006,9011,9013,9016,9018,9021,9023,9035, 9038,9041,9042 RET.
30	GE	U23B	9100-9129	75/03-75/06	9103,9118 WRK/RET. 9109,9116 RET.
10	GE	B23-7	9130-9139	79/12-80/01	ASSEMBLED IN BRAZIL, 9134 RET.
6	GE	B23-7	9140-9145	80/08-80/09	
32	GE	B23-7	9146-9177	80/11-81/01	9161,9163,9165,9166,9169 RET.
3	GE	B23-7	9178-9180	81/06	
20	EMD	GP38-2	9200-9219	75/06	HI-NOSE, STEAM GEN. 9201,9203 RET.
80	EMD	GP38-2	9220-9299	75/10-75/12	9626-9629,9642,9658,9674,9680,9683,9692, 9694,9695 RET.

NDEM-NATIONAL RAILWAYS OF MEXICO, cont'd

QTY.	BLDR.	MODEL	DELV.NO.	BLDR.DATE	NOTES
17	GE	U36C	9300-9316	75/01-75/02	
10	GE	C36-7	9317-9326	79/03	
15	GE	C36-7	9327-9341	80/03-80/05	ASSEMBLED IN BRAZIL
1	EMD	GP38-2	9400	75/12	
4	EMD	GP38-2	9401-9404	75/08	ASSEMBLED IN MEX. BY NDEM
10	EMD	GP38-2	9405-9414	79/03	9411 RET.
53	MLW	M424W	9500-9552	80/07-81/05	
6	GE	C30-7	9600-9605	80/07-80/08	
40	GE	C30-7	9607-9646	80/08-81/01	9617 RET.
6	GE	C30-7	9647-9652	81/04-81/05	
28	GE	C30-7	9653-9680	81/07-81/12	
25	EMD	MP15AC	9801-9825	82/07-82/09	
9	EMD	GP38-2	9901-9909	82/06-82/07	HI-NOSE
13	GE	B23-7	10001-013	80/10-81/02	(KITS)
33	GE	B23-7	10014-046	81/01-81/12	(KITS), 10031,10045 RET.
6	GE	B23-7	10047-052	81/12-82/01	(KITS)
29	GE	C30-7	11001-029	81/09	
10	GE	C30-7	11030-039	82/02-82/03	
29	GE	C30-7	11040-068	82/06-82/07	(KITS), 11065 RET.
30	GE	C30-7	11069-098	84/09-85/01	(KITS)
30	GE	C30-7	11099-128	83/04-83/06	SHIPPED 84/07
20	GE	C30-7	11129-148	86/02-86/05	(KITS)
12	GE	C30-7	11149-160	88/09-88/12	(KITS) MAY HAVE SOME REMFG.PARTS
6	GE	C30-7	11161-166	89/01-89/03	(KITS) MAY HAVE SOME REMFG.PARTS
6	GE	B23-7	12001-006	82/02-82/03	(KITS) 12004 WRK/RET.
5	GE	B23-7	12007-011	82/04-82/05	(KITS)
4	EMD	SD40-2	13001-004	86/02	LAST SD40-2's BUILT

NLG-NORTH LOUISANA & GULF RAILROAD CO.

4	EMD	MP15DC	42-45	75/11	

NOPB-NEW ORLEANS PUBLIC BELT RAILROAD

9	EMD	SW1000	101-106	71/07-71/08	
2	EMD	SW1500	151-152	71/08	
1	EMD	SW1500	153	71/08	

NP-NORTHERN PACIFIC RAILROAD CO.

10	GE	U33C	3300-3309	69/07	TO BN 5715-5724,PNC SCR.84
10	EMD	SD45	3620-3629	68/04-68/05	TO BN 6420-6429,RET'D LESSOR

NSR-NEWBURGH & SOUTH SHORE RAILWAY CO.

2	ALCO	T6	1016-1017	69/01	TO MKC IN 81,LAST ALCO BUILT
1	EMD	SW1001	1018	69/12	
1	EMD	SW1001	1019	71/07	
1	EMD	SW1001	1020	72/04	TO BS 226, 80/12
2	EMD	SW1001	1021-1022	75/03	

NW-NORFOLK & WESTERN
1787, EMD, SD45
BLT. 70/03
HAGERSTOWN, MD. 78/06

QTY.	BLDR.	MODEL	DELV.NO.	BLDR.DATE	NOTES
NW-NORFOLK & WESTERN RAILWAY CO.					
15	EMD	SD40	1610-1624	71/05	
11	EMD	SD40-2	1625-1635	73/09	
17	EMD	SD40-2	1636-1652	74/07	
25	EMD	SD45	1765-1789	70/02-70/03	MOST RET.SOME TO VMV,THEN NDM,SEE P.131
25	EMD	SD45	1790-1814	69/12	MOST RET.SOME TO VMV,THEN NDM,SEE P.131
25	EMD	GP38AC	4100-4124	71/08-71/10	4110 RET.IN 1980
35	EMD	GP38AC	4125-4159	71/06-71/11	
66	EMD	SD40-2	6073-6138	75/02-75/05	
50	EMD	SD40-2	6139-6188	78/04-78/06	
19	EMD	SD40-2	6189-6207	80/12	
6	EMD	SD50	6500-6505	80/11-80/12	
3	GE	U30C	8000-8002	74/03-74/04	DELV. W/LO-NOSE
35	GE	C30-7	8003-8037	78/11-78/12	
45	GE	C30-7	8038-8082	79/07-79/10	8075 RET.IN 1980
50	GE	U30B	8465-8514	70/08-71/01	MOST TO NDM M/79,REST RET.BY L/86,P.159
6	GE	C36-7	8500-8505	81/03	(2nd)
20	GE	C36-7	8506-8525	82/05-82/06	(2nd)
25	GE	U30B	8515-8539	71/05-71/11	MOST TO NDM M/79,REST RET.BY L/86,P.159
5	GE	C36-7	8526-8530	82/06	
12	GE	C36-7	8531-8542	84/05	DELV. NS
2	GE	C39-8	8550-8551	84/01	DELV. NS, GE PROTOTYPES
12	GE	C39-8	8552-8563	84/10-84/11	DELV. NS
50	GE	C39-8	8564-8613	85/04-85/10	DELV. NS
NYSW-NEW YORK, SUSQUEHANNA & WESTERN RAILWAY CORP.					
4	GE	DASH840B	4002-4008	88/06	EVEN NUMBERS ONLY
20	GE	DASH840B	4010-4048	89/04-89/05	EVEN NUMBERS ONLY

QTY.	BLDR.	MODEL	DELV.NO.	BLDR.DATE	NOTES

ONR-ONTARIO NORTHLAND RAILWAY

5	GMD	SD40-2	1730-1734	73/03	
3	GMD	SD40-2	1735-1737	74/01	
4	GMD	GP38-2	1800-1803	74/11	
4	GMD	GP38-2	1804-1807	82/11-82/12	
2	GMD	GP38-2	1808-1809	84/09	
4	GMD	GP38-2	2000-2003	83/03	

PBR-PATAPSCO & BACK RIVERS RAILROAD CO.

2	EMD	SW1500	160-161	69/09	SOLD TO CI RE# 17,18

PC-PENN CENTRAL
3173, EMD, GP40
BLT. 68/10
BLUE ISLAND, IL. 74/10

PC-PENN CENTRAL TRANSPORTATION CO.

					ALL TO CR SAME# UNLESS NOTED
50	GE	U23B	2700-2749	72/08-72/10	2732 SCR.2739 SCR.85
27	GE	U23B	2750-2776	73/08-73/10	
26	GE	U33B	2890-2915	68/09-68/11	RET.BY M/86, 6 TO IRRC
40	GE	U33B	2916-2955	68/11-68/12	RET.BY M/86, 9 TO BM
15	GE	U33B	2956-2970	70/05-70/06	ALL SCR. BY M/86
65	EMD	GP40	3105-3169	68/08-68/09	ALL RET.SOME TO MKT,DRGW
90	EMD	GP40	3170-3259	68/10-68/12	ALL RET.SOME TO KCS,BM
5	EMD	SD45	6235-6239	68/08	TO CNW 6562-6566
31	EMD	SD40	6240-6270	70/12-70/01	6253 SCR. 6265 SCR.88/04
14	EMD	SD40	6271-6284	71/01-71/02	
15	ALCO	C636	6330-6344	68/01-68/02	TO CR 6780-6794,ALL RET.
11	GE	U33C	6540-6550	68/02-68/04	CR 6845-55,6845 TO DH 650
4	GE	U33C	6551-6554	68/04	CR 6856-59,6856 TO DH 651
2	GE	U33C	6555-6556	68/04	CR 6860-61,6860 TO DH 652
2	GE	U33C	6557-6558	68/04	CR 6861-62,6862 TO DH 653
1	GE	U33C	6559-6560	68/04,68/08	CR 6864,65,TO DH 654,655

PC-PENN CENTRAL TRANSPORTATION CO. cont'd

QTY.	BLDR.	MODEL	DELV.NO.	BLDR.DATE	NOTES
3	GE	U33C	6561-6563	68/08	CR 6866-68,6866 TO DH 656 6867 TO IRRC,REST ALL RET.
19	GE	U23C	6700-6718	70/10-70/11	TO CR 6900-18,6913 SCR.85
35	EMD	SD38	6925-6959	70/04	
140	EMD	GP38	7675-7814	69/06-69/11	MOST RET.SOME TO PW,PLE,HL
10	EMD	GP38	7815-7824	69/11	MOST RET.SOME TO B&P,PLE
43	EMD	GP38	7825-7867	70/05-70/06	MOST BN 2155-89,7856 SCR.
36	EMD	GP38	7868-7903	71/01-71/02	7877,7900 SCR.
4	EMD	GP38	7904-7907	71/03	
32	EMD	GP38	7908-7939	71/02-71/03	7928,7929 SCR.
100	EMD	GP38-2	7940-8039	72/05-72/08	RET'D LESSOR,EMD,RE#740-839
114	EMD	GP38-2	8040-8153	73/01-73/03	8080,8101,8114 SCR.
9	EMD	GP38-2	8154-8162	73/10	
10	EMD	SW1500	9500-9509	71/02	
50	EMD	SW1500	9510-9559	72/02-72/03	
24	EMD	SW1500	9560-9583	73/09-73/10	

PCN-POINT COMFORT & NORTHERN RAILWAY CO.

3	EMD	MP15DC	11-13	74/11
2	EMD	MP15DC	14-15	80/11

PGE-PACIFIC GREAT EASTERN
702, MLW, C630
BLT. 69/07
LILOOET, BC. 73/06

PGE-PACIFIC GREAT EASTERN RAILWAY CO.

4	MLW	C630	701-704	69/07	TO BCOL SAME #
5	MLW	M630	705-709	70/12	TO BCOL SAME #
7	MLW	M630	710-716	71/12	TO BCOL SAME #,711 SCR.
6	MLW	M630	717-722	72/12	TO BCOL SAME #

QTY.	BLDR.	MODEL	DELV.NO.	BLDR.DATE	NOTES

PLE-PITTSBURGH & LAKE ERIE RAILROAD CO.

QTY.	BLDR.	MODEL	DELV.NO.	BLDR.DATE	NOTES
10	EMD	SW1500	1534-1543	73/05	1535,39,40,SOLD TO DOMINION TERM.ASSOCIATES,001.002.003
10	EMD	SW1500	1544-1553	72/09-72/10	1544,45,50,52 TO PEAKER SER
10	EMD	SW1500	1554-1563	71/12	4 SOLD KODAK,WEIRTON STL.87
10	EMD	MP15DC	1574-1583	74/06-74/07	TO UP 1200's MIXED,85/1 RE# 1000's,THEN 1300-1309
15	EMD	MP15DC	1584-1598	75/05	1584,87,88,96,98 TO UP 85/3 RE# 1010-1014,THEN 1310-14
6	EMD	GP38-2	2051-2056	77/06	TO GTW 5844-5849 85/06
10	EMD	SW1500	9280-9289	71/01	RE# 1573-1564,IN REVERSE

PRR-PENNSYLVANIA RAILROAD

QTY.	BLDR.	MODEL	DELV.NO.	BLDR.DATE	NOTES
38	EMD	SD45	6170-6207	67/12-68/01	6207 LAST NEW PRR,ALL TO PC-CR SAME#
27	EMD	SD45	6208-6234	68/01	DELV.IN PC SCHEME,ALL TO PC-CR SAME#

PRSL-PENNSYLVANIA-READING-SEASHORE LINES

QTY.	BLDR.	MODEL	DELV.NO.	BLDR.DATE	NOTES
5	EMD	GP38	2005-2009	69/04	T/PC-CR 7665-69,7669 SCR.
5	EMD	GP38	2010-2014	70/07-70/08	TO PC-CR 7670-7674

PRTD-PORTLAND TRACTION CO.

QTY.	BLDR.	MODEL	DELV.NO.	BLDR.DATE	NOTES
2	ALCO	T6	46-47	68/02	BOTH SOLD BY 1984

PW-PROVIDENCE & WORCESTER RAILROAD CO.

QTY.	BLDR.	MODEL	DELV.NO.	BLDR.DATE	NOTES
1	GE	U18B	1801	76/10	
2	MLW	M420RW	2001-2002	74/02	
3	MLW	M420RW	2003-2005	75/05	
1	EMD	GP38-2	2006	80/02	
2	EMD	GP38-2	2007-2008	80/12	
1	EMD	GP38-2	2009	82/09	
1	GE	B23-7	2201	78/03	

QNSL-QUEBEC, NORTH SHORE & LABRADOR RAILWAY CO.

QTY.	BLDR.	MODEL	DELV.NO.	BLDR.DATE	NOTES
6	GMD	SD40	200-205	68/07	
6	GMD	SD40	200-205	68/12-69/01	204,205 TO CP 5400,01 IN 85
15	GMD	SD40	206-220	71/06	206-218 TO CP 5403-14 IN 85
20	GMD	SD40-2	221-240	72/03-72/04	
20	GMD	SD40-2	241-260	73/03-73/04	
4	GMD	SD40-2	261-264	75/05	

RDG-READING CO.

QTY.	BLDR.	MODEL	DELV.NO.	BLDR.DATE	NOTES
24	EMD	SW1001	2601-2624	73/10-73/11	TO PC-CR 9401-9424
1	EMD	SW1001	2625	73/11	TO PC-CR 9400
10	EMD	SW1500	2761-2770	69/06-69/07	TO PC-CR 9611-9620
10	EMD	MP15	2771-2780	74/12	TO PC-CR 9621-9630
20	EMD	GP39-2	3401-3420	74/11-74/12	TO DH 7401-7420
5	EMD	GP40-2	3671-3675	73/12	TO CR 3275-3279

QTY.	BLDR.	MODEL	DELV.NO.	BLDR.DATE	NOTES

RFP-RICHMOND, FREDERICKSBURG & POTOMAC RAILROAD CO.

7	EMD	GP40-2	141-147	72/09	

RI-ROCK ISLAND
4711, EMD, GP40
BLT. 70/04
DENVER, CO. 79/09

RI-CHICAGO, ROCK ISLAND & PACIFIC RAILROAD CO.

10	GE	U33B	190-199	69/05	RET.TO LESSOR,ALL SCR.
5	GE	U33B	285-289	69/01	RET.TO LESSOR,ALL SCR.
10	GE	U33B	290-299	68/07-68/09	RET.TO LESSOR,ALL SCR.
15	EMD	GP40	382-396	69/01	RET.TO LESSOR,SOME TO NJT & EUKA
15	EMD	GP38-2	4300-4314	76/08-76/09	TO MP 2238-2251,TO UP SAME#
11	EMD	GP38-2	4315-4325	76/09-76/10	TO MP 2252-2263,TO UP SAME#
26	EMD	GP38-2	4326-4351	76/10-76/11	TO MP 2264-2289,TO UP SAME#
4	EMD	GP38-2	4352-4355	76/11	TO PLE 2057-2060
12	EMD	GP38-2	4368-4379	78/11	TO GTW 5850-5861
18	GE	U30C	4582-4599	73/10-73/12	RETURN TO LESSOR, SCR.
20	EMD	GP40	4700-4719	70/03-70/04	TO UP 631-650,SOME TO PNC 85
10	EMD	SD40-2	4790-4799	73/12	TO ICG 6040-6049,TO EMD,E/89

RS-ROBERVAL & SAGUENAY RAILWAY CO.

2	MLW	M420TR	26-27	72/04	

RSP-ROSCOE, SNYDER & PACIFIC RAILWAY

1	EMD	SW1500	500	69/09	
1	EMD	SW1500	600	70/06	

RSS-ROCKDALE, SANDOW & SOUTHERN RAILROAD CO.

3	EMD	MP15	13-15	74/11	

QTY.	BLDR.	MODEL	DELV.NO.	BLDR.DATE	NOTES

RT-RIVER TERMINAL RAILWAY CO.

2	EMD	SW1001	101-102	68/09	
2	EMD	SW1001	103-104	75/09	
2	EMD	SW1001	105-106	76/12	
1	EMD	SW1001	107	78/04	
1	EMD	SW1001	108	78/12	

SAN-SANDERSVILLE RAILROAD CO.

1	EMD	SW1500	300	70/05	

SBC-SONORA BAJA CALIFORNIA
2106, EMD, GP40-2
BLT. 72/10
MEXICALI, MX. 89/02
PHOTO: JAMES D. BRADLEY

SBC-FERROCARRIL SONORA BAJA CALIFORNIA (MEXICO)

3	EMD	GP40-2	2107-2109	73/12	HI-NOSE, STEAM GEN,TO NDM 7038-7040
3	EMD	GP40-2	2110-2112	76/08	TO NDM 7041-7043
2	EMD	GP40-2	2309-2310	79/11	(2nd) TO NDM 7029-7030(2nd)
2	EMD	GP40-2	2309-2310	72/10	RE# 2104,2105,HI-NOSE,NDM 7035,7036
1	EMD	GP40-2	2311	80/11	(2nd) TO NDM 7031(2nd)
1	EMD	GP40-2	2311	72/10	RE# 2106,HI-NOSE STM.GEN.TO NDM 7037
1	EMD	GP40-2	2312	81/07	TO NDM 7032(2nd)
2	EMD	GP40-2	2313-2314	82/06	TO NDM 7033,7034(2nd)

SBD-SEABOARD SYSTEM RAILROAD, INC.

15	EMD	MP15T	1200-1214	84/10-84/11	TO CSXT SAME #
8	EMD	MP15T	1215-1222	85/03	TO CSXT SAME #
19	EMD	MP15T	1223-1241	85/11-85/12	TO CSXT SAME #
75	GE	B36-7	5806-5880	85/02-85/06	TO CSXT SAME #
45	GE	B36-7	5881-5925	85/07-85/09	TO CSXT SAME #

SBD-SEABOARD SYSTEM RAILROAD,INC. cont'd

QTY.	BLDR.	MODEL	DELV.NO.	BLDR.DATE	NOTES
25	EMD	SD50	8500-8524	83/01-83/02	DELV FL-SBD TO CSXT SAME#
2	EMD	SD50	8525-8526	84/03	TO CSXT SAME #
26	EMD	SD50	8527-8552	84/02-84/03	TO CSXT SAME #
7	EMD	SD50	8596-8602	84/06	TO CSXT SAME #
21	EMD	SD50	8603-8623	85/01-85/02	TO CSXT SAME #

SCL-SEABOARD COAST LINE
501, EMD, GP38-2
BLT. 73/03
DOLTON,IL. NEW I/T,73/03

SCL-SEABOARD COAST LINE RAILROAD CO.

12	GE	U18B	250-261	73/12	TO CSXT 1888-1899
25	GE	U18B	300-324	73/03-73/05	CSXT 1900-22,SCR.305,313
19	GE	U18B	325-343	73/11-73/12	TO CSXT 1923-1941
49	GE	U18B	344-392	74/08-74/11	TO CSXT 1942-1990
25	EMD	GP38-2	500-524	73/03-73/04	TO CSXT 2500-2524
31	EMD	GP38-2	525-555	73/10-73/11	TO CSXT 2525-2555
30	EMD	GP40	1566-1595	69/12-70/01	TO CSXT 6721-6750,6723 REBLT.SLUG 2207
37	EMD	GP40	1596-1632	70/05-70/06	TO CSXT 6751-57,6759-86 1602,6758 OFF ROSTER
3	EMD	GP40	1633-1635	71/09	TO CSXT 6787-6789
21	EMD	GP40-2	1636-1656	72/04	TO CSXT 6346-6365 1653 OFF ROSTER
17	GE	U33B	1719-1735	67/12-68/01	1719 WRK.TO RI SLUG 282 IN 78.TO CSXT 5600-15,5600,02 04,06,07,10,11,SCR.BY 87/02
12	GE	U33B	1736-1747	69/01	TO CSXT 5617-5627 1736(5616) RET.86/09
28	GE	U36B	1748-1775	70/05-70/08	TO CSXT 5700-5727
1	GE	U36B	1776	71/06	DELV.R/W/B,TO CSXT 5728
1	GE	U36B	1777	70/08	TO CSXT 5729
35	GE	U36B	1778-1812	71/03-71/08	TO CSXT 5730-5763,1801 SCR.
22	GE	U36B	1813-1834	71/09-71/12	TO CSXT 5764-5784,1814 SCR.

SCL-SEABOARD COAST LINE RAILROAD CO. cont'd

QTY.	BLDR.	MODEL	DELV.NO.	BLDR.DATE	NOTES
21	GE	U36B	1835-1855	72/01-72/03	TO CSXT 5785-5805
14	EMD	SD45	2010-2023	68/09-68/10	TO SBD-CSXT 8910-8923, 8912 RET. 87/02
14	EMD	SD45	2024-2037	71/09	TO SBD-CSXT 8924-8937
7	EMD	SD45	2038-2044	71/10	CRR 3625-31,CSXT 8938-8944
15	EMD	SD45-2	2045-2059	74/08-74/09	TO SBD-CSXT 8950-8964
10	GE	MATE-4	3200-3209	71/08-71/10	TO SBD-CSXT 5200-5209
15	GE	MATE-4	3210-3224	72/09-72/12	TO SBD-CSXT 5210-5224
20	EMD	MP15AC	4000-4019	77/10	FL-SBD TO CSXT 1150-1169
25	EMD	MP15AC	4200-4224	78/02	FL-SBD TO CSXT 1170-1194
15	GE	B23-7	5100-5114	78/01-78/02	FL-SBD TO CSXT 3100-3114
10	GE	BQ23-7	5130-5139	78/10-79/01	FL-SBD TO CSXT 3000-3009
15	GE	B23-7	5140-5154	78/09	FL-SBD TO CSXT 3129-3143
10	GE	B30-7	5500-5509	80/03	FL-SBD TO CSXT SAME#
7	GE	B30-7	5510-5516	80/05	FL-SBD TO CSXT SAME#
1	EMD	GP38-2	6046	79/08	FL-WofA TO CSXT 2697
4	EMD	GP38-2	6047-6050	79/08	FL-SBD TO CSXT 2698-2701
1	EMD	GP38-2	6051	80/03	FL-GA.TO SBD/CSXT 2702
1	EMD	GP38-2	6052	80/03	FL-GA.TO SBD/CSXT 2703
2	EMD	GP38-2	6053-6054	80/03	FL-SBD TO CSXT 2604,2605
11	EMD	GP38-2	6055-6065	80/10	FL-SBD TO CSXT 2606-2616
5	EMD	GP40-2	6617-6621	80/06	FL-SBD TO CSXT 6383-6387
9	GE	C30-7	7016-7024	79/03	FL-SBD-TO CSXT SAME#
7	GE	C30-7	7025-7031	79/08	FL-SBD-TO CSXT SAME#
8	GE	C30-7	7052-7059	80/03	FL-SBD-TO CSXT SAME#
2	GE	C30-7	7060-7061	80/08	FL-SBD-TO CSXT SAME#
25	GE	C30-7	7070-7094	81/10-81/11	FL-SBD-TO CSXT SAME#
27	EMD	SD40-2	8040-8066	79/07-79/09	FL-SBD-TO CSXT SAME#
8	EMD	SD40-2	8087-8094	80/05-80/06	FL-SBD-TO CSXT SAME#
1	EMD	SD40-2	8130	80/08	FL-SBD-TO CSXT SAME#

SLSF-ST LOUIS-SAN FRANCISCO RAILWAY CO.

25	EMD	GP15-1	100-124	77/08-77/09	TO BN 1375-1399
2	EMD	SD38-2	296-297	79/06	TO BN 6260-6261
2	EMD	SD38-2	298-299	79/06	TO BN 6262-6263, LAST PROD.
16	EMD	SW1500	315-330	68/10	TO BN 20-35
16	EMD	SW1500	331-346	69/12-70/01	TO BN 36-51
6	EMD	SW1500	347-352	72/03-72/04	TO BN 52-57
8	EMD	SW1500	353-360	73/01	TO BN 58-65
5	EMD	MP15DC	361-365	75/03	TO BN 4000-04,RE#1000-04
18	EMD	GP38-2	400-417	73/06-73/07	TO BN 2255-2272
8	EMD	GP38-2	418-425	73/07	TO BN 2273-2280
21	EMD	GP38-2	426-446	74/08	TO BN 2281-2301
12	EMD	GP38-2	447-458	75/01	TO BN 2302-2313
1	EMD	GP38-2	459	76/11	TO BN 2314
1	EMD	GP38-2	460	76/11	TO BN 2315, WRK/REBLT TO GP38-2B 2601
18	EMD	GP38-2	461-478	76/11-76/12	TO BN 2316-2333
21	EMD	GP38AC	633-653	71/02-71/03	TO BN 2110-2129,651 WRK/SCR.74/09
6	EMD	GP38AC	654-659	71/04	TO BN 2130-2135
1	EMD	GP38AC	660	71/04	TO BN 2136, WRK/REBLT TO GP38B 2600, REBLT W/CAB AND RE# BACK TO 2136 E/89.

SLSF-ST LOUIS-SAN FRANCISCO RAILWAY CO. cont'd

QTY.	BLDR.	MODEL	DELV.NO.	BLDR.DATE	NOTES
2	EMD	GP38AC	661-662	71/04	TO BN 2137-2138
15	EMD	GP38-2	663-677	72/03	TO BN 2334-2347,674 SCR.
5	EMD	GP38-2	678-682	72/03	TO BN 2348-2352
17	EMD	GP38-2	683-699	72/11-72/12	TO BN 2353-2369
25	EMD	GP40-2	750-774	79/04-79/06	TO BN 3040-3064
4	GE	U30B	832-835	68/11	TO BN 5770-5773,ALL RET.86
8	GE	U30B	836-843	69/08-69/09	TO BN 5774-5781,ALL RET.86
10	GE	U30B	844-853	73/04-73/05	TO BN 5782-5791,5786 RET.87

SLSF-FRISCO
857, GE, U30B
BLT. 74/09
KANSAS CITY, MO. 80/11

QTY.	BLDR.	MODEL	DELV.NO.	BLDR.DATE	NOTES
4	GE	U30B	854-857	74/08-74/09	TO BN 5792-5794,856 WRK/SCR
5	GE	U30B	858-862	75/03	TO BN 5795-5799
8	GE	B30-7	863-870	77/12	TO BN 5485-5492
12	EMD	SD45	914-925	68/02	TO BN 6661-6673,ALL RET.
3	EMD	SD45	926-928	68/10	TO BN 6674-6675,926 SCR. ALL NOW RET.OR SCR.
14	EMD	SD45	929-942	69/09-69/10	TO BN 6676-6689,ALL RET.6677 TO WC,6683 TO VMV IN 86
5	EMD	SD45	943-947	69/12	TO BN 6690-6694,ALL RET.6690 TO WC SAME#.
1	EMD	SD45	948	71/09	TO BN 6695, RET.
8	EMD	SD40-2	950-957	78/07	TO BN 6840-6847

SM-ST MARYS RAILROAD CO.

QTY.	BLDR.	MODEL	DELV.NO.	BLDR.DATE	NOTES
1	EMD	SW1500	503	71/06	
1	EMD	MP15DC	504	74/10	
1	EMD	MP15DC	505	76/06	

QTY.	BLDR.	MODEL	DELV.NO.	BLDR.DATE	NOTES
SMA-SAN MANUEL ARIZONA RAILROAD CO.					
2	EMD	GP38-2	16-17	74/10	
SOO-SOO LINE RAILROAD CO.					
10	EMD	SD40	736-745	69/04-69/05	RE# 6600-6608,736 SCR.79
4	EMD	SD40	746-749	70/03	RE# 6609-6612
7	EMD	SD40	750-756	71/05	RE# 6613-6619
5	EMD	SD40-2	757-761	72/03	RE# 6620-6624
5	EMD	SD40-2	762-766	73/01	RE# 6625-6628,766 SCR.79
8	EMD	SD40-2	767-774	73/11	RE# 6629-6636
11	EMD	SD40-2	775-785	74/10	RE# 6637-6646,782 SCR.84
1	EMD	SD40-2	786	74/10	RE# 6647
3	EMD	SD40-2	787-789	75/10	RE# 6648-6650
7	EMD	GP38-2	790-796	77/09-77/10	RE# 4400-4406
3	EMD	GP38-2	797-799	78/04-78/05	RE# 4407-4409,4408 SCR.82

SOO-SOO LINE
809, GE, U30C
BLT. 68/06
CHICAGO, IL. 68/09

10	GE	U30C	800-809	68/04-68/06	SCRAPPED IN 84
6	EMD	GP38-2	4410-4415	78/10	
20	EMD	GP38-2	4416-4435	79/05-79/07	4430 WRK/SCR. 82
8	EMD	GP38-2	4436-4443	80/06	
7	EMD	GP38-2	4444-4450	81/02	
2	EMD	GP38-2	4451-4452	83/03	
21	EMD	SD60	6000-6020	87/08-87/11	
21	GMD	SD60	6021-6041	89/03-89/04	
1	EMD	SD40-2	6600	79/12	WRK/SCR. T/I FOR 6617
1	EMD	SD40-2	6601	79/12	RE# 6651
12	EMD	SD40-2	6602-6613	80/04	6605 WRK/82,SCR/84,RE# 6652-6662
3	EMD	SD40-2	6614-6616	81/03	RE# 6663-6665
1	EMD	SD40-2	6617	83/04	RE# 6666
6	EMD	SD40-2	6618-6623	84/07	RE# 6667-6672

SOU-SOUTHERN RAILWAY CO.

QTY.	BLDR.	MODEL	DELV.NO.	BLDR.DATE	NOTES
30	EMD	SW1500	2300-2329	68/11-68/12	2322 WRK/SCR.79/06
3	EMD	SW1500	2330-2332	69/11	
5	EMD	SW1500	2333-2337	69/11	
5	EMD	SW1500	2338-2342	70/03	
5	EMD	SW1500	2343-2347	70/03	
26	EMD	MP15DC	2348-2373	77/06-77/07	
10	EMD	MP15DC	2374-2383	79/09-79/10	
10	EMD	MP15DC	2384-2393	79/11	
10	EMD	MP15DC	2394-2403	82/05-82/06	
32	EMD	MP15DC	2404-2435	82/04-82/05	
12	EMD	GP38	2716-2727	69/09-69/10	
25	EMD	GP38	2728-2752	69/09	2732 WRK/SCR.74/06
70	EMD	GP38	2753-2822	69/10-70/03	
28	EMD	GP38AC	2823-2850	71/04-71/10	2839 RE#2887 IN 79 ONLY
28	EMD	GP38AC	2851-2878	71/08-71/10	
5	EMD	SD45	3100-3104	70/03	(2nd),ALL TO HELM LEASING
10	EMD	SD45	3160-3169	70/03	3164 RET.87/08,3167 TO HLC, 3168, 3169 TO NDM 13063,64 SD45M.

SOU-SOUTHERN RY.
3171, EMD, SD40
BLT. 71/04
DOLTON,IL.NEW I/T, 71/04

QTY.	BLDR.	MODEL	DELV.NO.	BLDR.DATE	NOTES
14	EMD	SD40	3170-3183	71/04	
2	EMD	SD40	3184-3185	71/04	
15	EMD	SD40	3186-3200	71/12	3191,3198 WRK/SCR.74/10
8	EMD	SD40-2	3201-3208	72/12	
8	EMD	SD40-2	3209-3216	73/01	
24	EMD	SD40-2	3217-3240	73/09	3217 WRK/SCR. 74/10
3	EMD	SD40-2	3241-3243	74/01	
11	EMD	SD40-2	3244-3254	75/07	
33	EMD	SD40-2	3255-3287	78/01-78/02	
15	EMD	SD40-2	3288-3302	78/05-78/06	(RCT)
10	EMD	SD40-2	3303-3312	79/02-79/03	(RCT)
16	EMD	SD40-2	3313-3328	79/05-79/06	

SOU-SOUTHERN RAILWAY CO. cont'd

QTY.	BLDR.	MODEL	DELV.NO.	BLDR.DATE	NOTES
22	GE	B30-7A	3500-3521	82/04-82/05	
5	GE	U33C	3805-3809	70/04	RET.86/03,3809 TO PEABODY COAL CO.
5	GE	U33C	3810-3814	72/01	T/I TO GE 87/02
6	GE	B36-7	3815-3820	81/03	
5	GE	U23B	3900-3904	72/05	
10	GE	U23B	3905-3914	73/05	
20	GE	U23B	3915-3934	74/05-74/06	
20	GE	U23B	3935-3954	75/05-75/07	3940 WRK/RET. 81/09
15	GE	U23B	3955-3969	76/11-77/02	3967 WRK/SCR. 79/06
10	GE	B23-7	3970-3979	78/09	
10	GE	B23-7	3980-3989	79/01	
20	GE	B23-7	3990-4009	81/02-81/03	
14	GE	B23-7	4010-4023	81/03-81/04	
6	EMD	GP39X	4600-4605	80/11	GP49 PROTOTYPES,UPGRADED TO GP49's IN 82
10	EMD	GP38-2	5000-5009	72/01-72/02	
45	EMD	GP38-2	5010-5054	72/02-72/03	5021-5023 WRK/RET.88/04
4	EMD	GP38-2	5055-5058	72/12	

SOU-SOUTHERN RY.
5098, EMD, GP38-2
BLT. 73/10
BIRMINGHAM, AL. 81/04

45	EMD	GP38-2	5059-5103	73/08-73/10	
4	EMD	GP38-2	5104-5107	74/01	
31	EMD	GP38-2	5108-5138	74/01-74/02	
24	EMD	GP38-2	5139-5162	74/10-74/11	
9	EMD	GP38-2	5163-5171	75/08	
30	EMD	GP38-2	5172-5201	76/09-76/10	
24	EMD	GP38-2	5202-5225	76/12-77/01	
6	EMD	GP38-2	5226-5231	77/01	(RCT)
25	EMD	GP38-2	5232-5256	79/08-79/09	

SOU-SOUTHERN RAILWAY CO.cont'd

QTY.	BLDR.	MODEL	DELV.NO.	BLDR.DATE	NOTES
15	EMD	SD50	6506-6520	84/07	NS OWNED
5	EMD	SD50	6521-6525	84/07	NS OWNED
4	EMD	SD60	6550-6553	84/12	NS OWNED, TEST PROTOTYPES
10	EMD	SD60	6554-6563	85/06-85/07	NS OWNED, (RCT)
40	EMD	SD60	6564-6603	85/07-85/10	NS OWNED
25	EMD	SD60	6604-6628	86/02-86/03	NS OWNED
12	EMD	SD60	6629-6640	86/06-86/08	NS OWNED
10	EMD	SD60	6641-6650	86/08	NS OWNED
25	GMD	SD60	6651-6675	88/11/88/12	NS OWNED
3	EMD	GP40X	7000-7002	78/06	
14	EMD	GP50	7003-7016	80/09-80/11	(RCT)
47	EMD	GP50	7017-7063	80/08-80/11	
7	EMD	GP50	7064-7070	80/11-80/12	
2	EMD	GP50	7071-7072	80/12	
20	EMD	GP50	7073-7092	81/04-81/06	
25	GE	C39-8	8614-8638	86/05-86/07	NS OWNED
25	GE	C39-8	8639-8663	86/08-86/10	NS OWNED
25	GE	C39-8E	8664-8688	87/03-87/06	NS OWNED

SP-SOUTHERN PACIFIC
2699, EMD, MP15DC
BLT. 75/02
FT.WORTH, TX. 89/04

SP-SOUTHERN PACIFIC TRANSPORTATION CO.

18	EMD	SW1500	2493-2510	68/06-68/07	2505 TO WILSON L/86
30	EMD	SW1500	2523-2552	69/07-69/11	2529 RET.86,2541 RET.78/12
26	EMD	SW1500	2553-2578	70/01-70/04	2454,69,76,78,RET.E/86
22	EMD	SW1500	2591-2612	71/10-71/11	2594 TO WILSON L/86
67	EMD	SW1500	2613-2679	72/04-72/08	2625,40,43,47,52,63,65,75,RET.86
10	EMD	SW1500	2680-2689	73/04-73/05	
7	EMD	MP15DC	2690-2696	74/12	
5	EMD	MP15DC	2697-2701	75/01-75/02	(2nd)
30	EMD	MP15AC	2702-2731	75/08-75/09	(2nd)

SP-SOUTHERN PACIFIC TRANSPORTATION CO. cont'd

QTY.	BLDR.	MODEL	DELV.NO.	BLDR.DATE	NOTES
4	EMD	MP15AC	2732-2735	75/10	(2nd)
24	EMD	MP15AC	2736-2759	75/09	(2nd)
6	EMD	SD38-2	2971-2976	73/04	
3	EMD	GP40P-2	3197-3199	74/11	RE# 7600-7602 (2nd)
45	EMD	GP38-2	4800-4844	80/05-80/07	
15	GE	B23-7	5100-5114	80/05-80/06	
18	EMD	SD39	5300-5317	68/08-68/10	(2nd)5301,05-07,11-13 SCR.
8	EMD	SD39	5318-5325	70/04	(2nd)ALL TO HL,4 TO CBRY
2	EMD	GP40X	7200-7201	78/02	(RCT)
2	EMD	GP40X	7230-7231	78/02	(RCR)
8	EMD	GP40-2	7240-7247	84/11	7241 WRK/RET M/87

SP-SOUTHERN PACIFIC
7618, EMD, GP40-2
BLT. 78/03
FT.WORTH, TX. 81/07

QTY.	BLDR.	MODEL	DELV.NO.	BLDR.DATE	NOTES
20	EMD	GP40-2	7608-7627	78/02-78/04	7612 RET.79/07,7618 RET.87
20	EMD	GP40-2	7658-7677	80/03	7659 RET.
16	GE	B36-7	7754-7769	84/11-84/12	
4	GE	B30-7	7800-7803	77/12-78/01	
20	GE	B30-7	7804-7823	78/03	7810 RET.79/07
30	GE	B30-7	7824-7853	79/02-79/03	
30	GE	B30-7	7854-7883	79/03-79/05	
30	GE	U30C	7900-7929	68/02-68/06	7900-7927,7929 T/I GE 84
7	GE	U30C	7930-7936	69/10	ALL T/I GE 84
20	EMD	GP40-2	7940-7959	80/04-80/05	EQUIPPED FOR SLUG MASTERS
40	GE	B39-8E	8000-8039	87/08-87/09	
70	EMD	SD40T-2	8230-8299	80/03-80/07	
7	EMD	SD40T-2	8300-8306	74/06-74/07	(2nd)(RCT)8302 RET.80/03
15	EMD	SD40T-2	8307-8321	78/02-78/04	(RCT)
15	EMD	SD40T-2	8327-8341	79/03-79/05	(RCT)
7	EMD	SD40T-2	8350-8356	74/06-74/07	(RCR)
15	EMD	SD40T-2	8357-8371	78/02-78/03	(RCR)
15	EMD	SD40T-2	8377-8391	79/05-79/07	(RCR)
10	EMD	SD40	8479-8488	68/04-68/06	REBLT.TO SD40R, 7300's

SP-SOUTHERN PACIFIC TRANSPORTATION CO. cont'd

QTY.	BLDR.	MODEL	DELV.NO.	BLDR.DATE	NOTES
10	EMD	SD40T-2	8489-8498	78/01-78/02	
75	EMD	SD40T-2	8499-8573	78/11-79/03	8507 WRK.TO HL, L/86
15	GE	U33C	8585-8599	74/12-75/01	8586 RET.80,8587 RET.78/09
30	GE	U33C	8600-8629	69/01-69/04	8610,8629 SCR.85, 8626 TO ATSF SLUG 144
15	GE	U33C	8630-8644	69/04-69/05	8644 TO ATSF SLUG 143, 8638 RET.78, 8642 WRK/SCR.69/09
2	GE	U33C	8645-8646	69/10	ALL RET.BY L/88
41	GE	U33C	8647-8687	70/02-70/06	ALL RET.BY L/88, 8686 RET. 78/05
26	GE	U33C	8688-8713	71/10-71/12	ALL RET.8691 RET.79, 8694 RET.78
14	GE	U33C	8714-8727	71/12-72/01	ALL RET.8718 WRK.TO NDEM 8987,86/2
10	GE	U33C	8728-8737	72/01-72/02	ALL RET.BY L/88,8734 RET. 78/08
30	GE	U33C	8738-8767	72/02-72/05	ALL RET.BY L/88,8756 TO GE,STORAGE
10	GE	U33C	8768-8777	73/01-73/02	ALL RET.BY L/88,8771,8772 TO GE,STORAGE
8	GE	U33C	8778-8785	73/06-73/07	ALL RET.BY L/88
11	GE	U33C	8786-8796	74/02-74/04	ALL RET.BY L/88
29	EMD	SD45	8935-8963	68/02-68/05	MOST RET.BY 87,8939 TO WC VIA WILSON,88
49	EMD	SD45	8982-9030	68/12-69/03	8992,8993,8999,9016,9023,9027 RET.
6	EMD	SD45	9031-9036	69/03-69/04	9032,RET.80,MOST RET.BY 87
15	EMD	SD45	9037-9051	69/03	9041,9043,9049 SCR.

SP-SOUTHERN PACIFIC
9074, EMD, SD45
BLT. 69/03
GRAND JUNCTION, CO. 88/07

QTY.	BLDR.	MODEL	DELV.NO.	BLDR.DATE	NOTES
35	EMD	SD45	9069-9103	69/03-69/04	9063,9069,9080,9091,9094 SCR. 9093 TO WC VIA WILSON 88/03
20	EMD	SD45	9104-9123	69/10-69/12	9110,9120,9121 SCR. MOST RET.
17	EMD	SD45	9124-9140	69/12-70/03	9128 TO PNC 86,9135 SCR.73/07, 9136 RET.9138 TO NDM SD40-2 VIA VMV 88/12
11	EMD	SD45	9141-9151	70/03	9141,9143,9144,9146-9151 TO NRE 9141,9143,9144,9146-9150 TO UTAH RR.

SP-SOUTHERN PACIFIC TRANSPORTATION CO. cont'd

QTY.	BLDR.	MODEL	DELV.NO.	BLDR.DATE	NOTES
43	EMD	SD45T-2	9166-9208	72/02-72/03	9174 SCR.76/07,9205 RET.78
52	EMD	SD45T-2	9209-9260	72/04-72/06	9220 WRK/REBLT TO 9314
12	EMD	SD45T-2	9302-9313	73/09	
29	EMD	SD45T-2	9315-9343	74/01-74/02	
27	EMD	SD45T-2	9344-9370	75/01-75/02	9354 RET.80
3	EMD	SD45X	9500-9502	70/08-70/09	(2nd) ALL SCR.84
20	GMD	GP60	9600-9619	87/12-88/03	

SP-SOUTHERN PACIFIC
9618, GMD, GP60
BLT. 88/02
TUSCON, AZ. 88/12
PHOTO: JAMES D. BRADLEY

SPS-SPOKANE, PORTLAND & SEATTLE RAILWAY CO.

1	ALCO	C415	100	68/11	BN 4010,TO AQUITANE(CANADA)
1	ALCO	C415	101	68/12	BN 4011,TO AQUITANE(CANADA)
6	ALCO	C636	330-335	67/12-68/01	TO BN 4360-4365 RET. SEE P.93
4	ALCO	C636	340-343	68/11	TO BN 4366-4369 RET. SEE P.93

SSDK-SAVANNAH STATE DOCKS RAILROAD CO.

2	EMD	SW1001	1001-1002	78/04	

SSW-ST LOUIS SOUTHWESTERN RAILWAY CO.(COTTON BELT)

12	EMD	SW1500	2481-2492	68/04-68/06	2487 RET.86, 2497 TO NRE
12	EMD	SW1500	2511-2522	69/03-69/04	2512 WILSON,T/NHN 1500,2518 WILSON L/86
4	EMD	SW1500	2579-2582	70/01	
8	EMD	SW1500	2583-2590	71/12	
26	EMD	GP40-2	7248-7273	84/10-84/11	
30	EMD	GP40-2	7628-7657	79/01-79/02	7650 WRK/SCR.M/87
4	GE	B36-7	7770-7773	80/01	3600HP B/P SAYS B30-7, 7771 WRK/REBLT. TO"B"UNIT IN 82.
26	GE	B30-7	7774-7799	80/03-80/04	

SSW-ST LOUIS SOUTHWESTERN RAILWAY CO.(COTTON BELT)

QTY.	BLDR.	MODEL	DELV.NO.	BLDR.DATE	NOTES
12	EMD	SW1500	2481-2492	68/04-68/06	2487 RET.86, 2497 TO NRE
12	EMD	SW1500	2511-2522	69/03-69/04	2512 WILSON,TO NHN 1500
4	EMD	SW1500	2579-2582	70/01	2518 TO WCL
8	EMD	SW1500	2583-2590	71/12	
26	EMD	GP40-2	7248-7273	84/10-84/11	
30	EMD	GP40-2	7628-7657	79/01-79/02	7650 WRK/SCR.M/87
4	GE	B36-7	7770-7773	80/01	3600HP B/P SAYS B30-7,7771 WRK/REBLT TO"B"UNIT IN 82.
26	GE	B30-7	7774-7799	80/03-80/04	
35	GE	DASH840B	8040-8074	88/07-88/11	
5	EMD	SD40T-2	8322-8326	78/01	(RCT)
5	EMD	SD40T-2	8372-8376	78/01-78/02	(RCR)
18	EMD	SD45	8964-8981	68/02-68/06	8971 WRK/RBLT RE# 9156,RET IN 85,8964-66,70,75,79,80, SCR.BY 87
17	EMD	SD45	9052-9068	68/11-69/01	9056 SCR.76,9063 SCR.73, 9054,57,60,66 SCR.BY M/87
4	EMD	SD45	9152-9155	70/01	9152,54,SCR.80,9155 BY 86
9	EMD	SD45T-2	9157-9165	72/07	
41	EMD	SD45T-2	9261-9301	73/02-73/03	
34	EMD	SD45T-2	9371-9404	75/03-75/06	9379 WRK/SCR. 75/08
15	GMD	GP60	9620-9634	88/09-88/10	

SSW-COTTON BELT
9620, GMD, GP60
BLT. 88/09
PHOENIX, AZ. 88/12
PHOTO: JAMES D. BRADLEY

TAG-TENNESSEE, ALABAMA & GEORGIA RAILWAY CO.

1	EMD	GP38	1	68/02	RE# 80, TO SOU 2879

QTY.	BLDR.	MODEL	DELV.NO.	BLDR.DATE	NOTES

TASD-TERMINAL RAILWAY ALABAMA STATE DOCKS

2	EMD	SW1500	681-682	68/07	
1	EMD	MP15DC	761	76/08	
2	EMD	MP15DC	771-772	77/10	
2	EMD	MP15DC	801-802	80/10	
1	EMD	MP15AC	803	80/10	
2	EMD	MP15DC	821-822	82/06	

TCT-TEXAS CITY TERMINAL
35, EMD, MP15DC
BLT. 82/11
TEXAS CITY, TX. 83/02

TCT-TEXAS CITY TERMINAL RAILWAY CO.

3	EMD	MP15DC	35-37	82/11	BUILT TO MP SPECIFICATIONS

TM-TEXAS MEXICAN RAILWAY CO.

1	EMD	GP38	859	71/08	
1	EMD	GP38	860	71/08	
2	EMD	GP38-2	861-862	74/09	
1	EMD	GP38-2	863	78/06	
1	EMD	GP38-2	864	79/09	
1	EMD	GP38-2	865	80/07	
1	EMD	GP38-2	866	80/11	
1	EMD	GP38-2	867	85/05	LAST GP38-2 BUILT

TN-TEXAS & NORTHERN RAILWAY CO.

2	EMD	MP15DC	998-999	75/12	

QTY.BLDR.MODEL DELV.NO. BLDR.DATE NOTES

TOE-TEXAS, OKLAHOMA & EASTERN RAILROAD CO.

1	EMD	GP40	D12	71/03	
1	EMD	GP40	D13	71/10	
1	EMD	GP40	D14	71/09	
1	EMD	GP40-2	D15	72/12	
1	EMD	GP40-2	D16	73/11	
1	EMD	GP40-2	D20	74/09	

TPW-TOLEDO, PEORIA & WESTERN RAILROAD CO.

4	EMD	GP38-2	2001-2004	77/05	TO ATSF 3561-64,RE# 2370-2373
7	EMD	GP38-2	2005-2011	78/10	TO ATSF 3565-71,RE# 2374-2380
2	EMD	SW1500	303-304	68/02	303 TO NASA SAME#, 304 TO VTR
2	EMD	SW1500	305-306	70/05	TO NASA SAME# VIA CCX

TRRA-TERM.RR.ASSOCIATION OF ST.LOUIS
1517, EMD, SW1500
BLT. 72/10
DOLTON,IL.NEW I/T, 72/11

TRRA-TERMINAL RAILROAD ASSOCIATION OF ST LOUIS

6	EMD	SW1500	1506-1511	69/11	
6	EMD	SW1500	1512-1517	72/10	

UP-UNION PACIFIC RAILROAD CO.

25	EMD	GP38-2	2000-2024	74/03-74/04	
15	EMD	GP38-2	2025-2039	74/05	2026 WRK/RET 87/04
20	EMD	GP38-2	2040-2059	75/04	
15	GE	C30-7	2415-2429	78/06-78/07	2425 WRK/RET 87/02
30	GE	C30-7	2430-2459	78/12-79/01	2432 WRK/SCR 86/10
40	GE	C30-7	2460-2499	80/01-80/02	2498 WRK/SCR.
40	GE	C30-7	2500-2539	80/08-80/10	2536 SCR.86/10,2539 88/07
20	GE	U30C	2810-2829	72/04-72/06	MOST RET.OR SCR.
30	GE	U30C	2830-2859	73/02-73/05	MOST RET.OR SCR.

UP-UNION PACIFIC RAILROAD CO.

QTY.	BLDR.	MODEL	DELV.NO.	BLDR.DATE	NOTES
10	GE	U30C	2860-2869	73/06	2860,63,2866-68 RET.85,2860,2864 RET.88
35	GE	U30C	2870-2904	74/03-74/07	MOST RET.OR SCR.
15	GE	U30C	2905-2919	75/04-75/06	MOST RET.OR SCR.2918 TO WILSON L/88
40	GE	U30C	2920-2959	76/07-76/10	MOST RET.2956 TO GE 3002,C30-S7 DEMO,89
15	GE	C30-7	2960-2974	77/07-77/09	RE# 2400-2414
40	EMD	SD40	3083-3122	71/08-71/10	3102 RET.88/09,3119 SCR.3084,3092 T/VMV
50	EMD	SD40-2	3123-3172	72/01-72/03	3146 SCR.
30	EMD	SD40-2	3173-3202	72/06-72/08	
37	EMD	SD40-2	3203-3239	73/04-73/05	
3	EMD	SD40-2	3240-3242	73/05	RE# 8000-8002,RE# BACK TO ORIG.# IN 80
32	EMD	SD40-2	3243-3274	74/06-74/07	RE# 8003-8034,RE# BACK TO ORIG.# IN 80
13	EMD	SD40-2	3275-3287	74/07	
17	EMD	SD40-2	3288-3304	75/03-75/04	

UP-UNION PACIFIC
3400, EMD, SD40-2
BLT. 77/05
PROVO, UT. 88/07

75	EMD	SD40-2	3335-3409	77/02-77/05	3336 SCR.
79	EMD	SD40-2	3410-3488	78/03-78/05	
10	EMD	SD40-2	3489-3498	78/12	
75	EMD	SD40-2	3499-3573	79/01-79/03	
10	EMD	SD40-2	3574-3583	79/07	
1	EMD	SD45	3600	68/03	RE# 50(2nd)ALL RET.
39	EMD	SD45	3601-3939	68/03-68/04	RE# 1-39(2nd)RET.BY 83. 34,14,15,13,8, 37 REBLT.W/SULZER ENG.IN 80/82,RE# 60-65,RET.83, 26 TO NDM 13076,SD45M 88/12
10	EMD	SD45	3640-3649	68/03	RE# 40-49(2nd)ALL RET.BY 83
50	EMD	SD40-2	3609-3658	79/09-79/12	(2nd),3612 RET. L/87
110	EMD	SD40-2	3659-3768	80/01-80/03	
36	EMD	SD40-2	3769-3804	80/10-80/11	
4	EMD	SD40-2	3805-3808	80/11	
20	GE	U50C	5000-5019	69/10-71/02	ALL SCR. BY 1978
20	GE	U50C	5020-5039	71/05-71/11	ALL SCR. BY 1978

UP-UNION PACIFIC RAILROAD CO. cont'd

UP-UNION PACIFIC RAILROAD CO.
6082, EMD, SD60
BLT. 88/05
FT.WORTH, TX. 88/10

QTY.	BLDR.	MODEL	DELV.NO.	BLDR.DATE	NOTES
60	EMD	SD60	6000-6059	86/02-86/05	
25	EMD	SD60	6060-6084	88/02-88/06	
25	GMD	SD60M	6085-6109	89/01-89/02	1st MAJOR U.S.RR.TO BUY CANADIAN
50	GMD	SD60M	6110-6159	89/04-89/06	STYLE COMFORT CAB.
56	GMD	SD60M	6160-6215	89/07-89/08	
1	EMD	DDA40X	6900	69/04	ALL DDA40X's RET.IN 85,
2	EMD	DDA40X	6901-6902	69/06	SOME DONATED AS FOLLOWS:
2	EMD	DDA40X	6903-6904	69/07	6903 SCR.74/04,6921 IN 78
4	EMD	DDA40X	6905-6908	69/08	6900 TO CITY OF OMAHA,NE.
4	EMD	DDA40X	6909-6912	69/09	6901 TO CITY OF POCOTELLO,ID.
4	EMD	DDA40X	6913-6916	69/10	6911 TO MUSEUM MEXICO CITY,MX
4	EMD	DDA40X	6917-6920	69/11	6913 TO AGE OF STEAM MUS.DALLAS,TX.
4	EMD	DDA40X	6921-6924	69/12	6915 TO MUSEUM. POMONA,CA.
3	EMD	DDA40X	6925-6927	70/06	6916 TO CITY OF OGDEN,UT.
4	EMD	DDA40X	6928-6931	70/07-70/08	6922 TO CITY OF NO.PLATTE,NE.
3	EMD	DDA40X	6932-6934	70/12	6925 TO DSRC, STORED
					6930 TO MUSEUM, KANSAS CITY,MO.
3	EMD	DDA40X	6935-6937	71/01	6936 KEPT FOR CO.PR.USE.
5	EMD	DDA40X	6938-6942	71/06-71/07	6938 AWAITING DISPOSITION.
4	EMD	DDA40X	6943-6946	71/08-71/09	6944 TO MUSEUM, ST LOUIS,MO.
					6946 TO MUSEUM, PORTOLA,CA
30	EMD	SD40-2	8035-8064	76/07-76/09	RE# 3305-3334 IN 1980,
					3309 SCR. 85/12
10	EMD	SD40-2	8065-8074	77/05	RE# 3400-3409 IN 1980
25	EMD	SD40-2	8075-8099	79/07-79/08	RE# 3584-3608(2nd)
1	EMD	GP40X	9000	77/12	RE# 90(2nd),RE# 954
1	EMD	GP40X	9001	78/02	RE# 91(2nd),RE# 955
4	EMD	GP40X	9002-9005	78/03	RE# 92-95(2nd),RE# 956-959

UNION PACIFIC RAILROAD CO. cont'd

QTY.	BLDR.	MODEL	DELV.NO.	BLDR.DATE	NOTES
75	GE	DASH840C	9100-9174	87/11-88/02	
10	GE	DASH840C	9175-9184	88/07-88/08	
1	GE	DASH840C	9185	88/08	GE RETAINED 1st AS DEMO UNIT.
1	GE	DASH840C	9185	88/11	(2nd) REPLACEMENT FOR ABOVE UNIT.
64	GE	DASH840C	9186-9249	88/08-88/10	
35	GE	DASH840C	9250-9284	88/11-88/12	
65	GE	DASH840C	9285-9349	88/12-89/03	

URR-UNION RAILROAD CO.

5	EMD	SW1500	1-5	72/11	
4	EMD	SW1500	6-9	73/09	
5	EMD	MP15DC	10-14	74/07	
7	EMD	MP15DC	15-21	75/06-75/07	
3	EMD	MP15DC	22-24	76/03	
2	EMD	MP15DC	25-26	76/12	
7	EMD	MP15DC	27-33	77/02	
3	EMD	SW1001	101-103	76/03	ALL TO BS, 85/11

VIA-VIA RAIL CANADA

20	GMD	F40PH-2	6400-6419	86/11-87/01	
10	GMD	F40PH-2	6420-6429	87/07-87/08	
26	GMD	F40PH-2	6430-6458	89/04-89/05	
21	BBD	LRC(B)	6900-6920	81/02-82/06	6906 WRK/83, SCR/85
10	BBD	LRC(B)	6921-6930	83/10-84/10	

VTR-VERMONT RAILWAY, INC.

1	EMD	GP38-2	201	72/12	
1	EMD	GP38-2	202	74/10	

WM-WESTERN MARYLAND RAILWAY CO.

WM-WESTERN MARYLAND
3799, EMD, GP40
BLT. 71/08
BALTIMORE, MD. 78/06
see p. 69 for roster

WM-WESTERN MARYLAND RAILWAY, cont'd

QTY.	BLDR.	MODEL	DELV.NO.	BLDR.DATE	NOTES
5	EMD	GP40	3795-3799	71/08	CS SAME#,TO CSXT 6570-6574
5	EMD	GP40-2	4257-4261	77/02	CS SAME#,TO CSXT 6156-6160
10	EMD	GP40-2	4312-4321	78/11	CS SAME#,TO CSXT 6211-6220
15	EMD	GP40-2	4352-4366	79/01-79/02	CS SAME#,TO CSXT 6251-6265
5	EMD	GP40-2	4367-4371	79/02	4367 WRK/SCR.80, TO CS SAME#, THEN TO CSXT 6266-6269
1	EMD	SD40	7445	69/06	RE# 7545,TO CSXT 8396
4	EMD	SD40	7446-7449	69/07	RE#7546-7549,TO CSXT 8397-8400
2	EMD	SD40	7495-7496	68/11	RE#7595,7596,TO CSXT 8437,8438

WP-WESTERN PACIFIC
2259, GE, U23B
BLT. 72/05
WENDOVER, NV. 73/05

WP-WESTERN PACIFIC RAILROAD CO.

4	GE	U30B	756-759	68/09	RE#3056-3059,ALL RET.BY 83
10	GE	U30B	760-769	69/04-69/05	RE#3060-3069,ALL RET.BY 83
3	EMD	SW1500	1501-1503	73/05	TO UP 1315-1317
15	GE	U23B	2251-2265	72/05-72/06	ALL RET.BY 87/09. 2263,2251,2257 TO GE DEMO's 2000-2002, B23-S7, 89/04
10	EMD	GP40	3517-3526	70/08	TO HL,CMNW 3000-3009
1	EMD	GP40	3527	71/08	WRK/SCR 80/04
1	EMD	GP40	3528	71/08	TO UP 676,GATX,CMNW 3010
2	EMD	GP40	3529-3530	71/08	TO GATX, CMNW 3011,3012
3	EMD	GP40	3531-3533	71/08	UP679-81,GATX,CMNW3013-15
2	EMD	GP40	3534-3535	71/08	TO GATX, CMNW 3016-3017
1	EMD	GP40	3536	71/08	TO UP 684,GATX,CMNW 3018
1	EMD	GP40	3537	71/08	TO GATX, CMNW 3019
1	EMD	GP40	3538	71/09	TO UP 686,GATX,CMNW 3020
1	EMD	GP40	3539	71/09	TO GATX, CMNW 3021

WP-WESTERN PACIFIC RAILROAD CO. cont'd

QTY.	BLDR.	MODEL	DELV.NO.	BLDR.DATE	NOTES
1	EMD	GP40	3540	71/09	WRK/SCR. 80/04
2	EMD	GP40	3541-3542	71/09	TO GATX. THEN CMNW 3022-3023
1	EMD	GP40	3543	71/09	TO UP 690,TO GATX, THEN CMNW 3024
1	EMD	GP40	3544	71/09	TO GATX, THEN CMNW 3025
5	EMD	GP40-2	3545-3549	79/07	TO MP 900-904, TO UP SAME#
10	EMD	GP40-2	3550-3559	80/04	TO MP 905-914, TO UP SAME#

WP-WESTERN PACIFIC
3529, EMD, GP40
BLT. 71/08
SALT LAKE CITY, UT. 82/04

WPY-WHITE PASS & YUKON RAILROAD CO.

7	MLW	DL535E	101-107	69/05	102,105 OFF ROSTER
3	MLW	DL535E	108-110	71/12	
4	MLW	DL35E(W)	111-114	82/07	NEVER SHIPPED, RR SHUTDOWN, STORED AT PLT.

WRyA-WESTERN RAILWAY OF ALABAMA

1	EMD	GP40	702	68/07	TO CS-SBD-CSXT 6791
2	EMD	GP40	703-704	69/01	TO CS-SBD-CSXT 6792,6793
3	EMD	GP40	705-707	70/05	TO CS-SBD-CSXT 6794-6796
1	EMD	GP40-2	708	74/11	TO CS-SBD 6642,TO CSXT 6388

WYS-WYANDOTTE SOUTHERN RAILROAD CO.

1	GE	SL110	101	76/12	

TRANSIT AND COMMUTER RAILROADS, 1968-1989.

CALT-CALTRANS
909, EMD, F40PH-2
BLT. 85/04
SAN FRANCISCO, CA. 86/06

QTY.	BLDR.	MODEL	DELV.NO.	BLDR.DATE	NOTES
CALT-CALTRANS (CALIFORNIA DEPT. OF TRANSPORTATION,SAN FRANCISCO)					
18	EMD	F40PH-2	900-917	85/03-85/06	
2	EMD	F40PH-2	918-919	87/12	
CDOT-CONNECTICUT DEPT. OF TRANSPORTATION					
1	BUDD	SPV2000	50	80/04	
GOT-GOVERMENT OF ONTARIO TRANSIT (GO TRANSIT,TORONTO)					
6	GMD	F40PH	510-515	78/04-78/05	
16	GMD	F59PH	520-535	88/10-88/12	
4	GMD	GP40-2W	707-710	75/09-75/10	
4	GMD	GP40-2W	9808-9811	73/12	
3	GMD	GP40-2W	9812-9814	74/11	
MBTA-MASSACHUSETTS BAY TRANSPORTATION AUTHORITY (BOSTON)					
13	EMD	F40PH	1000-1012	78/09-78/11	
5	EMD	F40PH	1013-1017	80/11	
10	EMD	F40PH-2	1018-1027	86/	
18	EMD	F40PH-2C	1050-1067	87/07-87/11	CUMMINS HEP POWERED
8	EMD	F40PH-2C	1068-1075	88/02-88/04	CUMMINS HEP POWERED
MDOT-MARYLAND DEPT. OF TRANSPORTATION (WASHINGTON,DC)					
4	EMD	AEM7	4900-4903	86/08-86/12	ASEA COMPONENTS

QTY.	BLDR.	MODEL	DELV.NO.	BLDR.DATE	NOTES

MTA-METROPOLITAN TRANSIT AUTHORITY (NEW YORK)

10	BUDD	SPV2000	290-299	81/09-81/11	

NJT-NEW JERSEY TRANSIT
4113, EMD, F40PH
BLT. 81/10
HARRISON, NJ. 87/09
PHOTO: JAMES D. BRADLEY

NJT-NEW JERSEY TRANSIT (NEW YORK)

17	EMD	F40PH	4113-4129	81/10-81/12	

NSMTD-NORTH SUBURBAN MASS TRANSIT DISTRICT (CHICAGO)

13	EMD	F40C	40-52	74-03/74-05	RE# 600-612 IN 86
2	EMD	F40C	53-54	74/05	RE# 613-614 IN 86

RTA-REGIONAL TRANSPORTATION AUTHORITY, (METRA) CHICAGO

28	EMD	F40PH	100-127	77/09-77/12	
22	EMD	F40PH	128-149	79/11-80/01	
24	EMD	F40PH	150-173	83/02-83/04	
7	EMD	F40PH-2	174-180	88/12-89/03	

SEPTA-SOUTHEASTERN PENNSYLVANIA TRANSPORTATION AUTHORITY (PHILADELPHIA)

7	EMD	AEM7	2301-2307	87/10-87/12	ASEA COMPONENTS

INDUSTRIES AND NON-COMMON CARRIERS, 1968-1989

QTY.	BLDR.	MODEL	DELV.NO.	BLDR.DATE	NOTES

AEPX-AMERICAN ELECTRIC POWER SERVICE CORP.

1	GE	110T	1085	74/08	
1	GE	SL110	N/A	88/	

ALAB-ALABAMA BY-PRODS.
1000, EMD, SW1000
BLT. 71/07
DOLTON,IL.NEW I/T, 71/08

ALAB-ALABAMA BY-PRODUCTS

1	EMD	SW1001	1000	71/07	

ALCO-AMERICAN LOCOMOTIVE CO.

3	ALCO	C636	636-1,2,3	68/11	DEMO's,TO QUE.CARTIER 79,78,77

ALCT-ALCOA TERMINAL (ALCOA ALUMINIUM)

1	EMD	MP15DC	7:3	80/02	
1	EMD	SW1500	9	70/06	
1	EMD	MP15DC	10	79/11	

ALGO-ALGOMA STEEL (CANADA)

1	GE	SL70	7	75/08	
2	GE	SL110	61	75/01	

ALLE-ALLEGHANY LUDLUM

1	GE	SL85	21	75/04	
1	GE	SL85	22	77/04	
1	GE	SL75	23	78/02	

QTY.BLDR.MODEL DELV.NO. BLDR.DATE NOTES

ALLP-ALLEGHANY POWER SYSTEM, WILLOW ISLAND, W.V.

QTY.	BLDR.	MODEL	DELV.NO.	BLDR.DATE	NOTES
1	GE	SL144	1	78/02	

ALMA-ALMACENES (MEXICO)

QTY.	BLDR.	MODEL	DELV.NO.	BLDR.DATE	NOTES
1	GE	100T	NONE	68/04	

ALTO-ALTOS HORNOS (MEXICO)

QTY.	BLDR.	MODEL	DELV.NO.	BLDR.DATE	NOTES
1	EMD	SW1000	132	68/10	
1	GE	80T	133	69/01	
2	EMD	GP38	135-136	71/06	
1	EMD	SW1000	137	72/09	
1	GE	80T	138	72/06	
1	EMD	GP38-2	141	74/01	
1	EMD	SW1001	142	74/08	
1	EMD	GP38-2	145	75/11	
3	EMD	MP15	146-148	75/11	
1	GE	SL85	150	77/06	
3	EMD	SW1001	151-153	78/04	
3	EMD	SW1001	154-156	78/11	
2	EMD	GP38-2	157-158	78/10	
1	EMD	MP15DC	159	78/12	
3	EMD	SW1001	159-161	79/06	159 2nd
2	EMD	SW1001	164-165	80/12	
1	EMD	MP15DC	166	80/11	
2	EMD	GP38-2	167-168	80/10	

AMCX-AMOCO CHEMICALS CO.

QTY.	BLDR.	MODEL	DELV.NO.	BLDR.DATE	NOTES
1	EMD	SW1001	SE3	78/12	

AMER-AMERICAN STEEL FOUNDRIES

QTY.	BLDR.	MODEL	DELV.NO.	BLDR.DATE	NOTES
2	EMD	SW1001	9G9-9G10	79/06	

AOCX-ALUMINUM CO. OF AMERICA

QTY.	BLDR.	MODEL	DELV.NO.	BLDR.DATE	NOTES
1	EMD	MP15DC	7	80/02	

APWX-APPALACHIAN POWER CO.

QTY.	BLDR.	MODEL	DELV.NO.	BLDR.DATE	NOTES
1	GE	65T	2	69/01	
1	GE	SL144	1	76/11	

ARGO-ARGO CORN INDUSTRIES

QTY.	BLDR.	MODEL	DELV.NO.	BLDR.DATE	NOTES
2	EMD	SW1000	68-69	69/03	

ARIZ-ARIZONA PUBLIC SERVICE CO.

QTY.	BLDR.	MODEL	DELV.NO.	BLDR.DATE	NOTES
1	EMD	MP15DC	2	77/06	

QTY.	BLDR.	MODEL	DELV.NO.	BLDR.DATE	NOTES

ARMC-ARMCO STEEL CO.

QTY.	BLDR.	MODEL	DELV.NO.	BLDR.DATE	NOTES
1	GE	SL115	12	76/11	KANSAS CITY PLANT
1	EMD	GP38-2	B84	75/09	
1	EMD	SW1001	E150	74/10	
2	EMD	SW1001	E151-E152	75/09	
3	EMD	SW1001	E153-E155	75/10	
3	EMD	SW1001	E156-E158	76/08	
3	EMD	SW1001	E159-E161	77/10	MIDDLETOWN PLANT
2	EMD	SW1001	E162-E163	78/11	MIDDLETOWN PLANT
2	EMD	SW1001	E164-E165	79/12	MIDDLETOWN PLANT
2	EMD	SW1001	E166-E167	80/11	MIDDLETOWN PLANT
2	EMD	SW1001	E168-E169	81/04	MIDDLETOWN PLANT
2	EMD	SW1500	701-702	72/10	
2	EMD	SW1500	703-704	73/08	
1	EMD	SW1500	705	73/12	
1	EMD	SW1001	1215	81/04	ASHLAND PLANT
1	EMD	SW1001	11838	80/11	HOUSTON PLANT
1	EMD	SW1001	11839	81/06	HOUSTON PLANT
1	EMD	SW1001	11840	82/06	HOUSTON PLANT

BBD-BOMBARDIER, INC. (CANADA)

QTY.	BLDR.	MODEL	DELV.NO.	BLDR.DATE	NOTES
1	BBD	HR412W	7000	82/05	PROTOTYPE TEST UNIT

BOAR-BOARD OF PUBLIC UTILITIES, KANSAS CITY, MO.

QTY.	BLDR.	MODEL	DELV.NO.	BLDR.DATE	NOTES
1	GE	SL110	846	84/06	

BPPX-INTERNATIONL MINING & CHEMICALS CORP.(IMC)

QTY.	BLDR.	MODEL	DELV.NO.	BLDR.DATE	NOTES
1	EMD	MP15DC	18	76/01	
1	EMD	MP15DC	19	80/11	

BRAZ-BRAZOS ELECTRIC POWER CO-OP.

QTY.	BLDR.	MODEL	DELV.NO.	BLDR.DATE	NOTES
1	GE	SL115	NONE	78/08	

BREX-BIG RIVERS ELECTRIC CORP.

QTY.	BLDR.	MODEL	DELV.NO.	BLDR.DATE	NOTES
1	GE	SL144	1	83/09	

BRFD-BRANTFORD STEAM RAILROAD

QTY.	BLDR.	MODEL	DELV.NO.	BLDR.DATE	NOTES
1	EMD	SW1001	7357	76/07	OWNED BY NEW HAVEN TRAP ROCK
1	GE	SL85	7358	84/05	OWNED BY NEW HAVEN TRAP ROCK
1	GE	SL85	N/A	88/04	OWNED BY NEW HAVEN TRAP ROCK

BSCX-BETHLEHEM STEEL CORP.

QTY.	BLDR.	MODEL	DELV.NO.	BLDR.DATE	NOTES
1	GE	80T	N/A	70/02	

CELU-CELULOSA de CHIHUAHUA
1811, EMD, SW1000
BLT. 71/08
DOLTON,IL.NEW I/T, 71/08

QTY.	BLDR.	MODEL	DELV.NO.	BLDR.DATE	NOTES
CELU-CELULOSA de CHIHUAHUA S.A.(MEXICO)					
1	EMD	SW1000	1811	71/08	
CEME-CEMENTOS ANAHUAC (MEXICO)					
1	EMD	SW1000	NONE	71/04	
1	GE	SL85	NONE	77/06	
1	GE	SL85	NONE	82/12	
CEMM-CEMENTOS y MAYA (MEXICO)					
1	GE	SL85	NONE	82/01	
CEMN-CEMENTOS y MEXICO (MEXICO)					
1	GE	SL115	NONE	81/01	
CENT-CENTRAL HUDSON POWER CO.					
1	GE	SL110	NONE	86/04	
CHAM-CHAMPION INTERNATIONAL					
1	EMD	SW1001	06056	79/07	
CHEV-CHEVROLET MOTOR DIVISION of GENERAL MOTORS					
1	EMD	SW1001	96	72/04	TONAWANDA,NY.ENGINE PLT.

QTY.	BLDR.	MODEL	DELV.NO.	BLDR.DATE	NOTES

CILC-CENTRAL ILLINOIS LIGHT CO. PEORIA, IL.

1	GE	SL110	NONE	75/07	

CIPX-CENTRAL ILLINOIS PUBLIC SERVICE

1	GE	110T	NONE	70/12	

CITI-CITIZENS GAS & COKE

1	GE	80T	3	72/04	

CITY-CITY OF SIKESTON, MO.

1	GE	SL110	1	80/06	

CLEV-CLEVELAND ELECTRIC ILLUMINATING

1	GE	SL110	15	84/06	
1	GE	SL110	18	78/03	
9	EMD	GP38-2	100-108	75/09	

COOR-COORS BREWING CO. BOULDER, CO.

1	EMD	SW1001	998 (2nd)	80/12	

CPCX-CORN PRODUCTS CO.

2	EMD	SW1000	68-69	69/05	

CPOX-CONSUMER'S POWER CO.

1	GE	SL125	NONE	79/02	

CPRX-CAROLINA POWER & LIGHT, ROXBORO, N.C.

1	GE	SL110	NONE	79/03	

CSNX-CITIES SERVICE CO.

1	EMD	SW1500	108	70/05	
1	EMD	MP15DC	109	74/04	

DEEX-DETROIT EDISON

6	EMD	SD40	001-006	70/04-70/05	003,004,006 TO MEC 600-602,87/01
6	GE	U30C	007-012	72/02-72/03	012 TO MEC 640, 86/02,RE# 663
2	EMD	SD40	013-014	72/02	014 TO MEC 603 IN 1986
3	EMD	SD40	015-017	72/07	017 TO MEC 604 IN 1986, LAST SD40's BUILT.
5	GE	U30C	018-022	75/07	
1	EMD	SW1001	217	68/09	

QTY.	BLDR.	MODEL	DELV.NO.	BLDR.DATE	NOTES

DELM-DELMARVA POWER & LIGHT

2	GE	SL100	3,7	77/06	

DIAM-DIAMOND SHAMROCK

1	GE	SL110	NONE	75/05	SOLD TO UNION CARBIDE

DKPX-DUKE POWER CO.

1	GE	SL82	83	80/11	ALLEN PLT. BELMONT, NC.
1	GE	80T	102	70/12	MARSHALL PLT. CATAWBA,NC.
1	GE	80T	103	72/05	
2	GE	80T	104-105	73/05	BELLOWS CREEK PLANT,NC.

DOT-US.DEPT.OF TRANS.
001, GE, U30C
BLT. 71/06
DOLTON,IL.NEW I/T, 71/06

DOT-U.S.DEPARTMENT OF TRANSPORTATION

1	GE	U30C	001	71/06	
1	EMD	GP40-2	003	78/11	

DOWX-DOW CHEMICAL CO.

3	EMD	SW1001	1001-1003	80/12	FREEPORT,TX.
2	EMD	SW1001	1008-1009	80/12	PLAQUEMINE,LA.
1	EMD	MP15T	957	87/05	

EACX-EASTERN ASSOCIATED COAL, WHARTON, WV.

1	GE	SL110	NONE	76/01	
1	GE	SL110	NONE	77/04	

QTY.	BLDR.	MODEL	DELV.NO.	BLDR.DATE	NOTES

EDSX-EXXON COMPANY, USA. BATON ROUGE, LA.

1	GE	SL144	3	81/08	

EKPC-EAST KENTUCKY POWER

1	GE	SL110	1	75/06	MARYSVILLE, KY.
1	EMD	SW1001	2	80/06	

EMD-ELECTRO-MOTIVE
114, EMD, SW1500
BLT. 71/04
LA GRANGE, IL. 72/09

EMD-ELECTRO-MOTIVE DIVISION, GENERAL MOTORS

4	EMD	SD60	EMD1-EMD4	84/05-84/07	PROTOTYPE TEST UNITS,1,2,4, TO CR 6840,6842,6841
3	EMD	GP60	EMD5-EMD7	85/10	PROTOTYPE TEST UNITS
3	EMD	GP59	EMD8-10	85/06	SOLD TO SOU(NS)4606-4608
10	EMD	GP40	11-20	69/04-69/05	TO PC 3260-3269
1	EMD	GP40	21	69/05	TPW 1000,ATSF 3461,SCR/84
5	EMD	GP40	22-26	69/05	TO PC 3270-3274
1	EMD	SW1500	109	70/03	PLT.SWITCHER,TO IHB 9222
1	EMD	SW1500	110	68/11	PLT.SWITCHER,TO IU 27
1	EMD	SW1500	111	71/12	PLT.SWITCHER,TO IU 29
1	EMD	SW1500	112	71/05	PLT.SWITCHER,TO IU 28
1	EMD	SW1500	113	71/04	PLT.SWITCHER,TO ETR 187
1	EMD	SW1500	114	71/04	PLT.SWITCHER,TO GRR 1010
1	EMD	MP15AC	115	75/10	PLANT SWITCHER
1	EMD	MP15AC	116	78/07	PLANT SWITCHER
1	EMD	SW1001	117	79/12	PLANT SWITCHER

EMD-ELECTRO-MOTIVE DIVISION, GENERAL MOTORS, cont'd

EMD-ELECTRO-MOTIVE
EMD5, EMD, GP60
BLT. 85/10
PHOENIX, AZ. 89/02
PHOTO: JAMES D. BRADLEY

QTY.	BLDR.	MODEL	DELV.NO.	BLDR.DATE	NOTES
1	EMD	GM6C	1975	75/04	6000HP C-C ELECTRIC DEMO
1	EMD	GM10B	1976	76/08	10000HP B-B-B ELEC. DEMO
4	EMD	GP40	2068-2071	69/05	TO MILW 2068-2071, 2070,2071 TO CCX IN 84
1	EMD	SD45X	4201	70/06	SOLD TO SP 9503, SCR.84
2	EMD	SD45X	4202-4203	71/02	TO SP 9504-9505,9504 SCR.84 9505 WRK/RET.78/06, TO MK, REBLT.TO SD40M, MK 8301.
1	EMD	SD45X	5740	70/06	DEMO UNIT

EMPI-EMPIRE REEVES STEEL

1	GE	110T	NONE	73/01	

ETCX-TENNESSEE EASTMAN CO.

1	EMD	SW1500	1	73/12	KINGSPORT,TN.PLANT
1	EMD	MP15DC	2	75/11	KINGSPORT,TN.PLANT

EWSX-INDIANAPOLIS POWER & LIGHT CO.

1	EMD	SW1001	NONE	82/03	

FERT-FERTIMEX (MEXICO)

7	GE	SL115	1-7	80/08-80/10	

FORD-FORD MOTOR CO.

5	EMD	SW1001	10014-10018	68/10	10015 SCR. 84
2	EMD	SW1001	10019-10020	73/10	
3	EMD	SW1001	10021-10023	75/12	

FRA-FEDERAL RAILROAD ADMINISTRATION

1	BUDD	SPV2000	T10	80/07

FUND-FUNDIDORA de FIERRO y ACERO (MEXICO)

1	GE	110T	8	68/01
1	GE	110T	9	71/05
2	GE	SL130	14-15	76/05,76/07
1	GE	SL110	16	77/03

GATX-GENERAL AMERICAN TRANSPORTATION CORP.

1	GE	SL85	46575	78/09
1	GE	SL85	46576	81/06

GECX-GENERAL ELECTRIC CORP.

1	GE	80T	N/A	70/12	
1	GE	SL110	1 (1st)	74/11	DEMO,TO ALGOMA STEEL 60
1	GE	SL110	1 (2nd)	76/06	DEMO,TO PULLMAN-SWINDELL
1	GE	SL144	2	78/02	DEMO,TO ALLP 1
1	GE	SL85	20	76/11	GE-SCHENECTADY
1	GE	SL85	21	78/12	GE-SCHENECTADY
2	GE	U36B	301-302	72/12	DEMO's, REBLT TO U30B, TO CO 8223,8224,TO CS/CSXT 5351,5352
2	GE	U36B	303-304	71/05	DEMO's, TO U30B, WP 770,771, RE# 3070,3071, SCR. 80/10
1	GE	C36-7	505	77/06	ENGR. DEPT. TEST UNIT
1	GE	B36-8	606	82/09	DEMO, REBLT. TO B39-8.5E IN 88, R# 809
1	GE	C36-8	607	83/03	TEST UNIT, REBLT TO C39-8
1	GE	DASH840B	8002	88/12	LEASED TO SP
6	GE	DASH840C	9350-9355	88/12	LEASED TO UP, WARRANTY PROTECTION UNITS

GLSX-GREAT LAKES STEEL CORP.

1	EMD	SW1001	58	71/10

GMCX-GENERAL MOTORS CORP.

1	EMD	SW1000	NONE	72/04	
1	EMD	SW1001	1971	71/08	DEFIANCE, OH. PLANT

GOCX-CHEVRON USA, INC.

1	EMD	MP15DC	101	79/09

GREE-GREENVILLE STEEL CAR CO.

1	GE	80T	3	74/02

QTY.	BLDR.	MODEL	DELV.NO.	BLDR.DATE	NOTES
GUAN-GUANOS Y FERILIZANTES (MEXICO)					
1	GE	SL110	NONE	77/05	
GUAX-GEORGIA POWER CO.					
1	EMD	SW1500	1401	69/05	HATCH PLANT, BAXLEY,GA.
1	EMD	SW1500	1402	71/08	YATES PLANT, NEWNAN,GA.
1	EMD	SW1500	1405	73/01	YATES PLANT, NEWNAN,GA.
2	EMD	SW1500	1503-1504	71/08	HAMMOND PLANT, ROME,GA.
HECX-HOOSIER ENERGY CO. MEROM, IN.					
1	GE	SL110	NONE	80/03	
HOJO-HOJOLATA y LAMINA, S.A. (MEXICO)					
4	GE	SL110	NONE	81/12	
1	GE	SL110	NONE	85/12	
1	GE	SL144	NONE	88/11	
HOUS-HOUSTON POWER & LIGHT CO.					
1	GE	SL65	1	82/10	
HOWE-HOWE COAL CO.					
1	EMD	SW1500	1	70/06	TO TOPCO, PORT ARTHUR, TX.
1	EMD	SW1500	2	70/05	TO KCS 4362
HPAX-HAMMERMILL PAPER CO.					
1	GE	SL110	16	80/01	
INCO-INTERNATIONAL NICKEL CO OF CANADA (CANADA)					
3	MLW	RS18	208-2,3,4	68/04-68/08	208-4 LAST MLW RS18 BUILT
INDI-INDIANA POWER & LIGHT					
1	GE	110T	NONE	73/03	
INDU-INDUSTRIAL MINERA (MEXICO)					
1	EMD	MP15DC	NONE	82/01	
1	EMD	MP15DC	383	79/09	
INLX-INLAND STEEL CO.					
1	EMD	SW1500	119	68/05	
2	EMD	SW1500	120-121	68/07,68/08	
2	EMD	SW1500	122-123	70/01	
2	EMD	SW1500	124-125	73/12	
2	EMD	SW1001	126-127	76/03	

IPPX-INTERMOUNTAIN POWER
1, EMD, SW1001
BLT. 85/04
SPRINGVILLE, UT. 88/07

QTY.	BLDR.	MODEL	DELV.NO.	BLDR.DATE	NOTES
IPPX-INTERMOUNTAIN POWER PROJECT					
1	EMD	SW1001	1	85/04	
IRON-IRON ORE CO OF CANADA (CANADA)					
1	GMD	SW1200MG	431506	68/03	CAROL LAKE, PQ.
3	GMD	SW1200MG	431507-09	71/10	CAROL LAKE, PQ.
ISCX-INTERLAKE STEEL CO.					
2	EMD	SW1001	17-18	74/10	
ITSE-ITSERCO, HYLSA, (MEXICO)					
3	GE	SL110	N/A	81/08	
1	GE	SL115	NONE	82/06	
JONE-JONES & LAUGHLIN STEEL					
1	EMD	SW1000	103	69/02	
KAIS-KAISER STEEL CO. FONTANA, CA.					
5	GE	U30C	1030-1034	68/03	STORED 86/03,PLT.SHUTDOWN

KCC-KENNECOTT COPPER CO.
786, EMD, GP39-2
BLT. 77/01
COPPERTON, UT. 80/06

QTY.	BLDR.	MODEL	DELV.NO.	BLDR.DATE	NOTES
KCC-KENNECOTT COPPER CORP.					
2	EMD	GP39	1-2	70/06	RE# 401,402,SOLD CBRY SAME#
1	EMD	GP39-2	3	80/12	
7	EMD	SD40-2	101-107	78/11	SOLD TO BCOL 736-742
3	EMD	MP15AC	120-122	78/12	HI-VISIBILITY WIDE CAB
2	EMD	MP15AC	701,704	78/12	701 RE# 915, 704 RE# 123
7	EMD	GP39-2	705-711	80/09	SPECIAL HI-VISIBILITY CAB
5	EMD	GP39-2	779-783	77/01	TO NRE,THEN MKT 380-384
1	EMD	GP39-2	784	77/01	RE# 910, HI-VISIBILITY CAB
1	EMD	GP39-2	785	77/01	TO NRE,THEN MKT 385
1	EMD	GP39-2	786	77/01	RE# 911. HI-VISIBILITY CAB
3	EMD	GP39-2	787-789	77/01	TO NRE,THEN MKT 386-388
10	EMD	GP39-2	790-799	78/10	SPECIAL HI-VISIBILITY CAB
1	EMD	GP39-2	905	76/12	
1	EMD	MP15DC	906	76/12	
1	EMD	GP39-2	910	80/12	
KCCX-KENNECOTT MINERALS DIVISION					
2	EMD	GP39-2	1-2	81/11	
KCDX-EASTMAN KODAK CO.					
1	EMD	SW1000	8	68/12	
1	EMD	MP15AC	10	81/04	
KCLX-KANSAS CITY POWER & LIGHT CO.					
1	GE	SL110	2	76/02	

QTY.	BLDR.	MODEL	DELV.NO.	BLDR.DATE	NOTES
KENT-KENTUCKY POWER					
1	GE	100T	103	69/08	
KEYS-KEYSTONE STEEL & WIRE					
2	GE	SL85	450-451	75/05,75/06	
KUCX-KENTUCKY UTILITIES					
1	GE	110T	NONE	71/03	E W BROWN STATION,BURGIN,KY.
LATC-LA TOLTECA CIA (MEXICO)					
1	GE	80T	NONE	68/09	

LMX-GEN.ELECTRIC LEASING
8560, GE, B39-8E
BLT. 87/11
IRVING, TX. 89/04

QTY.	BLDR.	MODEL	DELV.NO.	BLDR.DATE	NOTES
LMX-GENERAL ELECTRIC LEASING					
41	GE	B39-8E	8500-8540	87/05-87/07	LEASED TO BN, 8503,8540 WRK. RETURNED TO GE, REBLT. RE# GECX 8000,8001.
1	GE	B39-8E	8503(2nd)	88/03	WRECK REPLACEMENT, LEASED TO BN
1	GE	B39-8E	8540(2nd)	88/03	WRECK REPLACEMENT, LEASED TO BN
26	GE	B39-8E	8541-8566	87/10-87/11	LEASED TO BN
33	GE	B39-8E	8567-8599	88/03-88/04	LEASED TO BN
LOUI-LOUISVILLE GAS & ELECTRIC					
1	GE	110T	NONE	70/04	
1	GE	SL110	NONE	80/08	

QTY.	BLDR.	MODEL	DELV.NO.	BLDR.DATE	NOTES
LUKE-LUKENS STEEL					
1	GE	SL120	42	77/11	
MASS-MASSEY COAL CO.					
3	GE	SL110	SL1-SL3	82/09-82/12	
MOBX-MOBIL OIL CORP.					
1	GE	80T	N/A	71/04	
1	GE	SL110	117	81/05	BEAUMONT, TX.
MUSK-MUSKINGUM ELECTRIC					
2	GE	E50C	100,200	68/05	
NATI-NATIONAL HARBOURS BOARD (CANADA)					
2	EMD	SW1001	7601-7602	76/07	
4	GMD	MP15AC	8403-8406	84/08	

NORT-NW. STEEL & WIRE CO.
4, EMD, SW1001
BLT. 81/05
STERLING, IL. 88/09

NORT-NORTHWESTERN STEEL & WIRE CO.					
3	EMD	SW1001	2-4	81/05	
NYSX-NEW YORK STATE ELECTRIC & GAS CORP.					
1	GE	SL144	NONE	83/11	SOMERSET STATION

QTY.	BLDR.	MODEL	DELV.NO.	BLDR.DATE	NOTES

OLNX-OLIN CORP.

1	EMD	SW1001	1	82/06	

OPX-OHIO POWER CO.

1	GE	SL110	3	75/03	MITCHELL PLANT
2	GE	SL144	4,5	75/12,76/02	METROPOLIS, IL. PLANT

OWTX-SHAMROCK COAL CO.

8	EMD	SD40-2	9950-9957	79/09	LETTERED ONEIDA & WESTERN SOLD TO BCOL 743-750

OWY-OAKWAY LEASING
9021, EMD, SD60
BLT. 86/10
SIXELA, NM. 88/07

OWY-OAKWAY LEASING

100	EMD	SD60	9000-9099	86/10-86/12	LEASED TO BN

PACI-PACIFIC POWER

1	EMD	GP38AC	11	71/12	

PHDX-PHELPS DODGE CORP.

1	GE	80T	NONE	72/09	
1	GE	80T	NONE	74/07	
3	EMD	GP38-2	1-3	73/10	
1	EMD	GP38-2	4	77/03	
1	EMD	GP38-2	9	76/03	
1	EMD	GP39-2	33	81/08	AJO,AZ.TO MORENCI,RE# 63

PHDX-PHELPS DODGE CORP. cont'd

QTY.	BLDR.	MODEL	DELV.NO.	BLDR.DATE	NOTES
2	EMD	GP38	53-54	71/04	MORENCI MINES DIV.
2	EMD	GP38-2	55-56	76/03	MORENCI MINES DIV.
1	EMD	GP38-2	58	82/03	MORENCI MINES DIV.

PMEX-PETROLEOS MEXICANOS (MEXICO)

1	EMD	SW1001	5	86/06	
1	GE	SL85	12	75/05	
2	GE	SL125	13,14	76/01-76/02	
2	GE	SL115	18,19	77/07	
2	GE	SL144	20,21	78/08	
2	GE	SL115	22,23	78/12	
2	EMD	SW1001	24-25	80/08	
1	GE	SL144	0411-L	76/09	
1	GE	SL144	0412-L	76/09	

PORT-PORT OF TACOMA

1	GE	SL110	705	80/04	

PSCX-PUBLIC SERVICE CO. OF COLORADO

1	EMD	SW1001	15-1	73/10	(2nd)

PSIX-PUBLIC SERVICE CO. OF INDIANA

2	EMD	GP38-2	WG1-WG2	74/03	LETTERED AMAX COAL
1	EMD	SW1000	1	69/09	

QCMX-QUEBEC CARTIER MINING (CANADA)

3	MLW	M636	71-73	72/01-72/02	72 WRK/SCR.72/05
3	MLW	M636	74-76	73/10	
5	MLW	M636	81-85	75/03-75/04	

QITX-QUEBEC IRON & TITANIUM CORP. (CANADA)

1	EMD	MP15DC	10	80/10	ALLARD LAKE MINES
1	MLW	RS18	6	68/06	ALLARD LAKE MINES
1	EMD	MP15DC	9	77/03	ALLARD LAKE MINES

REPU-REPUBLIC STEEL, KITT, WV.

1	GE	SL110	NONE	76/06	SOLD TO STANDARD OIL CO.

RESE-RESERVE MINING CO.

9	EMD	SD38-2	1237-1245	78/10	

RMCX-REYNOLDS METALS CO.

1	GE	80T	NONE	68/09	

QTY.	BLDR.	MODEL	DELV.NO.	BLDR.DATE	NOTES

RWIX-ROCKWELL INTERNATIONAL

1	EMD	MP15AC	3727	83/12	HANFORD PLANT
1	EMD	MP15AC	3728	82/09	HANFORD PLANT

SANI-SANITARY DISTRICT OF CHICAGO

1	EMD	MP15DC	4	83/01	

SCEG-SOUTH CAROLINA ELECTRIC & GAS

1	GE	SL110	NONE	84/04	

SCWX-SOUTH CAROLINA PUBLIC SERVICE AUTHORITY

1	EMD	SW1001	1001	75/03	
2	EMD	SW1001	2001-2002	77/12	SUB-LETTERED FOR ECBR

SECX-SOUTH EAST COAL CO.

3	EMD	GP38-2	3821-3823	79/03	

SICA-SICARTSA (MEXICO)

3	EMD	SW1001	1-3	76/01	

SIGX-SOUTHERN INDIANA GAS & ELECTRIC CO.

1	GE	SL110	NONE	84/06	

SJGX-S.J.GROVES CONSTRUCTION CO.

2	GE	U33C	507-508	69/10	SOLD TO BN 5764-5765, SCR.86

SJMX-ST.JOE MINERALS CORP.

1	EMD	SW1001	1004	74/08	

SMCX-SAN MIGUEL ELECTRIC CO-OP,INC.

1	GE	SL115	NONE	78/09	SOLD, BRAZOS RIVER ELECTRIC

SMT-TRANS-ISTHMUS MULTIMODAL TRANSISTMICO (MEXICO)

8	GE	B23-7	1-01-1-08	81/01-81/02	OWNED BY NDEM, 1-08 WRK/RET. L/87.

SOUT-SOUTH CAROLINA ELECTRIC & GAS

1	GE	110T	NONE	69/09	WATEREE PLT. WATEREE,SC.
1	GE	SL110	NONE	84/04	

SPCX-SASKATCHEWAN POWER (CANADA)

2	EMD	SW1001	1001-1002	78/11	

QTY.	BLDR.	MODEL	DELV.NO.	BLDR.DATE	NOTES
SPEN-SPENO RAIL SERVICES CO.					
2	EMD	F40PH-2M	S1-S2	82/03	NON-TURBOCHARGED
2	EMD	F40PH-2M	S3-S4	85/11	NON-TURBO,RE# 212 & 201
SROX-U.S.DEPT.OF ENERGY, SAVANNAH RIVER PLANT					
1	GE	DASH840B	N/A	89/05	
SWIF-SWIFT, AGRICOLA, FL.					
1	EMD	MP15DC	1976	76/12	
TGSX-TEXAS GULF SULPHER CO. (CANADA)					
2	GMD	GP38-2	054-055	76/10	
TIMK-TIMKEN CO.					
1	GE	SL85	4845	77/12	
TMPX-TEXAS MUNICIPAL POWER AGENCY					
1	GE	SL125	NONE	79/12	
TPBX-TEXACO, INC.					
1	EMD	SW1001	24	75/12	
TUBO-TUBOS de ACEROS, TAMSA, (MEXICO)					
1	GE	SL125	5	81/03	
TUGX-TEXAS UTILITIES MINING CO.					
2	GE	SL65	NONE	76/11,77/02	
2	GE	U18B	101-102	74/03	RE# 2301,2302
1	GE	U23B	103	75/05	RE# 3305
3	GE	E25B	2304-2306	76/05	
2	GE	E25B	3301-3302	76/06	
2	GE	E25B	3303-3304	78/12,79/02	
1	GE	B23-7	3306	79/08	
1	GE	B23-7	3307	81/10	
USPF-U.S.PIPE & FOUNDRY					
4	EMD	SW1500	51-54	72/09	

QTY.	BLDR.	MODEL	DELV.NO.	BLDR.DATE	NOTES

USX-UNITED STATES STEEL CORP.

1	GE	110T	N/A	68/03	
1	EMD	SD38-2	1	75/12	CUMBERLAND MINE
2	EMD	SW1001	88,89	70/03	
1	EMD	SW1001	90	71/01	
1	EMD	MP15DC	170	76/05	FAIRFIELD WORKS, TO BS 370
1	GE	SL115	911	75/08	GARY WORKS
1	GE	SL115	912	76/02	GARY WORKS
6	EMD	SW1500	949-954	72/09	MINNESOTA TACONITE DIV.
11	EMD	MP15DC	955-965	76/05	MINNTAC MINE
3	EMD	MP15DC	966-968	76/08	MINNTAC MINE

VEPC-VEPCO, VIRGINA ELECTRIC POWER

1	GE	SL110	NONE	81/01	CHESTERFIELD POWER PLANT
1	GE	SL110	NONE	82/12	WHEELWRIGHT, VA. PLANT

WEPX-WISCONSIN ELECTRIC POWER CO.

1	EMD	SW1000	N/A	68/08	
1	GE	SL110	1	79/06	

WFAX-WESTERN FUELS ASSOCIATION, INC.

2	GE	E60C	WFU1-WFU2	83/08	DESERET WESTERN RR.

WRGX-W.R.GRACE CO.

1	EMD	SW1500	101	69/04	101 (2nd)
1	EMD	SW1500	102	68/03	102 (3rd)
2	EMD	MP15DC	121-122	75/08	
2	EMD	MP15DC	131-132	80/10	

WTCX-WEYERHAEUSER CO.

1	EMD	SW1500	306	68/05	
1	EMD	SW1500	307	72/12	

YANK-YANKEETOWN DOCK CORP.

2	EMD	SD38-2	20-21	72/11	
1	EMD	SD38-2	22	78/12	

YSTX-YOUNGSTOWN SHEET & TUBE CO.

2	EMD	SW1000	908-909	68/06	
1	EMD	SW1000	910	68/08	
1	EMD	SW1000	911	69/05	
2	EMD	SW1000	912-913	69/04	
3	EMD	SW1000	912-914	69/05-69/06	

THE BUILDERS, 1968-1989

ALCO PRODUCTS, SCHENECTADY, N.Y.
(FORMERLY AMERICAN LOCOMOTIVE WORKS)

MODEL C415
BURLINGTON NORTHERN
4010, ex SP&S 100
BLT. 68/11
PASCO, WA. 78/11

BLDR.DATE	RR.	QTY.	DELV.NO.	NOTES
MODEL C415, 1500 hp. BUILT 1966-1968				
68/07	CW	1	684	RELETTERED CM&E (CMER)
68/07	MCRR	1	701	OFF ROSTER
68/11	CLC	1	701	
68/11	SPS	1	100	TO BN 4010,TO AQUITANE (CANADA)
68/12	SPS	1	101	TO BN 4011,TO AQUITANE (CANADA)
MODEL C420, 2000 hp. BUILT 1963-1968				
68/08	LI	8	222-229	
MODEL C430, 3000 hp. BUILT 1966-1968				
68/02	GBW	1	315	STORED UNSERVICEABLE
MODEL C628, 2750 hp. BUILT 1963-1968				
68/02	NDEM	12	8310-8321	
68/02-68/03	NDEM	10	8322-8331	HAVE STEAM GENERATORS
68/12	FCP	4	607-610	607 RET. REST TO NDM 8335-8337

MODEL C636
BURLINGTON NORTHERN
4364, ex SP&S 334
BLT. 68/01
SPOKANE, WA. 78/04

MODEL C636, 3600 hp. BUILT 1967-1968

BLDR.DATE	RR.	QTY.	DELV.NO.	NOTES
67/12-68/01	SPS	6	330-335	TO BN 4360-4365, ALL RETIRED
68/01-68/02	PC	15	6330-6344	ORD.BY PRR, DEL.PC,TO CR 6780-6794, 6781,6782 TO AUSTRALA, 6792 TO DBT 1001, STOCKTON,CA. REST SCRAPPED.
68/05	IC	6	1100-1105	TO PNC 80/01
68/11	ALCO	3	636-1,2,3	DEMONSTRATORS,THEN SOLD TO QUEBEC CARTIER MINING 79,78,77.
68/11	SPS	4	340-343	TO BN 4366-4369, ALL RETIRED 4369 TO AUSTRALA IN 81

MODEL T6, 1000 hp. BUILT 1958-1969

BLDR.DATE	RR.	QTY.	DELV.NO.	NOTES
68/02	PRTD	1	46	SOLD 1984, TO JR MILLER, SEATTLE,WA.
68/02	PRTD	1	47	SOLD 1984, GILMORE STEEL, PORTLAND,OR.
68/07	MCRR	1	400	TO MKC, IN 1982
69/01	NSR	2	1016-1017	TO MKC, IN 1981, LAST ALCO'S BUILT

BBD-BOMBARDIER, INC. MONTREAL, PQ, CANADA
(FORMERLY MONTREAL LOCOMOTIVE WORKS)

BLDR.DATE	RR.	QTY.	DELV.NO.	NOTES

MODEL HR412W, 2000 hp. BUILT 1982

BLDR.DATE	RR.	QTY.	DELV.NO.	NOTES
81/09-81/11	CN	10	2580-2589	
82/05	BBD	1	7000	TEST BED,WITH SOME LRC TYPE PARTS

MODEL HR616W, 3000 hp. BUILT 1982

BLDR.DATE	RR.	QTY.	DELV.NO.	NOTES
82/02-82/08	CN	4	2100-2103	LEASED BACK TO BBD 83/02,TO BE DEMO's 7001-7004.
82/02-82/08	CN	16	2104-2119	

MODEL LRC(B)
VIA RAIL CANADA
6913, BLT. 81/09
WINDSOR, ON. 87/09

MODEL LRC(B), 3725 hp. BUILT 1980-1984

BLDR.DATE	RR.	QTY.	DELV.NO.	NOTES
80/02,80/06	AMTK	2	38-39	LEASED ONLY, RETURNED TO BBD 1982
81/02-82/06	VIA	21	6900-6920	6906 WRK.83, SCR.85
83/11-84/10	VIA	10	6921-6930	

THE BUDD COMPANY, PHILADELPHIA, PA.

MODEL SPV-2000,(SELF PROPELLED VEHICLE) BUILT 1980-1981

BLDR.DATE	RR.	QTY.	DELV.NO.	NOTES
80/04	CDOT	1	50	
80/04-80/07	AMTK	12	988-999	OWNED BY CDOT, SOME RETIRED
80/07	FRA	1	T10	
81/09-81/11	MTA	10	290-299	

EMD-ELECTRO-MOTIVE DIVISION of GENERAL MOTORS, LA GRANGE, IL.

MODEL AEM7
MARYLAND DEPT.of TRANS.
4903, BLT. 86/12
BALTIMORE, MD. 87/07
PHOTO: JAMES D. BRADLEY

BLDR.DATE	RR.	QTY.	DELV.NO.	NOTES
MODEL AEM7, 7000 hp. BUILT 1979-1988				
79/11-81/08	AMTK	30	900-929	BUDD & ASEA COMP.900,03,04, WRK.
81/09-82/07	AMTK	17	930-946	BUDD & ASEA COMPONENTS, 941 WRK.
86/08-86/12	MDOT	4	4900-4903	ASEA COMPONENTS
87/10-87/12	SEPT	7	2301-2307	ASEA COMPONENTS
88/09-88/12	AMTK	7	947-953	ASEA COMPONENTS
MODEL DDA40X, 6600 hp, BUILT 1969-1971				
				ALL DDA40X's RETIRED IN 1985
69/04	UP	1	6900	DONATED TO CITY OF OMAHA, NE.
69/06	UP	2	6901-6902	6901 TO CITY OF POCOTELLO, ID.
69/07	UP	2	6903-6904	6903 WRK/SCR.74/04
69/08	UP	4	6905-6908	
69/09	UP	4	6909-6912	6911 TO MUSEUM, MEXICO CITY, MEX.
69/10	UP	4	6913-6916	6913 TO AGE OF STEAM MUSEUM,DALLAS,TX.
				6915 TO MUSEUM, POMONA,CA.
				6916 TO CITY OF OGDEN, UT.
69/11	UP	4	6917-6920	
69/12	UP	4	6921-6924	6921 WRK/SCR. 78
				6922 TO CITY OF NORTH PLATTE, NE.
70/06	UP	3	6925-6927	6925 TO DSRC, STORED UNSERVICEABLE
70/07-70/08	UP	4	6928-6931	6930 TO MUSEUM, KANSAS CITY, MO.
70/12	UP	3	6932-6934	
71/01	UP	3	6935-6937	6936 RETAINED BY UP FOR CO.PR.USE

EMD-MODEL DDA40X, cont'd

MODEL DDA40X
UNION PACIFIC
6945, BLT. 71/09
LAS VEGAS, NV. 79/06

BLDR.DATE	RR	QTY.	DELV.NO.	NOTES
71/06-71/07	UP	5	6938-6942	6938 AWAITING DISPOSITION.
71/08-71/09	UP	4	6943-6946	6944 TO MUSEUM, ST LOUIS,MO.
				6946 TO MUSEUM, PORTOLA, CA.

MODEL F40C
NSMTD, (CHICAGO)
49, BLT. 74/05
ELGIN, IL. 75/08

MODEL F40C, 3200 hp, BUILT 1974

74/03-74/05	NSMT	13	40-52	RE# 600-612 IN 86
74/05	NSMT	2	53,54	RE# 613,614 IN 86

BLDR.DATE	RR	QTY.	DELV.NO.	NOTES

MODEL F40PH, 3000 hp, BUILT 1976-1988

BLDR.DATE	RR	QTY.	DELV.NO.	NOTES
76/03-76/04	AMTK	30	200-229	202 WRK & REBLT, MODIFIED W/AC TRACTION MOTORS.
77/07-77/10	AMTK	25	230-254	246 WRK/SCR.
77/09-77/12	RTA	28	100-127	
77/11-78/01	AMTK	15	255-269	
77/11-78/01	AMTK	10	270-279	
78/03-78/07	AMTK	14	280-293	
78/09-78/11	MBTA	13	1000-1012	
79/04-79/06	AMTK	10	300-309	
79/06-79/07	AMTK	6	294-299	

MODEL F40PH
AMTRAK
319, BLT. 79/08
SPOKANE, WA. 79/10

BLDR.DATE	RR	QTY.	DELV.NO.	NOTES
79/07-79/08	AMTK	12	310-321	
79/09-79/10	AMTK	7	322-328	
79/11-80/01	RTA	22	128-149	
80/08	AMTK	3	329-331	
80/08-80/11	AMTK	15	332-346	
80/11	MBTA	5	1013-1017	
80/11-80/12	AMTK	13	347-359	
80/12	AMTK	1	360	
81/04-81/08	AMTK	30	361-390	
81/10-81/12	NJT	17	4113-4129	
83/02-83/04	RTA	24	150-173	
85/08	AMTK	10	391-400	
87/11-88/02	AMTK	9	401-409	

BLDR.DATE	RR	QTY	DELV.NO.	NOTES
MODEL F40PH-2, 3200 hp. BUILT 1985-1988				
85/03-85/06	CALT	18	900-917	
86/	MBTA	10	1018-1027	
87/12	CALT	2	918-919	
87/07-87/11	MBTA	18	1050-1067	CUMMINS HEP POWERED (F40PH-2C)
88/02-88/04	MBTA	8	1068-1075	CUMMINS HEP POWERED (F40PH-2C)
88/12	RTA	7	174-180	
MODEL F40PH-2M, 2000 hp. 1982,1985				
82/03	SPEN	2	S1-S2	NON-TURBO,RE# 101 & 109
85/11	SPEN	2	S3-S4	NON-TURBO,RE# 212 & 201 SPECIAL ORDER FOR SPENO RAIL SERVICES
MODEL F45, 3600 hp. 1968-1971				
68/06	ATSF	20	1900-1919	RE# 5900-5919,REMFG.TO F45U 5950-5969
68/06-68/07	ATSF	20	1920-1939	RE# 5920-5939,REMFG.TO F45U 5970-5989
69/05-69/06	GN	6	427-432	TO BN 6600-6605, ALL SCR.
69/08	GN	8	433-440	TO BN 6606-6613,6609-6612 SCR. REST TO UTAH SAME#
70/07-70/09	BN	12	6614-6625	ORDERED BY GN, DELV.BN,ALL RET.BY 86/02
71/04-71/05	BN	20	6626-6645	ALL RET. 6640,6644,TO NYSW 86/11, 6640 RE# NYSW 6370, 6641 TO DOYLE McCORMACK 87/03 6635,6642 TO NRL.

MODEL FP45
MILWAUKEE ROAD
1, BLT. 68/12
BENSONVILLE, IL. 76/09

MODEL FP45, 3600 hp. 1967-1968				
68/12	MILW	5	1-5	ALL SCRAPPED
MODEL F69PH-AC, 3000 hp. 1989-				
89/04	AMTK	2	450,451	

BLDR.DATE	RR	QTY	DELV.NO.	NOTES
MODEL GA18, 1800 hp. BUILT 1968				
68/02	CHZ	1	800	ONLY ONE,BUILT FOR COAHUILA & ZACATECAS
MODEL GM6C, 6000 hp. BUILT 1975				
75/04	EMD	1	1975	C-C ELECTRIC DEMONSTRATOR
MODEL GM10B, 10000 hp. BUILT 1976				
76/08	EMD	1	1976	B-B-B ELECTRIC DEMONSTRATOR

MODEL GP15-1
MISSOURI PACIFIC
1711, BLT. 82/03
FT.WORTH, TX. 82/07

MODEL GP15-1, 1500 hp. BUILT 1976-1982

BLDR.DATE	RR	QTY	DELV.NO.	NOTES
76/06-76/07	CNW	25	4400-4424	
76/06-76/07	MP	15	1555-1569	TO UP SAME #
76/07	MP	5	1570-1574	SUB-LETTERED C&EI,TO UP SAME#
76/12	MP	15	1575-1589	TO UP SAME #
77/07	MP	25	1590-1614	TO UP SAME #
77/08-77/09	SLSF	25	100-124	TO BN 1375-1399
79/07-79/12	CR	100	1600-1699	
79/09-79/11	MP	30	1615-1644	TO UP SAME #
81/08	MP	20	1645-1664	TO UP SAME #
82/02-82/03	MP	40	1665-1704	TO UP SAME #
82/03	MP	10	1705-1714	TO UP SAME #

MODEL GP15-1(AC), 1500 hp, BUILT 1982

BLDR.DATE	RR	QTY	DELV.NO.	NOTES
82/11-82/12	MP	30	1715-1744	TO UP SAME #

MODEL GP15T(AC)
CO/CHESSIE SYSTEM
1517, BLT. 82/11
RIVERDALE, IL. 83/10

MODEL GP15T(AC), 1500 hp, BUILT 1982-1983

BLDR.DATE	RR	QTY.	DELV.NO.	NOTES
82/10-82/11	CO	25	1500-1524	CS TO CSXT SAME #
83/04	AN	3	720-722	

MODEL GP38, 2000 hp, BUILT 1966-1971

BLDR.DATE	RR	QTY.	DELV.NO.	NOTES
68/02	TAG	1	1	RE# 80, TO SOU 2879
68/06	AR	1	400	
69/04	PRSL	5	2005-2009	TO PC-CR 7665-7669, 7669 SCR.
69/06	MGA	5	2000-2004	
69/06-69/11	PC	140	7675-7814	CR SAME#, MOST RET. TO PLE,PW,NHL,NRE/87
69/08	GMO	20	701-720	TO ICG 9520-9539
69/09	DTI	2	205-206	TO GTW 6205-6206
69/09	SOU	25	2728-2752	2732 WRK/SCR.74/06
69/09-69/10	SOU	12	2716-2727	
69/10-70/03	SOU	70	2753-2822	
69/11	PC	10	7815-7824	CR SAME#, ALL RET. 7822 TO B&P, 7818,7824 TO PLE, 7816 TO SPENO MW111.
69/12	MKT	4	300-303	TO UP 1975-1978
70/02	BN	6	2072-2077	ORIGINALLY ORDERED BY SP&S, DELIVERED BN
70/05-70/05	DTI	8	207-214	TO GTW 6207-6214
70/05-70/06	PC	43	7825-7867	MOST SOLD TO BN 2155-2189, 7856 SCR.
70/06	ATSF	23	3500-3522	REMFG, RE# 2300-2322 GP38u
70/06	ATSF	1	3523	WRK/SCR. 73/04
70/06	ATSF	5	3524-3528	REMFG, RE# 2324-2328 GP38u
70/07-70/08	CO	6	4820-4829	TO CS SAME#, TO CSXT 2120-2125
70/07-70/08	PRSL	5	2010-2014	TO PC-CR 7670-7674
70/08	ATSF	19	3529-3547	REMFG, RE# 2329-2347 GP38u
70/08	ATSF	1	3548	REMFG, RE# 2348, SCR. 87/03
70/08	ATSF	1	3549	REMFG, RE# 2349 GP38u

MODEL GP38, cont'd

MODEL GP38
SANTA FE
3500, BLT. 70/06
CLEBURNE, TX. 81/08

BLDR.DATE	RR	QTY.	DELV.NO.	NOTES
70/08	CO	1	4826	WRK/RET. TO NRE 88/08
70/08	CO	3	4827-4829	TO CS SAME#, TO CSXT 2127-2129
70/08-70/12	BO	20	4800-4819	TO CS SAME#, TO CSXT 2100-2119, 4810 RET. 86/07, LATER TO NRL.
70/09	ATSF	2	3550-3551	REMFG, RE# 2350,2351, GP38u
70/09	ATSF	1	3552	WRK/SCR. 73/04
70/09	ATSF	8	3553-3560	REMFG, RE# 2353-2360, GP38u
71/01-71/02	PC	36	7868-7903	TO CR SAME#, 7877,7900 SCRAPPED
71/02-71/03	PC	32	7908-7939	TO CR SAME#, 7928,7929 SCRAPPED
71/03	PC	4	7904-7907	TO CR SAME#
71/04	PHDX	2	53-54	PHELPS-DODGE, MORENCI MINES DIV.
71/06	ALTO	2	135-136	ALTOS HORNOS (MEXICO)
71/06	FUS	2	512-513	TO BE RE# NDM 8255,8256.
71/08	TM	1	859	
71/08	TM	1	860	

MODEL GP38-2, 2000 hp, BUILT 1972-1985

BLDR.DATE	RR	QTY.	DELV.NO.	NOTES
72/01	LN	10	4050-4059	TO SBD SAME#, TO CSXT 2560-2569
72/01-72/02	MP	45	858-902	RE# 2009-2053, RET'D TO LESSOR L/87, THEN TO HL, SOME TO GTW.
72/01-72/02	SOU	10	5000-5009	
72/02-72/03	SOU	45	5010-5054	5021-5023 WRK/SCR. 88/04
72/03	LV	8	314-321	TO DH 7314-7321
72/03	SLSF	15	663-677	TO BN 2334-2347, 674 SCR. BEFORE RE#
72/03	SLSF	5	678-682	TO BN 2348-2352
72/04	LN	10	4060-4069	TO SBD SAME#, TO CSXT 2570-2579
72/04-72/08	GMO	15	740-754	TO ICG 9560-9574
72/05	BN	10	2078-2087	

MODEL GP38-2, cont'd

BLDR.DATE	RR	QTY	DELV.NO.	NOTES
72/05-72/08	PC	100	7940-8039	TO CR SAME#,RET'D LESSOR, EMD, 87/07, MOST LEASED TO BN, UP, RE# 740-839
72/08	BRC	6	490-495	
72/08	FUS	3	514-516	TO BE RE# NDM 9415,9416
72/08	LV	4	322-325	TO DH 7322-7325
72/09	MP	6	903-908	RE#2054-2059,TO UP 2380-2385,TO HL L/87
72/09-72/10	LN	20	4070-4089	TO SBD SAME#, TO CSXT 2580-2599
72/10	LN	5	4090-4094	TO SBD SAME#, TO CSXT 2600-2604
72/10	LN	1	4095	WRK/SCR. 80/01
72/10	LN	4	4096-4099	TO SBD SAME#, TO CSXT 2605-2608
72/10	MP	4	909-912	RE# 2060-2063,TO UP SAME #,TO HL L/87
72/10	MP	10	913-922	RE# 2064-2073,TO UP SAME #,TO HL L/87
72/11	SLSF	8	692-699	TO BN 2362-2369
72/11-72/12	SLSF	9	683-691	TO BN 2353-2361
72/12	DS	4	2000-2003	TO SBD 556-559, TO CSXT 2556-2559
72/12	EJE	4	700-703	(2nd) SOLD TO BS 700-703

MODEL GP38-2
MISSOURI-KANSAS-TEXAS
308, BLT. 72/12
DALLAS, TX. 84/01

BLDR.DATE	RR	QTY	DELV.NO.	NOTES
72/12	MKT	10	304-313	TO UP 2335-2344
72/12	SOU	4	5055-5058	
72/12	VTR	1	201	
73/01	MP	10	923-932	RE# 2074-2083, RET'D TO LESSOR, THEN LEASED BACK
73/01-73/03	PC	114	8040-8153	8080,8101,8114 SCRAPPED
73/02	LN	2	4100-4101	4100 TO SBD-CSXT 2609, 4101 SCR.80/05
73/02-73/03	LN	13	4102-4114	TO SBD SAME#,TO CSXT 2610-2622,4108 SCR
73/02-73/06	MP	27	933-959	RE# 2084-2110, RET'D TO LESSOR, THEN LEASED BACK
73/03	LN	10	4115-4124	TO SBD SAME#, TO CSXT 2623-2632
73/03-73/04	SCL	25	500-524	TO SBD SAME#, TO CSXT 2500-2524
73/05	ASAB	2	508-509	
73/05	MILW	6	350-355	TO SOO 4500-4505, RET'D TO LESSOR 89/01
73/06-73/07	SLSF	18	400-417	TO BN 2255-2272

MODEL GP38-2, cont'd

BLDR.DATE	RR	QTY	DELV.NO.	NOTES
73/07	SLSF	8	418-425	TO BN 2273-2280
73/08-73/09	LN	20	4125-4144	TO SBD SAME#,TO CSXT 2633-2652,4137 SCR
73/08-73/10	SOU	45	5059-5103	
73/10	EJE	1	704	(2nd) SOLD TO BS 704
73/10	PC	9	8154-8162	TO CR SAME #
73/10	PHDX	3	1-3	PHELPS-DODGE CORP.
73/10-73/11	SCL	31	525-555	TO SBD SAME#, TO CSXT 2525-2555
73/11	CW	2	2001-2002	
73/12	BM	12	201-212	212 RE# 200,206 RET.84, REST TO KCS 4012-4023, 88/07
74/01	ALTO	1	141	
74/01	KCS	10	4000-4009	
74/01-74/02	SOU	35	5104-5138	
74/03	PSIX	2	WG1-WG2	LETTERED AMAX COAL
74/03-74/04	UP	25	2000-2024	
74/05	UP	15	2025-2039	
74/08	MILW	10	356-365	TO SOO 4506-4515
74/08	MKT	4	314-317	TO UP 2345-2348
74/08	SLSF	21	426-446	TO BN 2281-2301
74/09	MP	10	2111-2120	TO UP SAME #
74/09	TM	2	861-862	
74/10	SMA	2	16-17	
74/10	VTR	1	202	
74/10-74/11	SOU	24	5139-5162	
74/11	BN	22	2088-2109	
74/11-74/12	ICG	40	9600-9639	
75/01	MP	12	2121-2132	TO UP SAME #
75/01	SLSF	12	447-458	TO BN 2302-2313
75/04	UP	20	2040-2059	
75/06	ASAB	1	510	
75/06	NDEM	20	9200-9219	HI-NOSE, STEAM GENERATOR
75/07	DTI	7	221-227	TO GTW 6221-6228
75/07	DTI	1	1776	R/W/B, RE# 228, TO GTW 6228
75/07	FUS	5	517-521	TO BE RE# NDM 9417-9421
75/08	NDEM	4	9401-9404	ASSEMBLED IN MEXICO BY NDEM
75/08	SOU	9	5163-5171	
75/09	ARMC	1	B84	ARMCO STEEL CO.
75/09	CLEV	9	100-108	CLEVELAND ELECTRIC ILLUMINATING
75/09	MSE	1	65	
75/10-75/12	NDEM	80	9220-9299	
75/11	ALTO	1	145	ALTOS HORNOS (MEXICO)
75/12	NDEM	1	9400	
76/01-76/02	LI	22	250-271	252 DELV. R/W/B
76/03	PHDX	1	9	PHELPS-DODGE CORP.
76/03	PHDX	2	55-56	PHELPS-DODGE CORP. MORENCI MINES DIV.
76/06	MKT	4	318-321	TO UP 2060-2063
76/07-76/08	MP	5	2133-2137	TO UP SAME #
76/08-76/09	RI	15	4300-4314	TO MP 2238-2251, TO UP SAME #
76/09-76/10	RI	11	4315-4325	TO MP 2252-2263, TO UP SAME #
76/09-76/10	SOU	30	5172-5201	
76/10-76/11	RI	26	4326-4351	TO MP 2264-2289, TO UP SAME #

MODEL GP38-2, cont'd

MODEL GP38-2
ROCK ISLAND
4352, BLT. 76/11
SILVIS, IL. 80/09

BLDR.DATE	RR	QTY.	DELV.NO.	NOTES
76/11	RI	4	4352-4355	TO PLE 2057-2060
76/11	SLSF	1	459	TO BN 2314
76/11	SLSF	1	460	TO BN 2315,WRK/REBLT TO GP38-2B 2601
76/11-76/12	SLSF	18	461-478	TO BN 2316-2333
76/12-77/01	SOU	24	5202-5225	
77/01	BAP	1	108	SOLD TO ARR 2001
77/01	SOU	6	5226-5231	(RCT)
77/03	LI	6	272-277	
77/03	PHDX	1	4	PHELPS-DODGE CORP.
77/05	ITC	4	2001-2004	TO NW 4160-4163
77/05	TPW	4	2001-2004	TO ATSF 3561-3564, RE# 2370-2373
77/06	CR	18	8163-8180	
77/06	PLE	6	2051-2056	TO GTW 5844-5849, 85/06
77/09-77/10	SOO	7	790-796	RE# 4400-4406
77/10	MP	10	2138-2147	TO UP SAME #
77/10-77/11	MP	10	2148-2157	TO UP SAME #
77/11	FEC	4	501-504	
78/04	FEC	6	505-510	
78/04	FEC	1	511	
78/04-78/05	SOO	3	797-799	RE# 4407-4409, 4408 SCR.
78/05-78/06	CR	21	8181-8201	
78/06	CRR	5	6000-6004	NEW FL,TO SBD/CSXT 2651-2655
78/06	KCS	2	4010-4011	
78/07-78/08	CR	22	8202-8223	
78/09	CR	32	8224-8255	
78/10	ALTO	2	157-158	ALTOS HORNOS (MEXICO)
78/10	SOO	6	4410-4415	
78/10	TPW	7	2005-2011	TO ATSF 3565-3571, RE# 2374-2380
78/11	BAP	1	109	SOLD TO ARR 2002
78/11	RI	12	4368-4379	TO GTW 5850-5861

MODEL GP38-2, cont'd

BLDR.DATE	RR	QTY.	DELV.NO.	NOTES
78/12	GTW	20	5812-5831	
79/02-79/03	CHP	10	900-909	(2nd) TO BE RE# NDM 9428-9437
79/02-79/04	LN	20	6011-6030	NEW FL, TO SBD/CSXT 2662-2681
79/03	NDEM	10	9405-9414	
79/03	SECX	3	3821-3823	SOUTH EAST COAL CO.
79/04	AWP	2	6007-6008	NEW FL,THEN SBD, TO CSXT 2658,2659
79/04	CRR	2	6005-6006	NEW FL,THEN SBD, TO CSXT 2656-2657
79/04	GA	2	6009-6010	NEW FL,THEN SBD, TO CSXT 2660-2661
79/04	MSE	1	66	
79/05-79/06	CR	26	8256-8281	
79/05-79/06	SOO	10	4416-4425	
79/07	SOO	10	4426-4435,	4430 WRK/SCR. 82
79/07-79/08	LN	14	6031-6044	NEW FL,THEN SBD, TO CSXT 2682-2695
79/08	CRR	1	6045	NEW FL,TO WofA,TO SBD, TO CSXT 2696
79/08	SCL	1	6046	NEW FL,TO WofA TO SBD, TO CSXT 2697
79/08	SCL	4	6047-6050	NEW FL,THEN SBD, TO CSXT 2698-2701
79/08-79/09	SOU	25	5232-5256	
79/09	TM	1	864	
79/11-79/12	CNW	26	4600-4625	ORIGINALLY ORDERED BY RI,DELV.CNW
79/12	CNW	9	4626-4634	ORIGINALLY ORDERED BY RI,DELV.CNW
80/01	GTW	5	5832-5836	
80/01-80/02	MP	40	2158-2197	TO UP SAME #
80/02	PW	1	2006	
80/03	SCL	1	6051	NEW FL,TO GA.TO SBD,TO CSXT 2702
80/03	SCL	1	6052	NEW FL,TO GA.TO SBD,TO CSXT 2703
80/03	SCL	2	6053-6054	NEW FL,THEN SBD, TO CSXT 2604,2605
80/04	CHP	2	910-911	HI-NOSE STEAM GEN. TO BE RE# NDM 9438,9439.
80/05-80/07	SP	45	4800-4844	
80/06	BN	5	2150-2154	OWNED BY FW&D
80/06	SOO	8	4436-4443	
80/07	TM	1	865	
80/07-80/08	MP	40	2198-2237	TO UP SAME #
80/08	ANR	1	2000	
80/10	ALTO	2	167-168	ALTOS HORNOS (MEXICO)
80/10	SCL	11	6055-6065.	NEW FL,THEN SBD, TO CSXT 2606-2616
80/11	TM	1	866	
80/12	PW	2	2007-2008	
81/01	CMER	1	810	LATER LETTERED FOR CHEHALIS WESTERN (CW)
81/01	CMER	3	817-819	LATER LETTERED FOR CHEHALIS WESTERN (CW)
81/01	CSS	10	2000-2009	
81/02	SOO	7	4444-4450	
81/02-81/03	MP	30	2290-2319	(2nd) TO UP SAME #
81/07-81/08	MP	15	2320-2334	(2nd) TO UP SAME #
81/08	FUS	3	528-530	TO BE RE# NDM 9422-9424
82/03	FUS	3	531-533	TO BE RE# NDM 9425-9427
82/03	PHDX	1	58	PHELPS-DODGE CORP. MORENCI MINES DIV.
82/06-82/07	NDEM	9	9901-9909	HI-NOSE
82/09	PW	1	2009	
83/03	SOO	2	4451-4452	
85/05	TM	1	867	

MODEL GP38AC
GULF,MOBILE & OHIO
724, BLT. 71/03
KANSAS CITY, MO. 78/06

BLDR.DATE	RR	QTY.	DELV.NO.	NOTES
MODEL GP38AC, 2000 hp, BUILT 1970-1971				
70/02	IC	10	9500-9509	TO MKT 325-334, M/86
70/02	IC	1	9510	RETIRED
70/02	IC	9	9511-9519	TO MKT 335,337-343, M/86, 9512 TO CMNW 2048 IN 87/04
70/06-70/07	LN	20	4000-4019	TO FL,THEN SBD 6221-6240,6221 WRK/SCR. 86/02, REST TO CSXT 2131-2149
71/02-71/03	SLSF	21	633-653	651 WRK/SCR. 74/09, TO BN 2110-2129
71/03-71/04	GMO	9	721-729	TO ICG 9540-9548
71/04	GMO	3	730-732	TO ICG 9549-9551
71/04	SLSF	6	654-659	TO BN 2130-2135
71/04	SLSF	1	660	TO BN 2136, WRK/REBLT TO GP38B 2600, REBLT W/CAB AND RE# BACK TO 2136 E/89
71/04	SLSF	2	661-662	TO BN 2137-2138
71/04-71/10	SOU	28	2823-2850	2839 RE#2887 IN 79 ONLY
71/05	LN	10	4020-4029	TO FL, THEN SBD 6241-6250, TO CSXT 2150-2159
71/05-71/06	LN	20	4030-4049	TO FL, THEN SBD 6251-6270, TO CSXT 2160-2179
71/06-71/11	NW	35	4125-4159	
71/07	BLE	6	864-869	
71/07	DTI	6	215-220	TO GTW 6215-6220
71/08-71/10	NW	25	4100-4124	4110 RETIRED
71/08-71/10	SOU	28	2851-2878	
71/11	GTW	12	5800-5811	5808 TO CV 88/12
71/12	GMO	1	733	TO ICG 9552
71/12	LV	4	310-313	TO CR 7656-7659
71/12	PACI	1	11	PACIFIC POWER CO.

BLDR.DATE	RR	QTY.	DELV.NO.	NOTES

MODEL GP39, 2300 hp, BUILT 1969-1970

BLDR.DATE	RR	QTY.	DELV.NO.	NOTES
69/05-69/07	CO	20	3900-3919	TO CS, TO CSXT 4280-4299
70/06	KCC	2	1-2	KENNECOTT COPPER CORP, RE# 401,402, TO CBRY SAME#
70/07	ASAB	1	507	

MODEL GP39-2
SANTA FE
3615, BLT. 74/08
FT.WORTH, TX. 81/05

MODEL GP39-2, 2300 hp, BUILT 1974-1984

BLDR.DATE	RR	QTY.	DELV.NO.	NOTES
74/08	ATSF	17	3600-3616	
74/11-74/12	RDG	20	3401-3420	TO DH 7401-7420
75/01	ATSF	10	3617-3626	REBLT, RE# TO 3400 CLASS,MIXED NO's
75/02	ATSF	13	3627-3639	REBLT, RE# TO 3400 CLASS,MIXED NO's
75/03	ATSF	8	3640-3647	REBLT, RE# TO 3400 CLASS,MIXED NO's
75/03	ATSF	1	3648	WRK/SCR 84/10
75/03	ATSF	3	3649-3651	REBLT, RE# TO 3400 CLASS,MIXED NO's
75/04	ATSF	14	3652-3665	REBLT, RE# TO 3400 CLASS,MIXED NO's
75/04	ATSF	1	3666	REBLT, RE# 3426, SCR.86/07
75/04	ATSF	2	3667-3668	REBLT, RE# TO 3400 CLASS,MIXED NO's
76/03-76/04	DH	20	7601-7620	TO BM 350-369 MIXED NO's, RET'D TO DH L/87, 7316 RET. IN 88.
76/12	KCC	1	905	KENNECOTT COPPER CORP.
77/01	KCC	5	779-783	TO NRE,THEN MKT 380-384,TO UP 2350-2354
77/01	KCC	1	784	RE# 910,ALL KCC 700's HI-VISABILITY CAB
77/01	KCC	1	785	TO NRE,THEN MKT 385, TO UP 2355
77/01	KCC	1	786	RE# 911, ALL 700's SOLD HAD CAB REBLT.
77/01	KCC	3	787-789	TO NRE,THEN MKT 386-388,TO UP 2356-2358
77/11	ATSF	14	3669-3682	3672 WRK/SCR 84/10
78/10	KCC	10	790-799	BUILT WITH SPECIAL HI-VISIBILITY CAB
79/06	ATSF	13	3683-3695	3692 WRK/SCR 83/11
80/04	ATSF	10	3696-3705	

MODEL GP39-2, cont'd

BLDR.DATE	RR	QTY.	DELV.NO.	NOTES
80/09	KCC	7	705-711	BUILT WITH SPECIAL HI-VISIBILITY CAB
80/12	KCC	1	3	KENNECOTT COPPER CORP.
80/12	KCC	1	910	KENNECOTT COPPER CORP.
81/03-81/04	BN	40	2700-2739	
81/08	PHDX	1	33	PHELPS-DODGE,AJO,AZ.TO MORENCI, RE# 63
81/11	KCCX	2	1-2	KENNECOTT MINERALS DIV.
84/03-84/06	MKT	20	360-379	HAVE GP49 CARBODIES, TO UP 2359-2378

MODEL GP39X, 2600 hp, BUILT 1980

80/11	SOU	6	4600-4605	GP49 PROTOTYPES, UPGRADED TO GP49 IN 82

MODEL GP40, 3000 hp, BUILT 1965-1971

68/01	MILW	10	2047-2056	RET'D LESSOR 84, 2053 SCR.84, 2050 TO MARC #75, REBLT TO GP39H-2 88/03.
68/02	CBQ	20	620-639	TO BN 3020-3039. 3024,3026-3030 REBLT. BY M-K TO GP40-2 3503-3508 IN L/88.
68/06	DTI	6	400-405	TO GTW 6400-6405
68/07	AWP	1	727	TO SBD-CSXT 6647
68/07	GA	2	753-754	TO SBD/CSX 6655,6656
68/07	WRyA	1	702	TO CS-SBD-CSXT 6791

MODEL GP40
MISSOURI-KANSAS-TEXAS
203, BLT. 68/08
FT.WORTH, TX. 89/01

68/08	MKT	16	194-209	
68/08-68/09	PC	65	3105-3169	TO CR SAME #,ALL RET. SOME TO DRGW,TOE, MKT,MARC,FDOT.
68/10	MKT	1	210	
68/10-68/12	PC	90	3170-3259	TO CR SAME #, MOST RET. SOME TO KCS,BM.
68/12	MILW	4	2057-2060	TO SOO 4231-4234

MODEL GP40, cont'd

BLDR.DATE	RR	QTY.	DELV.NO.	NOTES
68/12	MILW	5	2061-2065	TO SOO 4235-4239,4236,4238,4239 TO NRE 4239 TO UP 866, E/89.
68/12	MILW	2	2066-2067	TO SOO 4660,4240
69/01	AWP	2	728-729	TO SBD-CSXT 6648-6649
69/01	RI	15	382-396	RET'D LESSOR,US.LEASING,396 TO EUKA,384 389 REMFG.TO GP40FH-2,NJT 438,439,87/12
69/01	WRyA	2	703-704	TO CS-SBD-CSXT 6792,6793
69/02-69/04	BO	40	3700-3739	ALL TO GATX 85, 3701 SCR.86, see p. 16
69/04-69/05	EMD	10	11-20	BUILT AS LOANERS, TO PC/CR 3260-3269
69/05	EMD	1	21	BUILT AS LOANER, TO TPW 1000,THEN TO ATSF 3461, WRK/SCR/84
69/05	EMD	5	22-26	BUILT AS LOANERS, TO PC/CR 3270-3274
69/05	EMD	4	2068-2071	BUILT AS LOANERS, TO MILW 2068-2071 RET'D TO LESSOR,2070,2071 TO CCX IN 84

MODEL GP40
ILLINOIS CENTRAL
3061, BLT 69/08
MARKHAM, IL. 72/03

BLDR.DATE	RR	QTY.	DELV.NO.	NOTES
69/08	IC	10	3060-3069	
69/10	DRGW	5	3081-3085	
69/11	MKT	20	211-230	222 WRK/80, REBLT AS ROAD SLUG 501,TO UP S33, REST TO UP 581-599
69/12-70/01	SCL	30	1566-1595	TO SBD/CSXT 6721-6750, 6723 RET.87/02,TO SLUG 2207 88/12
70/02	IC	1	3070	REBLT RE# 3077 IN 1974
70/02	IC	4	3071-3074	3071 REBLT RE#3070(2nd),3072,3074,RET'D LESSOR HL,85
70/03-70/04	RI	20	4700-4719	TO UP 631-650,SOME TO PNC 85,MK IN 87
70/05	AWP	3	730-732	TO SBD-CSXT 6650-6652
70/05	WRyA	3	705-707	TO CS-SBD-CSXT 6794-6796
70/05-70/06	SCL	37	1596-1632	TO SBD/CSXT 6751-6786, 6758 RETIRED, 1602 RET. BEFORE RE#
70/08	WP	10	3517-3526	TO HL, TO CMNW 3000-3009

MODEL GP40, cont'd

BLDR.DATE	RR	QTY.	DELV.NO.	NOTES
70/12-71/02	BO	25	3740-3764	TO CS, TO CSXT 6516-6540
71/01-71/03	FEC	10	401-410	402 WRK/SCR. 79/07
71/02-71/03	BO	13	3765-3777	3773 RET.REST TO CSXT 6541-6552
71/03	BO	2	3778-3779	TO CS, TO CSXT 6553,6554
71/03	TOE	1	D12	
71/05	CO	6	4065-4070	TO CS, TO CSXT 6640-6645
71/05-71/08	CO	18	4071-4089	TO CS, TO CSXT 6826-6844
71/06	CHP	4	1000-1003	TO BE RE# NDM 8410-8413
71/06	CHP	4	1004-1007	TO BE RE# NDM 8414-8417
71/08	WM	5	3795-3799	TO CS, SAME#, TO CSXT 6570-74
71/08	WP	1	3527	WRK/SCR 80/04
71/08	WP	1	3528	TO UP 676, SOLD TO GATX, TO CMNW 3010
71/08	WP	2	3529-3530	TO UP 677,678,SOLD GATX, TO CMNW 3011,12
71/08	WP	3	3531-3533	TO UP 679-681,SOLD GATX, TO CMNW 3013-15
71/08	WP	2	3534-3535	TO UP 682,683,SOLD GATX, TO CMNW 3016-17
71/08	WP	1	3536	TO UP 684, SOLD TO GATX, TO CMNW 3018
71/08	WP	1	3537	TO UP 685, SOLD TO GATX, TO CMNW 3019
71/08-71/10	BO	55	4000-4054	CS, TO CSXT 6575-6629, 4039 SCR.87/02
71/09	SCL	3	1633-1635	TO SBD/CSXT 6787-6789
71/09	TOE	1	D14	
71/09	WP	1	3538	TO UP 686, SOLD TO GATX, TO CMNW 3020
71/09	WP	1	3539	TO UP 687, SOLD TO GATX, TO CMNW 3021
71/09	WP	1	3540	WRK/SCR. 80/04
71/09	WP	2	3541-3542	TO UP 688,689,SOLD GATX, TO CMNW 3022-23
71/09	WP	1	3543	TO UP 690, SOLD TO GATX, TO CMNW 3024
71/09	WP	1	3544	TO UP 691, SOLD TO GATX, TO CMNW 3025
71/10	TOE	1	D13	
71/10-71/11	BO	10	4055-4064	CS, TO CSXT 6630-6639
71/11	DRGW	8	3086-3093	
71/12	CO	15	3780-3794	TO CS/CSXT 6555-6569
71/12	CO	10	4090-4099	TO CS/CSXT 7845-6854

MODEL GP40-2, 3000 hp, BUILT 1972-1986

BLDR.DATE	RR	QTY.	DELV.NO.	NOTES
72/04	DRGW	12	3094-3105	
72/04	SCL	21	1636-1656	TO SBD SAME#, TO CSXT 6346-6365 1653 RET. BEFORE RE#
72/08-72/10	BO	63	4100-4162	4105 RET.4121 RET.87/07,4136 WRK/SCR. 87/06, TO CS SAME#, TO CSXT 6001-6062
72/09	BO	1	GM50	RE# 4164, TO CS 4164, TO CSXT 6063
72/09	BO	1	1977	(2nd)TO CS 4163, TO CSXT 6392
72/09	RFP	7	141-147	
72/10	DTI	8	406-413	TO GTW 6406-6413
72/10	SBC	2	2309-2310	RE# 2104,2105, TO BE RE# NDM 7035,7036, HI-NOSE.
72/10	SBC	1	2311	RE# 2106, TO BE RE# NDM 7037, HI-NOSE, STEAM.GEN.
72/11	CO	20	4165-4184	TO CS, TO CSXT 6064-6083, 4170 WRK/RET
72/11	FEC	5	411-415	
72/12	DRGW	10	3106-3115	
72/12	GA	2	755-756	TO SBD 6643,6644, TO CSXT 6389,6390
72/12	TOE	1	D15	
73/10	DTI	8	414-421	TO GTW 6414-6421
73/11	TOE	1	D16	
73/12	RDG	5	3671-3675	TO CR 3275-3279

MODEL GP40-2, cont'd

MODEL GP40-2
FLORIDA EAST COAST
417, BLT. 74/10
JACKSONVILLE, FL. 84/10

73/12	SBC	3	2107-2109	HI-NOSE, STEAM GEN. TO BE RE# NDM 7038-7040
74/09	DRGW	12	3116-3127	
74/09	TOE	1	D20	
74/10	FEC	3	416-418	
74/11	AWP	1	733	TO SBD 6645, TO CSXT 6391
74/11	DRGW	1	3128	
74/11	WRyA	1	708	TO CS-SBD 6642, TO CSXT 6388
75/04	ARR	6	3000-3005	3000 RE# 3006
75/04-75/06	BO	62	4185-4246	TO CS, TO CSXT 6084-6145
75/06	CHP	9	1008-1016	TO BE RE# NDM 7000-7008
76/01	CHP	2	1017-1018	TO BE RE# NDM 7009,7010
76/01	CHP	4	1019-1022	HI-NOSE, STEAM GEN. TO BE RE# NDM 7011-7014 (2nd)
76/05	ARR	5	3007-3011	
76/08	SBC	3	2110-2112	HI-NOSE, STEAM GEN. TO BE RE# NDM 7041-7043
77/02	BO	10	4247-4256	TO CS, TO CSXT 6146-6155
77/02	WM	5	4257-4261	TO CS SAME#, TO CSXT 6156-6160
77/04-77/05	CR	33	3280-3312	
77/12	BM	18	300-317	
78/01	CO	20	4262-4281	T/CS,TO CSXT 6161-80,4275 RET.87/07,REBLT.RE#6400-19
78/01-78/02	BO	21	4287-4307	TO CS, TO CSXT 6186-6206 4303 TO NRE/88. 6186,6187 REBUILT & RE# 6425,6426
78/02-78/03	CO	5	4282-4286	TO CS, TO CSXT 6181-6185, REBLT.& RE# 6420-6424
78/02-78/04	SP	20	7608-7627	7612 RET.79/07,7618 WRK/RET.M/87
78/03	BO	4	4308-4311	TO CS, TO CSXT 6207-6210
78/05-78/06	CR	33	3313-3345	3317,3319 SCR.
78/09	ARR	4	3012-3015	
78/11	DOT	1	003	U.S.DEPT.TRANSPORTATION
78/11	WM	10	4312-4321	TO CS SAME#, TO CSXT 6211-6220
79/01-79/02	SSW	30	7628-7657	7650 WRK/SCR M/87
79/01-79/02	WM	15	4352-4366	TO CS SAME#, TO CSXT 6251-6265
79/02	WM	1	4367	WRK/SCR. 80
79/02	WM	4	4367-4371	TO CS SAME#, TO CSXT 6266-6269
79/02-79/03	BO	30	4322-4351	TO CS SAME#, TO CSXT 6221-6250

MODEL GP40-2, cont'd

MODEL GP40-2
KANSAS CITY SOUTHERN
799, BLT. 79/08
SHREVEPORT, LA. 81/08

BLDR.DATE	RR	QTY.	DELV.NO.	NOTES
79/03-79/05	CR	40	3346-3385	
79/04-79/06	SLSF	25	750-774	TO BN 3040-3064
79/07	WP	5	3545-3549	TO MP 900-904, TO UP SAME #
79/08	KCS	2	798-799	SLUG MASTER EQUIPPED
79/10	FEC	5	419-423	423 WRK/REBLT TO 437, 87/12
79/11	DTI	4	422-425	TO GTW 6422-6425
79/11-79/12	SBC	2	2309-2310	(2nd), TO BE RE# NDM 7029,7030 (2nd).
79/12	SBC	2	2113-2114	TO BE RE# NDM 7033,7034 (2nd).
80/01	CO	20	4372-4391	TO CS SAME#, TO CSXT 6270-6289
80/01	FEC	1	424	
80/01-80/02	CR	18	3386-3403	3394 WRK/SCR. 88/01
80/02-80/03	CO	30	4392-4421	TO CS SAME#, TO CSXT 6290-6319
80/03	SP	20	7658-7677	7659 RET.
80/03-80/04	LN	17	6600-6616	TO SBD SAME#, TO CSXT 6366-6382
80/04	WP	10	3550-3559	TO MP 905-914, TO UP SAME#
80/04-80/05	SP	20	7940-7959	EQUIPPED FOR SLUG MASTERS
80/06	SCL	5	6617-6621	TO SBD SAME#, TO CSXT 6383-6387
80/08	FEC	5	425-429	
80/11	SBC	1	2311	(2nd), TO BE RE# NDM 7031 (2nd)
81/02	KCS	2	796-797	SLUG MASTER EQUIPPED
81/05-81/06	BO	26	4422-4447	TO CS SAME#, TO CSXT 6320-6345
81/07	CHP	7	1023-1029	TO BE RE# NDM 7015-7021 (2nd)
81/07	SBC	1	2312	TO BE RE# NDM 7032 (2nd)
82/03	CHP	7	1030-1036	TO BE RE# NDM 7022-7028 (2nd)

MODEL GP40-2, cont'd

BLDR.DATE	RR	QTY.	DELV.NO.	NOTES
82/06	SBC	2	2313-2314	TO BE RE# NDM 7033,7034 (2nd)
83/03	DRGW	2	3129-3130	
84/10-84/11	SSW	26	7248-7273	
84/11	SP	8	7240-7247	7241 WRK/RET. M/87
84/12	FEC	2	430-431	
85/12	FEC	1	432	
86/12	FEC	2	433-434	

MODEL GP40P, 3000 hp, BUILT 1968

68/10	CNJ	13	3671-3683	TO CR 4100-4112, TO NJT SAME #.

MODEL GP40P-2
SOUTHERN PACIFIC
3197, BLT. 74/11
SAN FRANCISCO, CA. 79/06

MODEL GP40P-2, 3000 hp, BUILT 1974

74/11	SP	3	3197-3199	3197, R/W/B IN 75/06,RE# 7600-7602 (2nd)

MODEL GP40X, 3500 hp, BUILT 1977-1978

77/12	UP	1	9000	RE# 90(2nd), RE# 954 IN 89
78/02	SP	2	7200-7201	(RCT)
78/02	SP	2	7230-7231	(RCR)
78/02	UP	1	9001	RE# 91(2nd), RE# 955 IN 89
78/03	UP	4	9002-9005	RE# 92-95(2nd), RE# 956-959 IN 89
78/04-78/05	ATSF	8	3802-3809	
78/06	ATSF	1	3800	(RCT)
78/06	ATSF	1	3801	(RCR)
78/06	SOU	3	7000-7002	

BLDR.DATE	RR	QTY.	DELV.NO.	NOTES
MODEL GP49, 2800 hp, 1983-1985				
83/08-83/09	ARR	4	2801-2804	
85/05	ARR	5	2805-2809	

MODEL GP50
CHICAGO & NORTH WESTERN
5075, BLT. 80/07
BOONE, IA. 80/09

MODEL GP50, 3500 hp, BUILT 1980-1985

80/05-80/09	CNW	50	5050-5099	5051 WRK/SCR. L/86
80/08-80/11	SOU	47	7017-7063	
80/09-80/11	SOU	14	7003-7016	(RCT)
80/11	MP	10	3500-3509	TO UP 50-59, RE# 960-969 IN 89
80/11-80/12	SOU	7	7064-7070	
80/12	BN	10	3100-3109	3100 DELIVERED IN SLSF PAINT SCHEME
80/12	SOU	2	7071-7072	
81/01	MP	16	3510-3525	TO UP 60-75, RE# 970-985 IN 89
81/01	MP	4	3526-3529	TO UP 76-79, RE# 986-989 IN 89
81/01-81/02	ATSF	7	3810-3822	EVEN NUMBERS ONLY (RCT)
81/01-81/02	ATSF	7	3811-3823	ODD NUMBERS ONLY (RCR)
81/03-81/04	ATSF	16	3824-3839	
81/04-81/06	SOU	20	7073-7092	
85/04	ATSF	15	3840-3854	
85/06-85/11	BN	48	3110-3157	
85/11	BN	5	3158-3162	5 MAN CREW CAB

MODEL GP59, 3800 hp, BUILT 1985

85/06	EMD	3	EMD 8-10	PROTOTYPES, SOLD TO SOU (NS) 4606-4608

MODEL GP60, 3800 hp, BUILT 1985

85/10	EMD	3	EMD5-EMD7	PROTOTYPE TEST UNITS, GP60 PRODUCTION TRANSFERRED TO GMD AFTER THESE UNITS.

MODEL MP15AC
MISSOURI-KANSAS-TEXAS
56, BLT. 80/09
KANSAS CITY, MO. 80/11

BLDR.DATE	RR	QTY.	DELV.NO.	NOTES
MODEL MP15AC, 1500 hp, BUILT 1975-1983				
75/08-75/09	SP	30	2702-2731	(2nd)
75/09	MILW	32	466-497	TO SOO 1532-1563
75/09	SP	24	2736-2759	(2nd)
75/10	EMD	1	115	PLANT SWITCHER
75/10	SP	4	2732-2735	(2nd)
76/01-76/02	MILW	32	434-465	TO SOO 1500-1531
77/03-77/04	LI	23	150-172	
77/10	SCL	20	4000-4019	TO FL/SBD SAME#, TO CSXT 1150-1169
78/02	SCL	25	4200-4224	TO FL/SBD SAME#, TO CSXT 1170-1194
78/03	LN	10	4225-4234	NEW FL, TO CSXT 1130-1139
78/07	EMD	1	116	PLANT SWITCHER, TO MOBX 116, IN 81/08
78/12	KCC	3	120-122	HI-VISIBILITY WIDE CAB
78/12	KCC	2	701,704	701 RE# 915, 704 RE# 123
80/09	GTRA	1	G1	GOLDEN TRIANGLE RR.OWNED BY WEYERHAUSER
80/09	MKT	4	56-59	TO UP 1393-1396
80/10	TASD	1	803	
81/04	KCDX	1	10	EASTMAN KODAK CO.
81/05	GRR	1	1013	WRK 85, SOLD TO NRE, NOW REBLT, FOR LEASE
82/07-82/09	NDEM	25	9801-9825	
82/09	RWIX	1	3728	HANFORD PLANT, ROCKWELL INTERNATIONL
83/12	RWIX	1	3727	HANFORD PLANT, ROCKWELL INTERNATIONL

MODEL MP15DC
MISSOURI PACIFIC
1543, BLT. 74/09
DOLTON, IL. 76/06

BLDR.DATE	RR	QTY.	DELV.NO.	NOTES
MODEL MP15DC, 1500 hp, BUILT 1974-1983				
74/02	MP	5	1530-1534	TO UP 1330-1334
74/04	CSNX	1	109	CITIES SERVICE CO.
74/06-74/07	PLE	10	1574-1583	TO UP 1274-84 MIXED NO's, LATER RE# 1000-1009 (2nd)
74/07	URR	5	10-14	
74/09	MP	5	1535-1539	TO UP 1335-1339
74/09	MP	5	1540-1544	TO UP 1340-1344
74/10	SM	1	504	
74/11	BXN	2	15-16	
74/11	PCN	3	11-13	
74/11	RSS	3	13-15	
74/12	RDG	10	2771-2780	TO PC 9621-9630, TO CR SAME#
74/12	SP	7	2690-2696	
75/01	LN	10	5030-5039	TO SBD 1140-1149, TO CSXT SAME#
75/01-75/02	SP	5	2697-2701	(2nd)
75/02	CNW	5	1302-1306	
75/02	MP	10	1545-1554	TO UP 1345-1354
75/03	CNW	10	1307-1316	
75/03	SLSF	5	361-365	TO BN 4000-4004, RE# 1000-1004
75/05	PLE	15	1584-1598	1584,1587,1588,1596,1598 TO UP 1010-1014(2nd) 85/03, RE# 1310-1314
75/06	BRC	2	533-534	534 DELIVERED RED/WHITE/BLUE
75/06-75/07	URR	7	15-21	
75/08	CI	2	19-20	
75/08	KCS	4	4363-4366	
75/08	MRS	2	251-252	
75/08	WRGX	2	121-122	W.R.GRACE CO.
75/11	ALTO	3	146-148	ALTOS HORNOS (MEXICO)
75/11	BCH	3	151-153	

MODEL MP15DC, cont'd

BLDR.DATE	RR	QTY.	DELV.NO.	NOTES
75/11	ETCX	1	2	TENNESSEE EASTMAN CO.KINGSPORT,TN.PLANT
75/11	NLG	4	42-45	
75/12	TN	2	998-999	
76/01	BPPX	1	18	INTERNATIONAL MINING & CHEMICALS CORP.
76/03	URR	3	22-24	
76/05	USX	1	170	U.S.STEEL, FAIRFIELD WORKS, TO BS 370
76/05	USX	11	955-965	U.S.STEEL, MINNTAC MINE
76/06	SM	1	505	
76/08	BS	2	260-261	
76/08	LEF	1	25	
76/08	TASD	1	761	
76/08	USX	3	966-968	U.S.STEEL, MINNTAC MINE
76/12	KCC	1	906	KENNECOTT COPPER CORP.
76/12	KCNW	1	1	
76/12	SWIF	1	1976	SWIFT & CO.
76/12	URR	2	25-26	
77/02	URR	7	27-33	
77/03	QITX	1	9	QUEBEC IRON & TITANIUM CORP.(CANADA) ALLARD LAKE MINES
77/06	ARIZ	1	2	ARIZONA PUBLIC SERVICE CO.
77/06-77/07	SOU	26	2348-2373	
77/10	LEF	1	26	
77/10	TASD	2	771-772	
78/12	ALTO	1	159	ALTOS HORNOS (MEXICO)
78/12	GRR	1	1011	
78/12	LEF	1	27	
79/09	GOCX	1	101	CHEVRON USA, INC.
79/09	INDU	1	383	INDUSTRIAL MINERA, (MEXICO)
79/09-79/10	SOU	10	2374-2383	
79/10	HBT	5	60-64	

MODEL MP15DC
HOUSTON BELT & TERMINAL
64, BLT. 79/10
HOUSTON, TX. 81/11

MODEL MP15DC, cont'd

MODEL MP15DC
SOUTHERN RY.
2387, BLT. 79/11
BIRMINGHAM, AL. 81/04

BLDR.DATE	RR	QTY.	DELV.NO.	NOTES
79/11	ALCT	1	10	ALCOA TERMINAL, (ALCOA ALUMINIUM)
79/11	LEF	1	28	
79/11	SOU	10	2384-2393	
80/02	ALCO	1	7:3	ALCOA TERMINAL, (ALCOA ALUMINIUM)
80/02	AOCX	1	7	ALUMINIUM CO. OF AMERICA, KNOXVILLE,TN
80/02	BRC	2	535-536	
80/09	GNA	1	80	
80/09	KCNW	1	2	
80/10	QITX	1	10	QUEBEC IRON & TITANIUM CORP.(CANADA) ALLARD LAKE MINES
80/10	TASD	2	801-802	
80/10	WRGX	2	131-132	W.R.GRACE CO.
80/10,80/11	GNWR	2	45-46	
80/11	ALS	1	1522	
80/11	ALTO	1	166	ALTOS HORNOS, (MEXICO)
80/11	BPPX	1	19	INTERNATIONAL MINING & CHEMICALS CORP.
80/11	GRR	1	1012	
80/11	PCN	2	14-15	
82/01	INDU	1	NONE	INDUSTRIAL MINERA (MEXICO)
82/01	MP	20	1356-1375	TO UP SAME #
82/04-82/05	SOU	32	2404-2435	
82/05-82/06	SOU	10	2394-2403	
82/06	TASD	2	821-822	
82/10-82/11	MP	17	1376-1392	TO UP SAME #
82/11	TCT	3	35-37	BUILT TO MP SPECIFICATIONS
83/01	MRS	1	254	
83/01	SANI	1	4	SANITARY DISTRICT OF CHICAGO

BLDR.DATE	RR	QTY.	DELV.NO.	NOTES

MODEL MP15T, 1500 hp, BUILT 1984-1985

BLDR.DATE	RR	QTY.	DELV.NO.	NOTES
84/10-84/11	SBD	15	1200-1214	TO CSXT SAME #
85/03	SBD	8	1215-1222	TO CSXT SAME #
85/11-85/12	SBD	19	1223-1241	TO CSXT SAME #
87/05	DOWX	1	957	DOW CHEMICAL CO.

MODEL SD38
Mc CLOUD RIVER RR.
37, BLT. 69/04
PROVO, UT. 88/07

MODEL SD38, 2000 hp, BUILT 1967-1970

BLDR.DATE	RR	QTY.	DELV.NO.	NOTES
69/04	MR	3	36-38	
69/07-69/08	DTI	3	250-252	TO GTW 6250-6252
70/01-70/02	EJE	6	650-655	
70/04	PC	35	6925-6959	TO TO CR SAME #

MODEL SD38-2, 2000 hp, BUILT 1972-1979

BLDR.DATE	RR	QTY.	DELV.NO.	NOTES
72/11	YANK	2	20-21	YANKEETOWN DOCK CORP.
72/12	BCH	2	382-383	
73/03-73/05	BLE	9	870-878	
73/04	SP	6	2971-2976	
74/01	EJE	4	656-659	
74/02	BLE	1	879	
74/05	CIM	6	70-75	
74/08	BCH	1	384	
74/08	MR	1	39	
75/01	CNW	10	6650-6659	
75/01	EJE	5	660-664	
75/01	LN	5	4500-4504	TO SBD SAME #,TO CSXT 2450-2454
75/03	DMIR	5	209-213	210 TO BLE, SAME#, 86/05
75/04	BLE	2	890-891	891 TO EJE, 86/05

MODEL SD38-2, cont'd

MODEL SD38-2
RESERVE MINING CO.
1239, BLT. 78/10
BABBITT, MN. 80/06

BLDR.DATE	RR	QTY.	DELV.NO.	NOTES
75/11	EJE	4	665-668	668 LATER PAINTED R/W/B
75/12	USX	1	1	U.S.STEEL, CUMBERLAND MINE
76/03	BLE	1	892	TO DMIR, SAME #, 86/05
78/10	RESE	9	1237-1245	RESERVE MINING CO.
78/12	YANK	1	22	YANKEETOWN DOCK CORP.
79/06	SLSF	2	296-297	TO BN 6260-6261
79/06	SLSF	2	298-299	TO BN 6262-6263

MODEL SD38AC, 2000 hp, BUILT 1971

BLDR.DATE	RR	QTY.	DELV.NO.	NOTES
71/06	DMIR	8	201-208	
71/07	BLE	6	864-869	864 RET.
71/07	DTI	2	253-254	TO GTW 6253-6254
71/10	BCH	1	381	

MODEL SD39, 2300 hp, BUILT 1968-1970

BLDR.DATE	RR	QTY.	DELV.NO.	NOTES
68/08-68/10	SP	18	5300-5317	(2nd), 5301, 5305-5307, 5311-5313, SCR.84
68/09	MNS	2	40-41	TO SOO 6240,6241
69/05	ATSF	12	4000-4011	REBLT, RE# 1556-1567
69/05	ITC	3	2301-2303	TO NW 2961-2963, TO BM 690-692
69/05	ITC	3	2304-2306	TO NW 2964-2966, 2964 TO ATSF SLUG 140, M/85 2965, 2966 TO MK 84, 2965 SCR. 2966 TO MEC 693
69/05-69/06	ATSF	8	4012-4019	(RCT), REBLT/RE# 1568-1575
70/04	SP	8	5318-5325	(2nd), ALL TO HL, 5320,5021,5023,5024, TO CBRY

BLDR.DATE	RR	QTY.	DELV.NO.	NOTES

MODEL SD40, 3000 hp, BUILT 1966-1972

BLDR.DATE	RR	QTY.	DELV.NO.	NOTES
68/01	IC	6	6000-6005	
68/01-68/02	MP	14	720-733	RE# 3020-3033,TO UP 4020-4033, 2 TO WC, 3021,25 RET.
68/03	NDEM	3	8500-8502	
68/04	CBQ	9	879-887	(C&S)TO BN 6339-6347,6340,6345 RET.B/87
68/04-68/06	SP	10	8479-8488	REBLT TO SD40R's,7300 CLASS MIXED NO's
68/05	NDEM	19	8503-8521	8513 WRK/SCR. 71/07
68/08	KCS	4	614-617	
68/08	KCS	2	618-619	(RCT)
68/08	KCS	2	620-621	(RCR)
68/09	CRR	1	3008	TO FL 8283, TO SBD/CSXT 8342
68/11	WM	2	7495-7496	RE# 7595,7596, TO CSXT 8437,8438
69/01-69/02	CRR	6	3009-3014	TO FL 8284-8289, TO SBD/CSXT 8343-8348
69/02	MP	20	734-753	RE# 3034-3053, RET'D LESSOR,NHL 86, 3045,3053,3036, 3048, REBLT. TO NDM SD40-2,s 13059-13062 88/06
69/04	BO	4	7497-7500	TO MK 84/07, 7497-7499 TO WFAX 1-3,7500 LEASED TO MKT, THEN SOO
69/04	CO	6	7501-7506	TO CS SAME #, TO CSXT 8360-8365
69/04	LN	5	1229-1233	TO SBD 8305-8309, TO CSXT SAME #
69/04-69/05	SOO	10	736-745	RE# 6600-6608, 736 SCR. IN 79
69/06	WM	1	7445	RE# 7545, TO CSXT 8396
69/07	WM	4	7446-7449	RE# 7546-7549, TO CSXT 8397-8400
69/08-69/10	GTW	12	5900-5911	5904-5911 ASSIGNED TO DWP
70/01	GTW	9	5912-5920	

MODEL SD40
MISSOURI PACIFIC
765, BLT. 70/01
DOLTON, IL. 72/01

BLDR.DATE	RR	QTY.	DELV.NO.	NOTES
70/01	MP	16	754-769	RE# 3054-3069, TO UP 4054-4069, 3055,3058 RET.88/11
70/03	SOO	4	746-749	RE# 6609-6612
70/04	LN	5	1234-1238	TO SBD 8310-8314, TO CSXT SAME#
70/04-70/05	DEEX	6	001-006	003,004,006 TO MEC 600-602
70/06	KCS	4	622-625	TO HL, THEN SOO 6400-6403
70/06	KCS	1	626	(RCT), TO HL, THEN SOO 6404
70/06	KCS	1	627	(RCR), TO HL, THEN SOO 6405

MODEL SD40, cont'd

BLDR.DATE	RR	QTY.	DELV.NO.	NOTES
70/06-70/07	CO	20	7507-7526	TO CS, TO CSXT 8366-8385, 7518 RET.86
70/08-70/09	GTW	9	5921-5929	
70/08-70/09	LN	10	1239-1248	TO SBD 8315-8324, TO CSXT SAME#
70/12-70/01	PC	31	6240-6270	TO CR SAME#, 6253 SCR. 6265 SCR.88/04
71/01-71/02	PC	14	6271-6284	TO CR SAME#
71/03	CO	10	7527-7536	TO CS SAME#, TO CSXT 8386-8395
71/03	KCS	4	628-631	
71/03	KCS	2	632-633	(RCT)
71/03	KCS	2	634-635	(RCR)
71/03	KCS	1	636	
71/03-71/04	MP	20	770-789	RE# 3070-3089, RET'D LESSOR 86/05, GATX,3070, 72,73,75-77,81,83,86,88 REBLT.TO BN SD40G's 7300-7309 IN M/89. 3071,74,78,80,82,84,85,87, 89, REBLT.TO NDM SD40-2's, 13049-13058.
71/04	SOU	14	3170-3183	
71/04	SOU	2	3184-3185	
71/05	LN	10	1249-1258	TO SBD 8325-8334, TO CSXT SAME#
71/05	NW	15	1610-1624	
71/05	SOO	7	750-756	RE# 6613-6619
71/06	CRR	5	3020-3024	TO FL 8295-8299, TO SBD/CSXT 8354-8358
71/06-71/07	CRR	5	3015-3019	TO FL 8290-8294, TO SBD/CSXT 8349-8353
71/08-71/10	UP	40	3083-3122	3119 SCR, 3084,3092 TO VMV
71/10	BN	1	6300	WRK & SCR. 87/05
71/10	BN	1	6301	TO MRL 201
71/10	BN	1	6302	WRK/REBLT TO SD40B 7600, TO SOO 6450
71/10	BN	3	6303-6305	6305 RET. 86/05
71/10	BN	3	6306-6308	TO MRL
71/10-71/11	BN	4	6309-6312	6310,6312 TO MRL, 6311 SCR. 85/09
71/11	BN	5	6313-6317	6315-6317 TO MRL 6314 RET. 87/02
71/11	BN	7	6318-6324	6320,6322,6324 TO MRL
71/11-71/12	NDEM	40	8536-8575	
71/12	SOU	15	3186-3200	3191,3198, WRK/SCR.74/10
72/02	DEEX	2	013-014	014 TO MEC 603 IN 1986
72/07	DEEX	3	015-017	017 TO MEC 604 IN 1986, 017 LAST BUILT

MODEL SD40-2, 3000 hp, BUILT 1972-1986

BLDR.DATE	RR	QTY.	DELV.NO.	NOTES
72/01	BN	1	6325	TEMPORAILY RE# 1976, THEN 1876, R-W-B
72/01	KCS	10	637-646	
72/01-72/02	BN	9	6326-6334	6330 RE-ENG. WITH CATAPILLER ENG.IN 87
72/01-72/03	UP	50	3123-3172	3146 SCR.
72/02	BN	2	6335-6336	RE# 6912-6913
72/02	BN	1	6337	RE# 6914, WRK/REBLT TO SD40-2B 7501
72/02	BN	2	6338-6339	RE# 6915-6916
72/03	SOO	5	757-761	RE# 6620-6624
72/03-72/05	BN	18	900-917	C&S OWNED, RE# 6348-6365
72/06-72/08	UP	30	3173-3202	
72/07-72/08	MILW	15	3000-3014	RE# 130-144, RET'D LESSOR 87, TO VMV, REBLT MK, TO NDM 13009-13048 MIXED #'s, IN 88.
72/07-72/08	MILW	1	3015	RE# 145, SCR.
72/08	MILW	25	3016-3040	RE# 146-170, RET'D LESSOR 87, TO VMV, REBLT MK, TO NDM 13009-13048 MIXED #'s, IN 88.
72/09	FUS	4	601-604	TO BE RE# NDM 13005-13008.

MODEL SD40-2, cont'd

BLDR.DATE	RR	QTY.	DELV.NO.	NOTES
72/11	KCS	6	647-652	
72/11	KCS	2	653-654	(RCT)
72/11	KCS	2	655-656	(RCR)
72/11-72/12	CP	30	5629-5658	5634 SCR.BY 79
72/12	NDEM	6	8710-8715	
72/12	SOU	8	3201-3208	
73/01	SOO	5	762-766	RE# 6625-6628, 766 SCR. 79
73/01	SOU	8	3209-3216	
73/03	BN	12	6340-6351	RE# 6800-6811, 6800 SCR.
73/03	BN	1	6352	RE# 6812, WRK/REBLT TO SD40-2B 7502
73/03-73/04	BN	11	6353-6363	RE# 6813-6823
73/03-73/04	BN	12	6364-6375	RE# 6900-6911
73/04-73/05	UP	37	3203-3239	
73/05	UP	3	3240-3242	RE# 8000-8002,RE# BACK 1980
73/07	MILW	5	21-25	TO SOO 6306-6309
73/07	MILW	5	26-30	TO SOO 6310-6314
73/07	MILW	11	171-181	TO SOO 6300 SERIES
73/08	CNW	10	6801-6810	
73/08	MP	5	790-794	RE# 3090-3094, TO UP 4090-4094
73/08-73/09	MP	20	795-814	RE# 3095-3114, TO UP 4095-4114
73/09	NW	11	1625-1635	
73/09	SOU	24	3217-3240	3217 WRK/SCR. 74/10
73/10-73/12	NDEM	40	8716-8755	
73/11	SOO	8	767-774	RE# 6629-6636
73/11-73/12	BN	13	6824-6836	
73/11-73/12	BN	12	6917-6928	6922 SCR. 6924 SCR.86/05

MODEL SD40-2
BURLINGTON NORTHERN
6927, BLT. 73/12
SPOKANE, WA. 76/06

MODEL SD40-2, cont'd

BLDR.DATE	RR	QTY.	DELV.NO.	NOTES
73/12	CNW	5	6811-6815	
73/12	RI	10	4790-4799	TO ICG 6040-6049, TO EMD IN E/89, LEASED TO UP
73/12-74/01	MP	24	816-839	SUB-LTR.T&P,RE# 3115-3138, TO UP 4115-4138
74/01	KCS	4	657-660	
74/01	KCS	3	661-663	(RCT)
74/01	KCS	3	664-666	(RCR)
74/01	SOU	3	3241-3243	
74/02	BN	8	918-925	C&S OWNED, RE# 6366-6373
74/02	BN	1	980	C&S OWNED, RE# 6850
74/02	BN	1	996	C&S OWNED, RE# 6950
74/02	MP	11	3139-3149	TO UP 4139-4149
74/02	MP	14	3150-3163	SUB-LTR C&EI, TO UP 4150-4163
74/02-74/04	CNW	50	6816-6865	
74/03	LN	2	1259-1260	TO SBD 8163,8164, TO CSXT SAME#
74/03	LN	18	1261-1278	TO SBD 8165-8181, TO CSXT SAME#, 1270 SCR
74/04	BN	10	6376-6385	6376 WRK & SCR. 85/02
74/05-74/06	MILW	28	182-209	ALL TO NDM, EXCEPT 185,194,195,199, 200,202, TO SOO 6383-6388

MODEL SD40-2
MILWAUKEE ROAD
187, BLT. 74/05
SPOKANE, WA. 79/05

BLDR.DATE	RR	QTY.	DELV.NO.	NOTES
74/06-74/07	UP	32	3243-3274	RE# 8003-8034, RE# BACK IN 1980
74/07	NW	17	1636-1652	
74/07	UP	13	3275-3287	
74/09	CNW	25	6866-6890	6870 WRK/RET. TO NRE
74/10	SOO	11	775-785	RE# 6637-6646, 782 RET.IN 82, SCR.84
74/10	SOO	1	786	RE# 6647
74/10-74/11	LN	30	3554-3583	TO SBD 8182-8211, TO CSXT SAME#
74/11	BN	10	950-959	C&S OWNED, RE# 7820-7829
74/12	BN	8	6700-6707	
75/01-75/02	CNW	35	6891-6925	6912 WRK/SCR. 80/12
75/02-75/03	MP	38	3164-3201	TO UP 4164-4201

MODEL SD40-2, cont'd

BLDR.DATE	RR	QTY.	DELV.NO.	NOTES
75/02-75/05	NW	66	6073-6138	
75/03-75/04	UP	17	3288-3304	
75/07	SOU	11	3244-3254	
75/08	MP	14	3202-3215	TO UP 4202-4215
75/10	SOO	3	787-789	RE# 6648-6650
75/12	ICG	4	6030-6033	
75/12	NDEM	12	8756-8767	
76/02-76/03	BN	35	6708-6742	6714 SCR.
76/03	BN	5	6743-6747	
76/03	BN	5	6748-6752	
76/07-76/09	MP	20	3216-3235	RE# 6000-6019, TO UP 3900-3935
76/07-76/09	UP	30	8035-8064	RE# 3305-3334 IN 1980
76/08	KCS	6	667-672	
76/08	KCS	2	673-674	(RCT)
76/08	KCS	2	675-676	(RCR)
76/11	BN	20	6753-6772	6760,6765,6767 SCR.
76/11	CNW	10	6926-6935	
77/01-77/02	BO	20	7600-7619	7603 RET.88/09 TO CSXT 8242-8244, 8246-8261
77/02-77/05	UP	75	3335-3409	3336 SCR.
77/05	BN	2	930-931	C&S OWNED, RE# 7800-7801
77/05	BN	5	932-936	C&S OWNED, RE# 7802-7806
77/05	BN	8	6773-6780	
77/05	UP	10	8065-8074	RE# 3400-3409 IN 1980
77/06	BN	13	937-949	C&S OWNED, RE# 7807-7819
77/06	BN	2	960-961	C&S OWNED, RE# 7830-7831
77/06	BN	10	8000-8009	
77/06-77/08	CR	46	6358-6403	
77/08-77/09	CR	37	6404-6440	
77/09	LN	22	3584-3605	FL TO SBD 8212-8233, TO CSXT SAME#
77/10	LN	4	3606-3609	(RCT) FL TO SBD 8234-8237,TO CSXT SAME#
77/10	LN	4	3610-3613	(RCR) FL TO SBD 8238-8241,TO CSXT SAME#
77/10-77/11	ATSF	30	5028-5057	5028,5034 WRK/RET.
77/11	ATSF	8	5020-5027	EVEN (RCT), ODD(RCR), 5024 RET.
77/11	BN	5	6781-6785	
77/11	BN	9	6791-6799	
77/11-77/12	BN	29	7000-7028	7019 SCR.
77/12	BN	5	6786-6790	
78/01-78/02	SOU	33	3255-3287	
78/02-78/03	BN	20	7029-7048	
78/03	BN	20	8010-8029	
78/03	KCS	3	677-679	(RCT)
78/03	KCS	3	680-682	(RCR)
78/03-78/04	BN	5	7049-7053	
78/03-78/05	UP	79	3410-3488	
78/04-78/06	NW	50	6139-6188	
78/05-78/06	SOU	15	3288-3302	(RCT)
78/06	BN	9	7054-7062	
78/06	KCS	4	683-686	683,684 HAVE (RCT),685,686 HAVE (RCR)
78/07	BN	12	7063-7074	
78/07	SLSF	8	950-957	TO BN 6840-6847
78/07-78/08	BN	24	7832-7855	C&S OWNED
78/08	MKT	7	600-606	TO UP 3809-3815

MODEL SD40-2, cont'd

BLDR.DATE	RR	QTY.	DELV.NO.	NOTES
78/08	MP	14	3252-3265	TO UP 4252-4265
78/09	MP	20	3216-3235	(2nd), TO UP 4216-4235
78/09	MP	16	3236-3251	TO UP 4236-4251
78/09-78/10	BN	13	7856-7868	C&S OWNED
78/09-78/11	CR	42	6441-6482	

MODEL SD40-2
SANTA FE
5209, BLT. 78/10
CLEBURNE, TX. 81/09

BLDR.DATE	RR	QTY.	DELV.NO.	NOTES
78/10	ATSF	14	5200-5213	5208 WRK/SCR 86/01
78/10	MKT	4	607-610	TO UP 3816-3819
78/10-78/12	BN	51	7075-7125	
78/11	KCC	7	101-107	KENNECOTT COPPER CORP, TO BCOL 736-742
78/12	UP	10	3489-3498	
79/01-79/02	BN	35	7126-7160	
79/01-79/03	UP	75	3499-3573	
79/02-79/03	SOU	10	3303-3312	(RCT)
79/03-79/04	BN	20	7869-7888	C&S OWNED
79/03-79/04	LN	34	8000-8033	FL TO SBD/CSXT SAME#
79/04	BN	6	7161-7166	
79/04-79/05	ATSF	13	5058-5070	
79/04-79/07	BN	35	7889-7923	C&S OWNED, 7899,7907 SCR.
79/05-79/06	MP	26	3266-3291	TO UP 4266-4291
79/05-79/06	SOU	16	3313-3328	
79/06	MP	34	6020-6053	TO UP 3920-3953
79/07	BN	1	8030	
79/07	MP	10	3292-3301	(2nd), TO UP 4292-4301
79/07	UP	10	3574-3583	
79/07-79/08	UP	25	8075-8099	RE# 3584-3608(2nd)
79/07-79/09	SCL	27	8040-8066	TO SBD/CSXT SAME#
79/07-79/10	CR	42	6483-6524	
79/08	LN	6	8034-8039	FL TO SBD/CSXT SAME#

MODEL SD40-2, cont'd

BLDR.DATE	RR	QTY.	DELV.NO.	NOTES
79/09	MKT	8	611-618	613 WRK/REBLT. RE# 637, TO UP 3844, REST TO UP 3820-3826
79/09	OWTX	8	9950-9957	SHAMROCK COAL CO, LETTERED ONEIDA & WESTERN, SOLD TO BCOL 743-750
79/09-79/10	ATSF	38	5071-5108	
79/09-79/12	BN	43	8031-8073	8043 SCR.
79/09-79/12	UP	50	3609-3658	(2nd),3617 RET. L/87
79/10	ATSF	8	5110-5124	EVEN (RCT), 5015 WRK/SCR. 86/03
79/10-79/11	LN	20	8067-8086	FL TO SBD/CSXT SAME#
79/11	ATSF	8	5109-5123	ODD (RCR)
79/12	MP	10	3302-3311	(2nd), TO UP 4302-4311
79/12	SOO	1	6600	WRK/SCR, TRADE IN FOR 6617
79/12	SOO	1	6601	RE# 6651

MODEL SD40-2
UNION PACIFIC
3765, BLT. 80/03
PROVO, UT. 88/07

BLDR.DATE	RR	QTY.	DELV.NO.	NOTES
80/01-80/03	UP	110	3659-3768	
80/01-80/04	BN	56	7236-7291	7241 SCR.
80/02	NDEM	10	8768-8777	
80/03-80/05	BN	17	7924-7940	C&S OWNED
80/04	MP	10	3312-3321	(2nd), TO UP 4312-4321
80/04	MP	20	6054-6073	TO UP 3954-3973
80/04	SOO	3	6602-6604	RE# 6652-6654
80/04	SOO	1	6605	WRK.82, SCR.84
80/04-80/05	SOO	8	6606-6613	RE# 6655-6662
80/05-80/06	LN	21	8095-8115	FL TO SBD/CSXT SAME#
80/05-80/06	SCL	8	8087-8094	FL TO SBD/CSXT SAME#
80/05-80/07	BN	92	8090-8181	
80/06	KCS	2	687-688	(RCT)
80/06	KCS	2	689-690	(RCR)
80/06	KCS	2	691-692	
80/07	MKT	10	619-628	628 WRK/SCR. 83/03, TO UP 3827-3835

MODEL SD40-2, cont'd

BLDR.DATE	RR	QTY.	DELV.NO.	NOTES
80/08	CRR	3	8127-8129	NEW FL, TO SBD/CSXT SAME#
80/08	LN	11	8116-8126	NEW FL, TO SBD/CSXT SAME#
80/08	SCL	1	8130	NEW FL. TO SBD/CSXT SAME#
80/08-80/09	NDEM	21	8778-8798	
80/09-80/10	ATSF	29	5141-5169	
80/10-80/11	UP	36	3769-3804	
80/11	ATSF	8	5126-5140	EVEN (RCT)
80/11	UP	4	3805-3808	
80/11-80/12	ATSF	8	5125-5139	ODD (RCR), 5037 SCR.78/03
80/12	NW	19	6189-6207	
81/03	SOO	3	6614-6616	RE# 6663-6665
81/09	CRR	1	8131	NEW FL, TO SBD/CSXT 8131
81/09	CRR	1	8132	NEW FL, TO SBD/CSXT 8132
81/09	MKT	8	629-636	TO UP 3836-3843
81/09-81/10	LN	30	8133-8162	FL TO CRR/SBD/CSXT SAME#
81/10-81/12	ATSF	23	5170-5192	
83/04	SOO	1	6617	RE# 6666
84/07	SOO	6	6618-6623	RE# 6667-6672
86/02	NDM	4	13001-13004	ORIGINALLY ORDERED BY FCP, DELV. NDM.

MODEL SD40A
ILLINOIS CENTRAL
6011, BLT. 69/08
BIRMINGHAM, AL. 81/04

MODEL SD40A, 3000 hp, BUILT 1969-1970

69/08-69/09	IC	13	6006-6018	6012 REBLT RE# 6024
70/01	IC	5	6019-6023	TO HL L/86, RE# 5019-5023

BLDR.DATE	RR	QTY.DELV.NO.		NOTES

MODEL SD40T-2, 3000 hp, BUILT 1974-1980

74/06-74/07	SP	7	8300-8306	2nd (RCT),8302 RET. 80/03
74/06-74/07	SP	7	8350-8356	(RCR)
74/10	DRGW	15	5341-5355	
75/07-75/08	DRGW	18	5356-5373	
77/01	DRGW	12	5374-5385	
78/01	SSW	5	8322-8326	(RCT)
78/01-78/02	SP	10	8489-8498	
78/01-78/02	SSW	5	8372-8376	(RCR)
78/02-78/03	SP	15	8357-8371	(RCR)
78/02-78/04	SP	15	8307-8321	(RCT)
78/08	DRGW	12	5386-5397	
78/11-79/03	SP	75	8499-8573	8507 WRK, TO HL L/86
79/03-79/05	SP	15	8327-8341	(RCT)
79/05-79/07	SP	15	8377-8391	(RCR)
80/03	DRGW	16	5398-5413	
80/03-80/07	SP	70	8230-8299	

MODEL SD40X
KANSAS CITY SOUTHERN
702, BLT. 79/09
SHREVEPORT, LA. 81/08

MODEL SD40X, 3500 hp, BUILT 1979

79/09	KCS	2	700-701	(RCT)
79/09	KCS	2	702-703	(RCR)

MODEL SD45, 3600 hp, BUILT 1965-1971

67/12-68/01	PRR	38	6170-6207	6207 LAST UNIT DELV.IN PRR SCHEME, ALL TO PC/CR S/#.
68/01	PRR	27	6208-6234	DELIVERED IN PC SCHEME, ALL TO PC/CR SAME #.
68/01-68/02	MILW	6	4000-4005	RE# 6-11, ALL SCR.
68/02	SLSF	12	914-925	TO BN 6661-6673, ALL RET. OR SCR.
68/02-68/05	SP	29	8935-8963	8939 RET.86/12, THEN TO WC VIA WILSON M/88, MOST RETIRED BY 1987.

MODEL SD45, cont'd

BLDR.DATE	RR	QTY.	DELV.NO.	NOTES
68/02-68/06	SSW	18	8964-8981	8971 WRK/REBLT RE# 9156, RET.85, 8964-8966,70,75,79,80,SCRAPPED BY 1987
68/03	DRGW	4	5337-5340	
68/03	UP	1	3600	RE# 50(2nd) NOW RETIRED
68/03-68/04	UP	39	3601-3939	RE# 1-39(2nd), 34,14,15,13,8,37 REBLT.W/SULZER ENG. IN 1980,81, THEN RE# 60-65, RET.82. 26 TO VMV 88/12, REBLT. TO SD40-2 STANDARDS, TO NDM 13076.
68/03	UP	10	3640-3649	RE# 40-49 (2nd), ALL RETIRED
68/03-68/05	DRGW	12	5325-5336	

MODEL SD45
NORTHERN PACIFIC
3620, BLT. 68/04
RIVERDALE,IL.NEW I/T, 68/04

BLDR.DATE	RR	QTY.	DELV.NO.	NOTES
68/04-68/05	NP	10	3620-3629	TO BN 6420-6429, ALL RET'D TO LESSOR
68/05	EL	14	3621-3634	TO CR 6086-6099, ALL RET. BY 86
68/07	GN	9	418-426	TO BN 6448-6456, TO CNW 6567-6575
68/08	PC	5	6235-6239	TO CR SAME#, TO CNW 6562-6566
68/09-68/10	SCL	14	2010-2023	SBD 8910-8923, TO CSXT SAME #, 8912 RET.87
68/10	SLSF	3	926-928	926 SCR. REST TO BN 6674-6675, ALL RET.
68/11-69/01	SSW	17	9052-9068	9056 SCR.76/03, 9063 SCR.73, 9054,9057, 9060,9066 SCRAPPED BY 1987
68/12	MILW	4	4006-4009	RE# 12-15, ALL SCR.
68/12-69/03	SP	49	8982-9030	8991,8992,8993,8999,9016,9023,9027 RET.
69/01	CBQ	15	516-530	BN 6457-6471, 6468 RET. REST TO CNW 6576-6589
69/01-69/02	CNW	41	937-977	942,945-947,953,960-963 RET. 86/07
69/03	SP	15	9037-9051	9041,9043,9049 SCR.
69/03-69/04	SP	6	9031-9036	
69/03-69/04	SP	35	9069-9103	9069,9080,9094 SCR. 9093 TO WC VIA WILSON 88/03
69/04	ATSF	2	5590-5591	REMFG. TO SD45U, 5386, 5388
69/04	ATSF	2	5592-5593	REMFG. TO SD45U, 5403, 5383
69/04	ATSF	2	5594-5595	REMFG. TO SD45U, 5400, 5397
69/04	ATSF	2	5596-5597	REMFG. TO SD45U, 5402, 5394
69/05	ATSF	2	5598-5599	REMFG. TO SD45U, 5384, 5399
69/05	ATSF	2	5600-5601	REMFG. TO SD45U, 5382, 5385

MODEL SD45, cont'd

BLDR.DATE	RR	QTY.	DELV.NO.	NOTES
69/04	ATSF	2	5590-5591	REMFG. TO SD45U, 5386, 5388
69/04	ATSF	2	5592-5593	REMFG. TO SD45U, 5403, 5383
69/04	ATSF	2	5594-5595	REMFG. TO SD45U, 5400, 5397
69/04	ATSF	2	5596-5597	REMFG. TO SD45U, 5402, 5394
69/05	ATSF	2	5598-5599	REMFG. TO SD45U, 5384, 5399
69/05	ATSF	2	5600-5601	REMFG. TO SD45U, 5382, 5385
69/05	ATSF	2	5602-5603	REMFG. TO SD45U, 5389, 5395
69/05	ATSF	2	5604-5605	REMFG. TO SD45U, 5396, 5401
69/05	ATSF	2	5606-5607	REMFG. TO SD45U, 5393, 5392
69/05	ATSF	2	5608-5609	REMFG. TO SD45U, 5391, 5381
69/05	ATSF	1	5610	WRK & SCRAPPED 78/03
69/05	ATSF	2	5611-5612	REMFG. TO SD45U, 5390, 5387
69/05	ATSF	2	5613-5614	REMFG. TO SD45U, 5404, 5398
69/09-69/10	SLSF	14	929-942	TO BN 6676-6689,ALL RET.6683 TO VMV 86,6677 TO WC S#

MODEL SD45
SOUTHERN PACIFIC
9121, BLT. 69/12
DALLAS, TX. 84/11

BLDR.DATE	RR	QTY.	DELV.NO.	NOTES
69/10-69/12	SP	20	9104-9123	9110,9120,9121 SCR.
69/12	NW	25	1790-1814	MOST RET.E/88, 1796,1809 REBLT.TO NDM SD40-2 13073,13067 VIA VMV L/88. 1801,1811 TO ST 683, 684 87/10. 1813 TO TAMPER INC #2, 88/01.
69/12	SLSF	5	943-947	TO BN 6690-6694 ALL RET.6690 TO WC SAME #.
69/12-70/03	SP	28	9124-9151	9135,9136,9145 RET. 9128 TO PNC, 9151 TO NRE, 9138 TO NDM SD40-2 13075, VIA VMV 88/12. 9141,9143,9144,9146-9150 TO UTAH RR.
70/01	SSW	4	9152-9155	9152,9154,9155 SCR. BY 1987
70/02-70/03	NW	25	1765-1789	MOST RET.E/88, 1771,1779 TO ST 681,682 87/10, 1780,1775,1787,1782,1781,1796,1785,REBLT BY VMV TO SD40-2, NDEM 13068-13072,13074, M/88.
70/03	SOU	5	3100-3104	(2nd) ALL TO HELM LEASING
70/03	SOU	10	3160-3169	3164 RET. 87/08, 3167 TO HLC, 3168,3169 TO NDM SD45M 13063,13064.

MODEL SD45, cont'd

BLDR.DATE	RR	QTY.	DELV.NO.	NOTES
70/06	ATSF	4	5615-5618	REMFG.TO SD45U 5379,5372,5380,5371
70/06	ATSF	4	5619-5622	REMFG.TO SD45U 5377,5374,5373,5375
70/06	ATSF	4	5621-5624	REMFG.TO SD45U 5373,5375,5378,5376
70/07-70/08	BN	20	6472-6491	ORDERED BY NP, RET'D.TO LESSOR IN 85. 6475,6480,6486,6489 TO NYSW
70/08	BN	6	6492-6497	ORDERED BY CB&Q, RET'D TO LESSOR M/86
71/05-71/08	BN	45	6498-6542	ALL RET. BY M/86, 6500,6503,6509,6513, 6514,6515,6521,6525,6542 TO NYSW
71/09	SCL	14	2024-2037	TO SBD 8924-8937, TO CSXT SAME #.
71/09	SLSF	1	948	TO BN 6695, RET.
71/10	BN	7	868-874	C&S OWNED, RE# 6570-6576, RET.BY L/86
71/10	SCL	7	2038-2044	TO CRR 3625-3631, TO CSXT 8938-8944
71/11-71/12	BN	25	6543-6567	ALL RET. BY M/86

MODEL SD45
BURLINGTON NORTHERN (C&S)
871, BLT. 71/10
SPOKANE, WA. 77/04

MODEL SD45-2, 3600 hp, BUILT 1972-1975

BLDR.DATE	RR	QTY.	DELV.NO.	NOTES
72/05	ATSF	1	5625	REBLT. WITH CAT.ENG.RE# 5855
72/05	ATSF	1	5626	REMFG. TO SD45-2B, RE# 5513
72/05	ATSF	6	5627-5632	REMFG. TO SD45-2u, 5800,7200 #'s MIXED
72/05	ATSF	1	5633	REMFG. TO SD45-2B, RE# 5515
72/05	ATSF	10	5634-5643	REMFG. TO SD45-2u, 5800,7200 #'s MIXED
72/05	ATSF	1	5644	WRK & SCR. 77/06
72/05	ATSF	6	5645-5650	REMFG. TO SD45-2u, 5800,7200 #'s MIXED
72/05	ATSF	1	5651	REMFG. TO SD45-2B, RE# 5510(2nd)
72/05	ATSF	6	5652-5657	REMFG. TO SD45-2u, 5800,7200 #'s MIXED
72/05	ATSF	1	5658	WRK & SCR. 77/11
72/05	ATSF	3	5659-5661	REMFG. TO SD45-2u, 5800,7200 #'s MIXED
72/10	EL	13	3669-3681	TO CR 6654-6666
72/11	CRR	10	3607-3716	TO FL 3607-3616, TO SBD/CSXT 8965-8974
73/05	ATSF	4	5662-5665	REMFG. TO SD45-2u, 5800,7200 #'s MIXED

MODEL SD45-2, cont'd

BLDR.DATE	RR	QTY.	DELV.NO.	NOTES
73/05	ATSF	1	5666	REMFG. TO SD45-2u, RE# 7205, WRK/REBLT. RE# 5805
73/05	ATSF	1	5687	WRK & SCR. 80/08
73/05	ATSF	12	5688-5699	REMFG. TO SD45-2u, 5800,7200 #'s MIXED
73/05	ATSF	2	5700-5701	REMFG. TO SD45-2B, RE# 5517,5514
73/05	ATSF	1	5702	REMFG. TO SD45-2u, RE# 5842
73/05	ATSF	1	5703	REMFG. TO SD45-2B, RE# 5512 (2nd)
73/05	ATSF	1	5704	REMFG. TO SD45-2u, RE# 5834
73/06	ATSF	9	5667-5675	REMFG. TO SD45-2u, 5800,7200 #'s MIXED
73/06	ATSF	1	5676	REMFG. TO SD45-2B, RE# 5511 (2nd)
73/06	ATSF	7	5677-5683	REMFG. TO SD45-2u, 5800,7200 #'s MIXED
73/06	ATSF	1	5684	REMFG. TO SD45-2B, RE# 5516
73/06	ATSF	2	5685-5686	REMFG. TO SD45-2u, RE# 7211,7212
74/02	CRR	8	3617-3624	TO FL 3617-3624, TO SBD/CSXT 8975-8982
74/05	ATSF	8	5705-5714	5706 WRK & SCR. 80/08
74/08-74/09	SCL	15	2045-2059	TO SBD 8950-8964, CSXT SAME#

MODEL SD45T-2
SOUTHERN PACIFIC
9242, BLT. 72/06
SPOKANE, WA. 77/02

MODEL SD45T-2, 3600 hp, BUILT 1972-1975

BLDR.DATE	RR	QTY.	DELV.NO.	NOTES
72/02-72/03	SP	43	9166-9208	9174 WRK/SCR. 76/07
72/04-72/06	SP	52	9209-9260	9220 WRK/REBLT RE# 9314
72/07	SSW	9	9157-9165	
73/02-73/03	SSW	41	9261-9301	
73/09	SP	12	9302-9313	
74/01-74/02	SP	29	9315-9343	
75/01-75/02	SP	27	9344-9370	9354 RET.80
75/03-75/06	SSW	34	9371-9404	9379 WRK/SCR. 75/08

MODEL SD45X, 4200 hp, BUILT 1970-1971

70/06	EMD	1	4201	SOLD TO SP 9503, SCR.84
70/06	EMD	1	5740	DEMO UNIT, STILL OWNED BY EMD.
70/08-70/09	SP	3	9500-9502	(2nd) SCR.IN 84
71/02	EMD	2	4202-4203	SOLD TO SP 9504-9505, 9504 SCR.84, 9505 RET.78/06, TO MK, REBLT TO SD40M 8301

MODEL SD50, 3500 hp, BUILT 1980-1988

80/11-80/12	NW	6	6500-6505	
81/05-81/06	KCS	10	704-713	
83/01-83/02	SBD	25	8500-8524	DELIVERED FL-SBD, TO CSXT SAME#
83/10-83/12	CR	40	6700-6739	
84/01-84/02	CO	23	8553-8575	DELIVERED CS, TO CSXT SAME#
84/02-84/03	SBD	26	8527-8552	TO CSXT SAME #
84/03	SBD	2	8525-8526	TO CSXT SAME #
84/04-84/06	CR	40	6740-6779	
84/06	SBD	7	8596-8602	TO CSXT SAME #
84/07	SOU	15	6506-6520	NS OWNED
84/07	SOU	5	6521-6525	NS OWNED
84/07-84/08	BO	20	8576-8595	DELIVERED CS, TO CSXT SAME#
84/08-84/09	DRGW	17	5501-5517	BUILT TO CSXT SPECS.
84/11-84/12	MP	60	5000-5059	TO UP SAME #, RATED AT 3600HP
85/01-85/02	SBD	21	8603-8623	TO CSXT SAME #
85/04-85/05	CR	25	6780-6804	
85/10-85/11	CO	20	8624-8643	DELIVERED CS, TO CSXT SAME#
85/11-85/12	CNW	35	7000-7034	
86/01-86/02	CR	30	6805-6834	

MODEL SD50
CHICAGO & NORTH WESTERN
7024, BLT. 85/12
CRESTON, IL. 88/09

BLDR.DATE	RR	QTY.	DELV.NO.	NOTES

MODEL SD60, 3800 hp, BUILT 1984-

BLDR.DATE	RR	QTY.	DELV.NO.	NOTES
84/05-84/07	EMD	4	EMD1-EMD4	PROTOTYPES. 1,2,4,TO CR 6840,6842,6841
84/12	SOU	4	6550-6553	NS OWNED, TEST PROTOTYPES
85/06-85/07	SOU	10	6554-6563	NS OWNED, (RCT)
85/07-85/10	SOU	40	6564-6603	NS OWNED
85/11	BN	3	8300-8302	PROTOTYPES, RETURNED EMD, TO LEASE UNITS
86/02-86/03	SOU	25	6604-6628	NS OWNED
86/02-86/05	UP	60	6000-6059	
86/06-86/08	SOU	12	6629-6640	NS OWNED
86/08	SOU	10	6641-6650	NS OWNED
86/08-86/10	CNW	55	8001-8055	
86/10-86/12	OWY	100	9000-9099	OAKWAY LEASING, LEASED TO BN
87/08-87/11	SOO	21	6000-6020	
88/02-88/06	UP	25	6060-6084	
89/06-89/07	CR	25	6845-6869	

MODEL SDL39
MILWAUKEE ROAD
584, BLT. 69/03
DUBUQUE, IA. 80/09

MODEL SDL39, 2300 hp, BUILT 1969-1972

BLDR.DATE	RR	QTY.	DELV.NO.	NOTES
69/03	MILW	5	581-585	581 SCR. REST TO WCL
72/11	MILW	5	586-590	ALL TO WCL

MODEL SDP40, 3000 hp, BUILT 1966-1970

BLDR.DATE	RR	QTY.	DELV.NO.	NOTES
68/05	NDEM	10	8522-8531	
70/05	NDEM	4	8532-8535	

BLDR.DATE	RR	QTY.	DELV.NO.	NOTES
MODEL SDP40F, 3000 hp, BUILT 1973-1974				
73/06	AMTK	11	500-510	TRADED TO EMD
73/06	AMTK	1	511	TO ATSF SDP40FU 5251
73/06-73/07	AMTK	14	512-525	TRADED TO EMD
73/07	AMTK	1	526	TO ATSF SDP40FU 5255
73/07	AMTK	13	527-539	TRADED TO EMD
74/03-74/05	AMTK	40	540-579	TRADED TO EMD,569 TO EMD TEST BED 134
74/05-74/06	AMTK	35	580-614	TRADED TO EMD,609 TO EMD TEST BED 169
74/06	AMTK	1	615	TO ATSF SDP40FU 5252
74/06-74/07	AMTK	5	617-621	TRADED TO EMD
74/07	AMTK	1	622	TO ATSF SDP40FU 5257
74/07	AMTK	5	623-627	TRADED TO EMD
74/07	AMTK	2	628-629	TO ATSF SDP40FU 5258,5262
74/07	AMTK	1	630	TO ATSF SDP40FU 5253
74/07	AMTK	1	631	TRADED TO EMD
74/07	AMTK	1	632	TO ATSF SDP40FU 5264
74/07	AMTK	1	633	TRADED TO EMD
74/07	AMTK	2	634-635	TO ATSF SDP40FU, 5261, 5254
74/07	AMTK	2	636-637	TRADED TO EMD
74/07	AMTK	2	638-639	TO ATSF SDP40FU, 5260, 5263
74/07	AMTK	1	640	TO ATSF SDP40FU, 5256
74/07	AMTK	2	641-642	TRADED TO EMD
74/08	AMTK	2	643-644	TO ATSF SDP40FU, 5250, 5266
74/08	AMTK	1	645	TO ATSF SDP40FU, 5267
74/08	AMTK	3	646-648	TRADED TO EMD
74/08	AMTK	1	649	TO ATSF SDP40FU, 5265
				ALL SDP40's EITHER TRADED TO EMD OR TO ATSF BY 84/09

MODEL SDP40F
AMTRAK
645, BLT. 74/08
NASHVILLE, TN. 74/08

BLDR.DATE	RR	QTY.	DELV.NO.	NOTES

MODEL SDP45, 3600 hp, BUILT 1967-1970

69/05	EL	2	3635-3636	TO CR 6667, 6668, TO NW SAME# IN 85
69/05	EL	1	3637	WRK.TO NW, REBLT.TO SLUG 9920,RE# 9950
69/05-69/06	EL	16	3638-3653	TO CR 6669-6684, TO NW SAME# IN 85
70/07-70/08	EL	15	3654-3668	TO CR 6685-6699, RET'D TO LESSOR 86, THEN TO VMV.

MODEL SW1000
HOUSTON,BELT & TERMINAL
42, BLT. 68/01
HOUSTON, TX. 81/11

MODEL SW1000, 1000 hp, BUILT 1966-1972

68/01	HBT	3	40-42	40 RET. TO NRE
68/04	DRGW	3	147-149	
68/06	YSTX	2	908-909	YOUNGSTOWN SHEET & TUBE CO.
68/08	WEPX	1	N/A	WISCONSIN ELECTRIC POWER CO.
68/08	YSTX	1	910	YOUNGSTOWN SHEET & TUBE CO.
68/10	ALTO	1	132	ALTOS HORNOS (MEXICO)
68/12	KCDX	1	8	EASTMAN KODAK CO.
69/01	BS	2	12-13	RE# 212,213
69/02	JONE	1	103	JONES & LAUGHLIN STEEL
69/03	ARGO	2	68-69	ARGO CORN INDUSTRIES
69/04	YSTX	2	912-913	YOUNGSTOWN SHEET & TUBE CO.
69/05	CPCX	2	68-69	CORN PRODUCTS CO.
69/05	YSTX	1	911	YOUNGSTOWN SHEET & TUBE CO.
69/05-69/06	YSTX	3	912-914	YOUNGSTOWN SHEET & TUBE CO.
69/09	PSIX	1	1	PUBLIC SERVICE CO. OF INDIANA
69/10	BS	1	14	SCR. 73
69/12	AEPX	1	1	AMERICAN ELECTRIC POWER SERVICE CORP.
70/11-71/01	BN	15	435-449	ORDERED BY CB&Q, DELIVERED BN 442 WRK/REBLT. INTO CABLESS B UNIT.
71/01	BS	1	15	SCR. 73
71/01-71/02	BN	8	427-434	

MODEL SW1000, cont'd

BLDR.DATE	RR	QTY.	DELV.NO.	NOTES
71/04	CEME	1	NONE	CEMENTOES ANAHUAC (MEXICO)
71/07-71/08	NOPB	9	101-106	
71/08	CELU	1	1811	CELULOSA de CHI (MEXICO)
71/10	BS	2	16-17	BOTH SCR. 73
72/01-72/02	BN	15	375-389	
72/04	GMCX	1	NONE	GENERAL MOTORS CORP.
72/09	ALTO	1	137	ALTOS HORNOS (MEXICO)
72/10	BN	5	390-394	

MODEL SW1001, 1000 hp, BUILT 1968-1986

BLDR.DATE	RR	QTY.	DELV.NO.	NOTES
68/09	DEEX	1	217	DETROIT EDISON
68/09	LT	1	1021	
68/09	RT	2	101-102	
68/10	FORD	5	10014-10018	FORD MOTOR CO. 10015 SCR. 84
69/12	NSR	1	1018	
70/02	MCRR	1	420	
70/03	USX	2	88-89	U.S.STEEL CORP.
71/01	USX	1	90	U.S.STEEL CORP.
71/07	ALAB	1	1000	ALABAMA BY-PRODUCTS
71/07	NSR	1	1019	
71/08	EJE	2	444,445	
71/08	GMCX	1	1971	GENERAL MOTORS CORP, DEFIANCE,OH. PLANT
71/10	GLSX	1	58	GREAT LAKES STEEL CORP.
72/04	CHEV	1	96	CHEVROLET MTR.DIV.TONAWANDA,NY.ENG.PLT
72/04	NSR	1	1020	TO BS 226, 80/02
73/02	ALQS	2	1000-1001	
73/02	CUVA	1	1051	
73/05	BS	2	18-19	RE# 218-219 IN 73/10
73/10	FORD	2	10019-10020	FORD MOTOR CO.
73/10	PSCX	1	15-1	(2nd) PUBLIC SERVICE CO. OF COLORADO
73/10-73/11	RDG	24	2601-2624	TO PC 9401-9424, TO CR SAME #
73/11	RDG	1	2625	TO PC 9400, TO CR SAME #
74/01	BS	5	220-224	
74/04,74/03	MCRR	2	421-422	
74/08	ALTO	1	142	ALTOS HORNOS (MEXICO)
74/08	SJMX	1	1004	ST.JOE MINERALS CORP.
74/09	CSL	2	28-29	
74/10	ARMC	1	E150	ARMCO STEEL CO.
74/10	BS	1	225	
74/10	CCR	1	1003	
74/10	ISCX	2	17-18	INTERLAKE STEEL CO.
75/03	ALQS	1	1002	SOLD TO RIVER TERMINAL, RE# 109
75/03	MCRR	1	423	
75/03	NSR	2	1021-1022	
75/03	SCWX	1	1001	SOUTH CAROLINA PUBLIC SERVICE AUTHORITY
75/09	ARMC	2	E151-E152	ARMCO STEEL CO.
75/09	RT	2	103-104	
75/10	ARMC	3	E153-E155	ARMCO STEEL CO.

MODEL SW1001, cont'd

MODEL SW1001
GALVESTON WHARVES
302, BLT. 75/10
GALVESTON, TX. 83/02

BLDR.DATE	RR	QTY.	DELV.NO.	NOTES
75/10	GWF	2	301-302	
75/12	FORD	3	10021-10023	FORD MOTOR CO.
75/12	TPBX	1	24	TEXACO, INC.
76/01	SICA	3	1-3	SICARTSA (MEXICO)
76/03	INLX	2	126-127	INLAND STEEL CO.
76/03	MCRR	2	424-425	DELV. R/W/B
76/03	URR	3	101-103	ALL TO BS 85/11
76/07	NATI	2	7601-7602	NATIONAL HARBOURS BOARD (CANADA)
76/07	BRFD	1	7357	OWNED,NEW HAVEN TRAP ROCK, DELV. R/W/B
76/08	ARMC	3	E156-E158	ARMCO STEEL CO.
76/12	RT	2	105-106	
77/03	LI	8	100-107	
77/10	ARMC	3	E159-E161	ARMCO STEEL CO. MIDDLETOWN PLANT
77/12	GWF	1	303	
77/12	SCWX	2	2001-2002	SOUTH CAROLINA PUBLIC SERVICE AUTHORITY SUB-LETTERED FOR ECBR
78/04	ALTO	3	151-153	ALTOS HORNOS (MEXICO)
78/04	RT	1	107	
78/04	SSDK	2	1001-1002	
78/11	ALTO	3	154-156	ALTOS HORNOS (MEXICO)
78/11	ARMC	2	E162-E163	ARMCO STEEL CO. MIDDLETOWN PLANT
78/11	SPCX	2	1001-1002	SASKATCHEWAN POWER (CANADA)
78/12	AMCX	1	SE3	AMOCO CHEMICALS CO.
78/12	RT	1	108	
79/06	ALTO	3	159-161	159 2nd, ALTOS HORNOS (MEXICO)
79/06	AMER	2	9G9-9G10	AMERICAN STEEL FOUNDRIES
79/07	CHAM	1	06056	CHAMPION INTERNATIONAL
79/12	ARMC	2	E164-E165	ARMCO STEEL CO. MIDDLETOWN PLANT
79/12	EMD	1	117	PLANT SWITCHER
80/01	CCR	1	1004	

MODEL SW1001, cont'd

BLDR.DATE	RR	QTY.	DELV.NO.	NOTES
80/06	EAST	1	2	EAST KENTUCKY POWER
80/07	GWF	2	304-305	
80/08	PMEX	2	24-25	PETROLEOS MEXICANOS, (MEXICO)
80/11	ARMC	2	E166-E167	ARMCO STEEL CO. MIDDLETOWN PLANT
80/11	ARMC	1	11838	ARMCO STEEL CO. HOUSTON PLANT
80/12	ALTO	2	164-165	ALTOS HORNOS (MEXICO)
80/12	COOR	1	998 (2nd)	COORS BREWING, GOLDEN, CO.
80/12	DOWX	3	1001-1003	DOW CHEMICAL CO.PLAQUEMINE, LA.
80/12	DOWX	2	1008-1009	DOW CHEMICAL CO.FREEPORT, TX.
81/04	ARMC	2	E168-E169	ARMCO STEEL CO. MIDDLETOWN PLANT
81/04	ARMC	1	1215	ARMCO STEEL CO. ASHLAND PLANT
81/05	CCR	1	1005	
81/05	NORT	3	2-4	NORTHWESTERN STEEL & WIRE CO.
81/06	ARMC	1	11839	ARMCO STEEL CO. HOUSTON PLANT
82/03	EWSX	1	NONE	INDIANAPOLIS POWER & LIGHT CO.
82/06	ARMC	1	11840	ARMCO STEEL CO. HOUSTON PLANT
82/06	OLNX	1	1	OLIN CORP.
85/04	IPPX	1	1	INTERMOUNTAIN POWER PROJECT
86/06	PMEX	1	5	PETROLEOS MEXICANOS, (MEXICO)

MODEL SW1500, 1500 hp, BUILT 1966-1974

BLDR.DATE	RR	QTY.	DELV.NO.	NOTES
68/02	KIT	2	70-71	
68/02	TPW	2	303-304	303 TO CHROME CRANKSHAFT ,304 TO VTR
68/03	BRC	2	531-532	
68/03	MTFR	1	302	
68/03	WRGX	1	102	102 (3rd), W.R.GRACE CO.
68/04-68/06	SSW	12	2481-2492	2487 TO NRE
68/05	INLX	1	119	INLAND STEEL CO.
68/05	WTCX	1	306	WEYERHAEUSER CORP.
68/06	CI	2	15-16	
68/06-68/07	IHB	6	9216-9221	9219-21 SLUG MASTER UNITS
68/06-68/07	SP	18	2493-2510	2505 TO WILSON L/86
68/07	TASD	2	681-682	
68/07-68/08	INLX	2	120-121	INLAND STEEL CO.
68/08	KCS	14	1504-1517	1509 SLUG MASTER, RE# 4324-4337
68/08-68/09	MKT	4	52-55	TO UP 1324-1327
68/09	CSL	1	30	
68/10	IU	1	26	
68/10	SLSF	16	315-330	TO BN 20-35
68/11	EMD	1	110	PLANT SWITCHER, SOLD TO IU 27
68/11-68/12	SOU	30	2300-2329	2322 WRK/SCR 79/06
69/03-69/04	SSW	12	2511-2522	2512 TO NHN 1500, 2518 TO WCL VIA WILSON L/86
69/04	MTFR	2	303-304	
69/04	WRGX	1	101	(2nd), W.R.GRACE CO.
69/05	ALS	6	1500-1505	
69/05	AN	4	712-715	
69/05	GUAX	1	1401	GEORGIA POWER CO. HATCH PLT. BAXLEY,GA.
69/06-69/07	RDG	10	2761-2770	TO PC 9611-9620, TO CR SAME#
69/07-69/11	SP	30	2523-2552	2529 RET. 86, 2541 RET. 78/12
69/09	PBR	2	160-161	SOLD TO CI RE# 17,18
69/09	RSP	1	500	

MODEL SW1500, cont'd

BLDR.DATE	RR	QTY.	DELV.NO.	NOTES
69/11	SOU	3	2330-2332	
69/11	SOU	5	2333-2337	
69/11	TRRA	6	1506-1511	
69/12	HBT	3	50-52	
69/12	LPN	1	130	
69/12-70/01	SLSF	16	331-346	TO BN 36-51
70/01	INLX	2	122-123	INLAND STEEL CO.
70/01	SSW	4	2579-2582	
70/01-70/04	SP	26	2553-2578	2454,2469,2476,2478 RET.L/86,2578 TO WC
70/02	ALS	6	1506-1511	
70/02	ITC	6	1509-1515	TO NW 2290-2296,2295 TO MRS 257,88/01
70/03	EMD	1	109	PLANT SWITCHER, TO IHB 9222
70/03	SOU	5	2338-2342	
70/03	SOU	5	2343-2347	
70/04	LN	10	5000-5009	TO SBD 1100-1109, TO CSXT SAME#
70/05	ADN	1	150	
70/05	CSNX	1	108	CITIES SERVICE CO.
70/05	HOWE	1	2	HOWE COAL CO. TO KCS 4362
70/05	MTFR	2	305-306	305 TO MTW 83, 83/10
70/05	SAN	1	300	
70/05	TPW	2	305-306	TO CHROME CRANKSHAFT FOR RESALE
70/06	ALCT	1	9	ALCOA TERMINAL, (ALCOA ALUMINIUM)
70/06	IHB	5	9223-9227	RESOLD TO PC ON DELV. TO CR SAME #
70/06	HOWE	1	1	TO TOPCO, PORT ARTHUR, TX.
70/06	RSP	1	600	

MODEL SW1500
APALACHICOLA NORTHERN
718, BLT. 70/09
ST.JOE, FL. 84/10

70/08-70/09	AN	4	716-719	
71/01	PLE	10	9280-9289	RE# 1573-1564, IN REVERSE ORDER
71/02	PC	10	9500-9509	
71/03	KIT	5	72-76	

MODEL SW1500, cont'd

BLDR.DATE	RR	QTY.	DELV.NO.	NOTES
71/04	EMD	1	113	PLANT SWITCHER TO ETR 107
71/04	EMD	1	114	PLANT SWITCHER, TO GRR 1010
71/04	KCS	6	1518-1523	RE# 4338-4343
71/04-71/05	KCS	8	1524-1531	RE# 4344-4351
71/05	ALS	6	1512-1517	
71/05	EMD	1	112	PLANT SWITCHER, TO IU 28
71/05-71/10	HBT	3	53-55	
71/06	SM	1	503	
71/07	CSL	1	31	
71/08	GUAX	1	1402	GEORGIA POWER CO. YATES PLT. NEWNAN,GA.
71/08	GUAX	2	1503-1504	GEORGIA POWER CO. HAMMOND PLT. ROME,GA.
71/08	LEF	1	23	OFF ROSTER

MODEL SW1500
NEW ORLEANS PUBLIC BELT
153, BLT. 71/08
NEW ORLEANS, LA. 84/10

BLDR.DATE	RR	QTY.	DELV.NO.	NOTES
71/08	NOPB	3	151-153	
71/10-71/11	SP	22	2591-2612	2594 SOLD TO WILSON L/86
71/11	LN	10	5010-5019	TO SBD 1110-1119, TO CSXT SAME#
71/12	EMD	1	111	PLANT SWITCHER, TO IU 29
71/12	PLE	10	1554-1563	1554,57,60,62,63 TO PEAKER SERVICES, 1559,1562,1557 TO WEIRTON STEEL 302-304 1560 TO KODAK 3 (2nd).
71/12	SSW	8	2583-2590	
72/01	KCS	10	1532-1541	RE# 4352-4361
72/02-72/03	PC	50	9510-9559	TO CR SAME#
72/03-72/04	SLSF	6	347-352	TO BN 52-57
72/04-72/08	SP	67	2613-2679	2640,2643,2663 TO NRE, 2652 TO WILSON 2625,2647,2652,2665,2675 RET. L/86.
72/09	KIT	3	77-79	
72/09	USPF	4	51-54	U.S.PIPE & FOUNDRY
72/09	USX	6	949-954	U.S.STEEL CO. MINNESOTA TACONITE DIV.
72/09-72/10	PLE	10	1544-1553	1544,1545,1550,1552 TO PEAKER SERVICES

MODEL SW1500, cont'd

BLDR.DATE	RR	QTY.	DELV.NO.	NOTES
72/10	ARMC	2	701-702	ARMCO STEEL CO.
72/10	TRRA	6	1512-1517	
72/11	ANR	1	1500	
72/11	LEF	1	24	OFF ROSTER
72/11	LN	10	5020-5029	TO SBD 1120-1129, TO CSXT SAME#
72/11	URR	5	1-5	
72/12	IU	3	30-32	
72/12	MP	4	1518-1521	TO UP 1318-1321, 1318,1319 TO CRL 18,19 L/88.
72/12	WTCX	1	307	WEYERHAEUSER CORP.

MODEL SW1500
BURLINGTON NORTHERN
321, BLT. 73/01
SPOKANE, WA. 79/04

73/01	BN	15	310-324	
73/01	GUAX	1	1405	GEORGIA POWER CO.YATES PLANT,NEWNAN,GA.
73/01	SLSF	8	353-360	TO BN 58-65
73/04-73/05	SP	10	2680-2689	
73/05	PLE	10	1534-1543	1535,1539,1540, TO DOMINION TERMINAL ASSOCIATES 001,002,003, 83/11.
73/05	WP	3	1501-1503	TO UP 1315-1317
73/08	ARMC	2	703-704	ARMCO STEEL CO.
73/08	MSE	1	64	
73/09	URR	4	6-9	
73/09-73/10	PC	24	9560-9583	TO CR SAME #
73/10	KIT	2	80-81	
73/12	ARMC	1	705	ARMCO STEEL CO.
73/12	ETCX	1	1	TENNESSEE EASTMAN CO. KINGSPORT,TN.
73/12	INLX	2	124-125	INLAND STEEL CO.
74/01	KIT	2	82-83	#82 IS LAST SW1500 BUILT

MODEL SW1504, 1500 hp, BUILT 1973

73/05-73/08	NDEM	60	8800-8859	ONLY PURCHASER OF THIS MODEL

GE-GENERAL ELECTRIC CO. ERIE, PA.

BLDR.DATE	RR	QTY.	DELV.NO.	NOTES
MODEL 65 TON, 550 hp, BUILT 1957-1974				
69/01	APWX	1	2	APPALACHIAN ELECTRIC POWER CO.
MODEL 80 TON, 600 hp, BUILT 1957-1974				
68/09	LATC	1	NONE	LA TOLTECA CIA (MEXICO)
68/09	RMCX	1	NONE	REYNOLDS METALS CO.
69/01	ALTO	1	133	ALTOS HORNOS (MEXICO)
70/02	BSCX	1	N/A	BETHLEHAM STEEL CORP.
70/12	DKPX	1	102	DUKE POWER CO.MARSHALL PLT.CATAWBA,NC
70/12	GECX	1	N/A	GENERAL ELECTRIC CO.
71/04	MOBX	1	N/A	MOBIL OIL CORP.
72/04	CITI	1	3	CITIZENS GAS & COKE
72/05	DKPX	1	103	DUKE POWER CO.
72/06	ALTO	1	138	ALTOS HORNOS (MEXICO)
72/09	PHDX	1	NONE	PHELPS-DODGE CORP.
73/05	DKPX	2	104,105	DUKE POWER CO. BELLOWS CREEK, NC.
74/02	GREE	1	3	GREENVILLE STEEL CAR CO.
74/07	PHDX	1	NONE	PHELPS-DODGE CORP.
MODEL 100 TON, 600 hp, BUILT 1957-1974				
68/04	ALMA	1	NONE	ALMACENES (MEXICO)
69/08	KENT	1	103	KENTUCKY POWER
71/03-71/04	AEPX	3	N/A	AMERICAN ELECTRIC POWER SERVICE CORP.
MODEL 110 TON, 600 hp, BUILT 1957-1974				
68/01	FUND	1	8	FUNDIDORA de FIERRO y ACERO (MEXICO)
68/01	NDEM	1	N/A	NATIONAL RAILWAYS OF MEXICO
68/03	USX	1	N/A	U.S.STEEL CORP.
69/09	SCWX	1	NONE	S.CAROLINA ELECTRIC & GAS, WATEREE SC
70/04	LOUI	1	NONE	LOUISVILLE GAS & ELECTRIC
70/12	CIPX	1	NONE	CENTRAL ILLINOIS PUBLIC SERVICE CO.
71/03	KUCX	1	NONE	KENTUCKY UTILITIES
71/05	FUND	1	9	FUNDIDORA de FIERRO y ACERO (MEXICO)
73/01	EMPI	1	NONE	EMPIRE REEVES STEEL
73/03	INDI	1	NONE	INDIANA POWER & LIGHT CO.
74/08	AEPX	1	1085	AMERICAN ELECTRIC POWER SERVICE CORP.

BLDR.DATE	RR	QTY.	DELV.NO.	NOTES

MODEL B23-7, 2250 hp, BUILT 1977-1984

BLDR.DATE	RR	QTY.	DELV.NO.	NOTES
77/09-77/11	CR	17	2800-2816	
78/01	MP	10	2287-2298	RE# 4600-4609, TO UP 100-109
78/01-78/02	SCL	15	5100-5114	DELV.FL,TO SBD SAME#, TO CSXT 3100-3114
78/02	LN	8	5115-5122	DELV.FL,TO SBD SAME#, TO CSXT 3115-3122
78/02	LN	1	5123	WRK/SCR. 82/01
78/02	LN	6	5124-5129	DELV.FL TO SBD SAME#, TO CSXT 3123-3128
78/03	PW	1	2201	
78/04-78/05	ATSF	14	6350-6363	MOST UPGRADED TO 3000 hp, RE# IN 7200 SERIES MIXED.
78/04-78/06	CR	40	1900-1939	1903-1909 TO MNCR 801-807
78/07-78/09	CR	27	1940-1966	
78/09	SCL	15	5140-5154	DELV.FL,TO SBD SAME#, TO CSXT 3129-3143
78/09	SOU	10	3970-3979	
78/10-78/11	MP	20	2299-2318	RE# 4610-4629, TO UP 110-129
79/01	SOU	10	3980-3989	
79/03-79/05	CR	25	1967-1991	

MODEL B23-7
SANTA FE
6383, BLT. 79/06
CLEBURNE, TX. 81/08

BLDR.DATE	RR	QTY.	DELV.NO.	NOTES
79/04-79/06	ATSF	26	6364-6389	MOST UPGRADED TO 3000 hp, RE# IN 7200 SERIES MIXED.
79/06-79/09	CR	32	1992-2023	
79/08	TUGX	1	3306	TEXAS UTILITIES MINING CO.
79/12	FUS	3	522-524	ASSEMBLED IN BRAZIL, 522,524 RET. 523 TO NDM 9181
79/12	MP	20	2319-2338	RE# 4630-4649, TO UP 130-159
79/12-80/01	NDEM	10	9130-9139	ASSEMBLED IN BRAZIL
80/04	ATSF	15	6390-6404	
80/04	MP	10	4650-4659	TO UP 150-159
80/05-80/06	SP	15	5100-5114	
80/06	MP	10	4660-4669	TO UP 160-169
80/08-80/09	NDEM	6	9140-9145	
80/10-81/02	NDEM	13	10001-10013	(KITS) ASSEMBLED BY NDEM
80/11-81/01	NDEM	32	9146-9177	

MODEL B23-7, cont'd

BLDR.DATE	RR	QTY.	DELV.NO.	NOTES
81/01-81/02	SMT	8	1-01/1-08	TRANS-ISTHMUS MULTIMODAL TRANSISTMICO (MEXICO) OWNED BY NDEM, 1-08 WRK/RET. L/87.
81/01-81/12	NDEM	33	10014-10046	(KITS) ASSEMBLED BY NDEM
81/02-81/04	SOU	34	3990-4023	
81/04-81/05	MP	15	4670-4684	TO UP 170-184
81/06	NDEM	3	9178-9180	
81/10	TUGX	1	3307	TEXAS UTILITIES MINING CO.
81/12-82/01	NDEM	6	10047-10052	(KITS) ASSEMBLED BY NDEM
82/02-82/03	NDEM	6	12001-12006	(KITS) ASSEMBLED BY NDEM
82/04-82/05	NDEM	5	12007-12011	(KITS) ASSEMBLED BY NDEM
84/04-84/05	ATSF	14	6405-6418	DELV. IN 84/12

MODEL BQ23-7, 2250 hp, BUILT 1978-1979

78/10-79/01	SCL	10	5130-5139	DELV.FL,TO SBD SAME#,TO CSXT 3000-3009

MODEL B30-7
COTTON BELT (SSW)
7795, BLT. 80/04
PHOENIX, AZ. 88/11
PHOTO: JAMES D. BRADLEY

MODEL B30-7, 3000 hp, BUILT 1977-1981

77/12	SLSF	8	863-870	TO BN 5485-5492, 5490 RET. 82/01
77/12-78/01	SP	4	7800-7803	
78/03	SP	20	7804-7823	7810 RET. 79/07
78/05	CO	10	8235-8244	DELV.CS, TO CSXT 5517-5526, 5517,5518, RET. 87/02, 5534 RET.86/02, 5535 87/02
79/02-79/05	SP	60	7824-7883	
79/06	CO	10	8255-8264	DELV. CS, TO CSXT 5537-5546
80/01	CO	14	8265-8278	DELV. CS, TO CSXT 5547-5560
80/03	SCL	10	5500-5509	DELV. FL, TO SBD/CSXT SAME#
80/03080/04	SSW	26	7774-7799	
80/05	SCL	7	5510-5516	DELV. FL, TO SBD/CSXT SAME#
81/03-81/05	CO	20	8279-8298	DELV. CS, TO CSXT 5561-5580

BLDR.DATE	RR	QTY.	DELV.NO.	NOTES

MODEL B30-7A, 3000 hp, BUILT 1981-1982

BLDR.DATE	RR	QTY.	DELV.NO.	NOTES
81/11-82/01	MP	35	4800-4834	TO UP 200-234
82/01-82/02	MP	14	4835-4848	TO UP 235-248
82/02	MP	6	4849-4854	TO UP 249-254
82/04-82/05	SOU	22	3500-3521	

MODEL B30-7A(B), 3000 hp, BUILT 1982-1983

BLDR.DATE	RR	QTY.	DELV.NO.	NOTES
82/06-82/09	BN	53	4000-4052	4051 WRK/SCR.
83/08-83/10	BN	67	4053-4119	

MODEL B30-7A(B)
BURLINGTON NORTHERN
4016, BLT. 82/07
FT.WORTH, TX. 82/12

MODEL B32-8, 3200 hp, BUILT 1984

BLDR.DATE	RR	QTY.	DELV.NO.	NOTES
84/01	BN	3	5497-5499	PROTOTYPE TEST UNITS

MODEL B36-7, 3600 hp, BUILT 1980-1985

BLDR.DATE	RR	QTY.	DELV.NO.	NOTES
80/01	SSW	4	7770-7773	7771 WRK/REBLT TO CABLESS BOOSTER IN 82
80/10-80/11	ATSF	16	7484-7499	7484,7486 (RCT),7485,7487 (RCR)
81/03	SOU	6	3815-3820	
83/10-83/12	CR	49	5000-5048	5017 WRK/SCR.88/01, 5045 SCR.
83/12	CR	11	5049-5059	
84/11-84/12	SP	16	7754-7769	
85/02-85/06	SBD	75	5806-5880	TO CSXT SAME#
85/07-85/09	SBD	45	5881-5925	TO CSXT SAME#

MODEL B36-8, 3600 hp, BUILT 1982

BLDR.DATE	RR	QTY.	DELV.NO.	NOTES
82/09	GECX	1	606	GENERAL ELECTRIC DEMO UNIT, NOW REBLT. TO B39-8.5E, RE# 809, HAS WIDE CAB

BLDR.DATE	RR	QTY.	DELV.NO.	NOTES

MODEL B39-8, 3900 hp, BUILT 1984

BLDR.DATE	RR	QTY.	DELV.NO.	NOTES
84/01	ATSF	1	7400	PROTOTYPE TEST UNIT (RCT)
84/09	ATSF	1	7402	PROTOTYPE TEST UNIT
84/12	ATSF	1	7401	PROTOTYPE TEST UNIT

MODEL B39-8E
SOUTHERN PACIFIC
8015, BLT. 87/08
SAN ANTONIO, TX. 88/06

MODEL B39-8E, 3900 hp, BUILT 1987-1988

BLDR.DATE	RR	QTY.	DELV.NO.	NOTES
87/05-87/07	LMX	41	8500-8540	GENERAL ELECTRIC LEASING CO. ALL LEASED TO BN, 8503,8540 WRK.87, REBLT,RE# GECX 8000, 8001, NOW LEASED TO BN.
87/08-87/09	SP	40	8000-8039	
87/10-87/11	LMX	26	8541-8566	ALL LEASED TO BN
88/03	LMX	1	8503	(2nd) WRECK REPLACEMENT,LEASED TO BN
88/03	LMX	1	8540	(2nd) WRECK REPLACEMENT,LEASED TO BN
88/03-88/04	LMX	33	8567-8599	ALL LEASED TO BN

MODEL C30-7, 3000 hp, BUILT 1976-1986

BLDR.DATE	RR	QTY.	DELV.NO.	NOTES
76/09	BN	1	5500	
76/12	BN	9	5501-5509	
77/04-77/07	BN	20	5510-5529	
77/07-77/09	UP	15	2960-2974	RE# 2400-2414
77/11	CR	10	6600-6609	
77/11-77/12	BN	15	5530-5544	
77/12	ATSF	10	8010-8019	
78/03-78/06	ATSF	38	8020-8057	
78/06-78/07	UP	15	2415-2429	
78/09-78/10	BN	22	5545-5566	
78/10	ATSF	6	8058-8063	

MODEL C30-7, cont'd

MODEL C30-7
NORFOLK & WESTERN
8031, BLT. 78/12
DECATUR, IL. 87/09

BLDR.DATE	RR	QTY.	DELV.NO.	NOTES
78/11-78/12	NW	35	8003-8037	
78/12	NDEM	1	6700	(2nd)
78/12-79/01	UP	30	2430-2459	
79/02	BN	15	5567-5581	
79/02-79/03	LN	16	7000-7015	DELV.FL, TO SBD/CSXT SAME#
79/03	SCL	9	7016-7024	DELV.FL, TO SBD/CSXT SAME#
79/04-79/05	ATSF	35	8064-8098	
79/05-79/06	BN	18	5582-5599	
79/06	BN	7	5001-5007	
79/07-79/10	NW	45	8038-8082	
79/08	SCL	7	7025-7031	DELV. FL, TO SBD, TO CSXT SAME#
79/09	BN	1	5000	
79/09	LN	20	7032-7051	DELV. FL. TO CSXT 7032-7044(2nd)
79/09	NDEM	9	6701-6709	(2nd), 6704 WRK/RET.
79/09-79/10	BN	39	5008-5046	
79/10-79/11	NDEM	21	6710-6730	6716,6737,6750,6759 WRK/RET.
79/11-79/12	NDEM	29	6731-6759	
79/12-80/01	NDEM	25	6760-6784	6763,6779, WRK/RET.
80/01-80/02	UP	40	2460-2499	2498 WRK/SCR.
80/02-80/03	BN	29	5047-5075	
80/03	SCL	8	7052-7059	DELV. FL, TO SBD, TO CSXT SAME#
80/03-80/05	BN	36	5076-5111	
80/05-80/06	ATSF	24	8099-8122	
80/06-80/07	BN	15	5112-5126	
80/07	NDEM	15	6785-6799	
80/07-80/08	NDEM	6	9600-9605	
80/08	LN	8	7062-7069	DELV. FL, TO SBD, TO CSXT SAME#
80/08	SCL	2	7060-7061	DELV. FL, TO SBD, TO CSXT SAME#

MODEL C30-7, cont'd

MODEL C30-7
BURLINGTON NORTHERN
5136, BLT. 81/04
FT.WORTH, TX. 82/05

BLDR.DATE	RR	QTY.	DELV.NO.	NOTES
80/08-80/10	UP	40	2500-2539	2539 WRK/SCR. 88/07
80/08-81/01	NDEM	40	9607-9646	
81/02-81/05	BN	15	5127-5141	5136 WRK & SCR.
81/04-81/05	NDEM	6	9647-9652	
81/05-81/07	ATSF	30	8123-8152	UNITS 8138-8152 EVEN# ONLY HAVE (RCT)
81/06-81/08	FCP	22	434-455	449 RET. TO BE RE# NDM 9667-9687
81/07-81/12	NDEM	28	9653-9680	
81/09	NDEM	29	11001-11029	
81/10-81/11	SCL	25	7070-7094	DELV FL. TO SBD, TO CSXT SAME#
82/02-82/03	NDEM	10	11030-11039	
82/06-82/07	NDEM	29	11040-11068	KITS ASSEMBLED IN MEXICO
82/12	ATSF	14	8153-8166	UNITS 8133-8151 ODD# ONLY HAVE (RCR)
83/04-83/06	NDEM	30	11099-11128	SHIPPED 84/07
84/09-85/01	NDEM	30	11069-11098	KITS ASSEMBLED IN MEXICO
86/02-86/05	NDEM	20	11129-11148	KITS ASSEMBLED IN MEXICO
86/05	FCP	4	456-459	NDEM OWNED, TO BE RE# NDM 11149-11152

MODEL C30-7A, 3000 hp, BUILT 1984

84/05-84/06	CR	50	6550-6599

MODEL C32-8, 3150 hp, BUILT 1984

84/09	CR	10	6610-6619

BLDR.DATE	RR	QTY.	DELV.NO.	NOTES
MODEL C36-7, 3600 hp, BUILT 1977-1985				
77/06	GECX	1	505	ENGR.DEPT. TEST UNIT
79/03	NDEM	10	9317-9326	
79/07	FCP	4	419-422	TO BE RE# NDM 9653-9656
79/10	FCP	11	423-433	433 RET. 82, TO BE RE# NDM 9657-9666
80/03-80/05	NDEM	15	9327-9341	BUILT IN BRAZIL
81/03	NW	6	8500-8505	(2ND)
82/05-82/06	NW	20	8506-8525	(2ND)
82/06	NW	5	8526-8530	
84/05	NW	12	8531-8542	DELV. NS
85/06	CR	25	6620-6644	
85/09-85/11	MP	60	9000-9059	TO UP SAME#, 9025 WRK/SCR 87/11, ALL RATED AT 3750 hp.

MODEL C36-7
MISSOURI PACIFIC
9047, BLT. 85/11
DALLAS, TX. 86/03

BLDR.DATE	RR	QTY.	DELV.NO.	NOTES
MODEL C36-8, 3600 hp, BUILT 1983				
83/03	GECX	1	607	TEST UNIT, NOW REBLT TO C39-8
MODEL C39-8, 3900 hp, BUILT 1984-1986				
84/01	NW	2	8550-8551	DELV. NS, GE PROTOTYPES
84/10-84/11	NW	12	8552-8563	DELV. NS
85/04-85/10	NW	50	8564-8613	DELV. NS
86/05-86/07	SOU	25	8614-8638	DELV. NS
86/06-86/08	CR	22	6000-6021	
86/08-86/10	SOU	25	8639-8663	DELV. NS
MODEL C39-8E, 3900 hp, BUILT 1987				
87/03-87/06	SOU	25	8664-8688	DELV. NS

MODEL DASH840B
COTTON BELT (SSW)
8049, BLT. 88/08
TUSCON, AZ. 88/12
PHOTO: JAMES D. BRADLEY

BLDR.DATE	RR	QTY.	DELV.NO.	NOTES
MODEL DASH 840B, 4000 hp, BUILT 1988-				
88/04-88/05	CR	30	5060-5089	
88/06	NYSW	4	4002-4008	EVEN NUMBERS ONLY
88/06	ATSF	20	7410-7429	
88/07-88/11	SSW	35	8040-8074	
88/12	GECX	1	8002	LEASED TO SP
89/04	ATSF	20	7430-7449	
89/04-89/05	NYSW	20	4010-4048	EVEN NUMBERS ONLY
89/05	SROX	1	N/A	U.S. DEPT. OF ENERGY, SAVANNAH RIVER PLT.
MODEL DASH 840C, 4000 hp, BUILT 1987-				
87/11-88/02	UP	75	9100-9174	
88/07-88/10	UP	75	9175-9249	9185 RETAINED BY GE AS DEMO UNIT.
88/11	UP	1	9185	(2nd) BUILT AS REPLACEMENT FOR 9185 (1st)
88/11-88/12	UP	50	9250-9284	
88/12	GECX	6	9350-9355	WARRANTY PROTECTION UNITS, LEASED TO UP
88/12-89/03	UP	65	9285-9349	
89/03-89/04	CR	25	6025-6049	
MODEL E25B, 2500 hp, BUILT 1976-1979				
76/05	TUGX	3	2304-2306	TEXAS UTILITIES MINING CO.
76/06	TUGX	2	3301-3302	TEXAS UTILITIES MINING CO.
78/12,79/02	TUGX	2	3303-3304	TEXAS UTILITIES MINING CO.
MODEL E50C, 5000 hp, BUILT 1968				
68/05	MUSK	2	100,200	MUSKINGUM ELECTRIC

BLDR.DATE	RR	QTY.	DELV.NO.	NOTES

MODEL E60C, 6000 hp, BUILT 1972-1983

72/12	BMLP	1	6000	RE# 6003, SHIPPED 73/04
72/12	BMLP	2	6001-6002	
76/09-76/10	BMLP	3	6004-6006	
82/09-83/12	NDEM	39	EA001-EA039	
83/08	WFAX	2	WFU1-WFU2	DESERET WESTERN RR.

MODEL E60CH, 6000 hp, BUILT 1975-1976

75/11-76/01	AMTK	11	965-975	967,971-973 TO NJT, SAME #,966,968 TO NAVAJO MINE RR IN 82

MODEL E60CP, 6000 hp, BUILT 1974-1976

74/10	AMTK	1	950	RE# 620
74/10	AMTK	1	951	RE# 957, THEN 604
74/10-75/11	AMTK	5	952-956	RE# 610,611,608,612,601
75/11	AMTK	1	957	RE# 951, THEN 609
75/11-76/10	AMTK	7	958-964	958-963 TO NJT, SAME #

MODEL E60CP
AMTRAK
960, BLT. 76/07
PHILADELPHIA, PA. 78/06

MODEL MATE-4, ROAD SLUG, BUILT 1971-1972

71/08-71/10	SCL	10	3200-3209	TO SBD 5200-5209, TO CSXT SAME#
72/09-72/12	SCL	15	3210-3224	TO SBD-5210-5224, TO CSXT SAME#

MODEL P30CH, 3000 hp, BUILT 1975-1976

75/08-76/01	AMTK	25	700-724	713 WRK/SCR. 77/12, 715 WRK/SCR. 79/10

MODEL SL65
HOUSTON POWER & LIGHT
NONE, BLT. 82/10
NEW, IN TRANSIT
WAXAHACHIE, TX. 82/11

BLDR.DATE	RR.	QTY.	DELV.NO.	NOTES
MODEL SL65, 550 hp, BUILT 1976-				
76/11	TUGX	1	NONE	TEXAS UTILITIES MINING CO.
77/02	TUGX	1	NONE	TEXAS UTILITIES MINING CO.
82/10	HOUS	1	1	HOUSTON POWER & LIGHT CO.
MODEL SL75, 600 hp, BUILT 1978-				
78/02	ALLE	1	23	ALLEGHANY LUDLUM
80/11	DKPX	1	83	DUKE POWER CO, ALLEN PLT.
MODEL SL85, 600 hp, BUILT 1975-				
75/04	ALLE	1	21	ALLEGHANY LUDLUM
75/05	PMEX	1	12	PEMEX, (MEXICO)
75/05-75/06	KEYS	2	450,451	KEYSTONE STEEL & WIRE
76/11	GECX	1	20	GENERAL ELECTRIC, SCHENECTADY PLT.
77/04	ALLE	1	22	ALLEGHANY LUDLUM
77/05	ALTO	1	150	ALTOS HORNOS (MEXICO)
77/06	CEME	1	NONE	CEMENTOS-ANAHUAC (MEXICO)
77/12	TIMK	1	4845	TIMKEN CO.
78/09	GATX	1	46575	GENERAL AMERICAN TRANSPORTATION CORP
78/12	GECX	1	21	GENERAL ELECTRIC CO, SCHENECTADY, NY.
80/03	EEC	2	21,22	EAST ERIE COMMERCIAL RAILROAD
81/06	GATX	1	46576	GENERAL AMERICAN TRANSPORTATION CORP.
82/01	CEME	1	NONE	CEMENTOS-ANAHUAC (MEXICO)
82/01	CEMM	1	NONE	CEMENTOS-MAYA (MEXICO)
84/05	BRFD	1	7358	BRANTFORD STEAM RAILROAD
88/04	BRFD	1	N/A	BRANTFORD STEAM RAILROAD

BLDR.DATE	RR.	QTY.	DELV.NO.	NOTES

MODEL SL87, 600 hp, BUILT 1975

BLDR.DATE	RR.	QTY.	DELV.NO.	NOTES
75/08	ALGO	1	7	ALGOMA STEEL (CANADA)

MODEL SL100, 600 hp, BUILT 1977

BLDR.DATE	RR.	QTY.	DELV.NO.	NOTES
77/06	DELM	2	3,7	DELMARVA POWER & LIGHT

MODEL SL110, 600 hp. BUILT 1974-

BLDR.DATE	RR.	QTY.	DELV.NO.	NOTES
74/11	GECX	1	1 (1st)	DEMO TO ALGOMA STEEL, (CANADA)
75/01	ALGO	1	61	ALGOMA STEEL, (CANADA)
75/03	OPX	1	3	OHIO POWER, MITCHELL PLT
75/05	DIAM	1	NONE	DIAMOND SHAMROCK
75/06	EKPC	1	1	EASTERN KENTUCKY POWER
75/07	CILC	1	NONE	CENTRAL ILLINOIS LIGHT CO.
76/01	EACX	1	NONE	EASTERN ASSOCIATED COAL CO.
76/02	KCLX	1	2	KANSAS CITY POWER & LIGHT
76/06	GECX	1	1 (2nd)	DEMO TO PULLMAN-SWINDEL, (MEXICO)
76/06	REPU	1	NONE	REPUBLIC STEEL CORP, KITT WV.
76/12	WYS	1	101	WYANDOTTE SOUTHERN RR CO.
77/03	FUND	1	16	FUNDIDORA de FIERRO y ACERO, (MEXICO)
77/04	EACX	1	NONE	EASTERN ASSOCIATED COAL CO.
77/05	GUAN	1	NONE	GUANOS y FERILIZANTES, (MEXICO)
77/05	USX	1	912	U.S. STEEL CORP.
78/03	CLEV	1	18	CLEVELAND ELECTRIC ILLUMINATING
78/10	MCSA	1	548	MCSA RR, TO CHAMPION INTERNATIONAL
79/03	CPRX	1	1	CAROLINA POWER & LIGHT
79/06	WEPX	1	1	WISCONSIN ELECTRIC POWER CO.
80/01	HPAX	1	16	HAMMERMILL PAPER CO. ERIE, PA.
80/04	PORT	1	705	PORT OF TACOMA
80/06	CITY	1	1	CITY OF SIKESTON, MO.
80/08	LOUI	1	NONE	LOUISVILLE GAS & ELECTRIC
81/01	VEPC	1	NONE	VEPCO, VIRGINA ELECTRIC POWER
81/05	MOBX	1	117	MOBIL OIL CORP. BEAUMONT, TX.
81/08	ITSE	3	N/A	ITSERCO, HYLSA, (MEXICO)
81/12	HOJO	4	NONE	HOJOLATA Y LAMINA (MEXICO)
82/09-82/12	MASS	3	SL1-SL3	MASSEY COAL CO. NEWPORT NEWS, VA.
82/12	VEPC	2	NONE	VEPCO,VA.ELECTRIC POWER,WHEELWRIGHT,VA
84/04	SCWX	1	NONE	SOUTH CAROLINA GAS & ELECTRIC
84/06	BOAR	1	846	BOARD OF PUBLIC UTILITIES,KANSAS CITY
84/06	CLEV	1	15	CLEVELAND ELECTRIC ILLUMINATING
84/06	SIGX	1	NONE	SOUTHERN INDIANA GAS & ELECTRIC
85/12	HOJO	1	NONE	HOJOLATA Y LAMINA, (MEXICO)
86/04	CENT	1	NONE	CENTRAL HUDSON POWER CO.
88/NA	AEPX	1	N/A	AMERICAN ELECTRIC POWER SERVICE CORP.MUSKINGUM,OH.

MODEL SL115, 600 hp, BUILT 1976-

BLDR.DATE	RR.	QTY.	DELV.NO.	NOTES
76/02	USX	1	911	U.S. STEEL CORP.
76/11	ARMC	1	12	ARMCO, KANSAS CITY
77/07	PMEX	2	18,19	PEMEX, PETROLEOS MEXICANO, (MEXICO)
78/08	SANM	1	NONE	SAN MIGUEL ELECTRIC,TO BRAZOS POWER CO

MODEL SL115, cont'd

BLDR.DATE	RR.	QTY.	DELV.NO.	NOTES
78/12	PMEX	2	22,23	PEMEX, PETROLEOS MEXICANO, (MEXICO)
80/03	HECX	1	1	HOOSIER ENERGY, CO. MEROM, IN.
80/08-80/10	FERT	7	1-7	FERTIMEX, (MEXICO)
81/01	CEMN	1	NONE	CEMENTOS, (MEXICO)
82/06	ITSE	1	1	ITSERCO, HYLSA, (MEXICO)

MODEL SL120, 1000 hp, BUILT 1977

77/11	LUKE	1	42	LUKENS STEEL, COATSVILLE, PA.

MODEL SL125, 1000 hp, BUILT 1976-

76/01	PMEX	1	13	PEMEX, PETROLEOS MEXICANO, (MEXICO)
76/02	PMEX	1	14	PEMEX, PETROLEOS MEXICANO, (MEXICO)
79/02	CPOX	1	NONE	CONSUMER'S POWER
79/12	TMPX	1	NONE	TEXAS MUNICPAL POWER AUTHORITY
81/03	TUBO	1	5	TUBOS de ACEROS de MEXICO, (MEXICO)
82/12	KNOR	1	207	KLAMATH NORTHERN RY. CO.

MODEL SL130, 1000 hp, BUILT 1976

76/05	FUND	1	14	FUNDIDORA de FIERRO y ACERO (MEXICO)
76/07	FUND	1	15	FUNDIDORA de FIERRO y ACERO (MEXICO)

MODEL SL136, 1000 hp, BUILT 1978

78/10	CNW	2	1198-1199	TO BN 1100,1101, 1101 LATER SOLD TO SEPX 1101

MODEL SL144, 1000 hp, BUILT 1975-

75/12,76/02	OPX	2	4,5	OHIO POWER, METROPOLIS, IL.
76/09	PMEX	1	0411-L	PEMEX, PETROLEOS MEXICANO, (MEXICO)
76/09	PMEX	1	0412-L	PEMEX, PETROLEOS MEXICANO, (MEXICO)
76/11	APWX	1	1	APPALACHIAN POWER CO.
78/02	GECX	1	2	DEMO TO ALLEGHENY POWER SYSTEM, WILLOW ISLAND, WV.
78/08	PMEX	2	20,21	PEMEX, PETROLEOS MEXICANO, (MEXICO)
81/08	EDSX	1	3	EXXON CO. USA, BATON ROUGE, LA.
83/09	BREX	1	1	BIG RIVERS ELECTRIC CORP.
83/11	NYSX	1	NONE	NEW YORK STATE ELECTRIC & GAS CORP.
88/11	HOJO	1	NONE	HOJOLATA y LAMINA S.A. (MEXICO)

MODEL U18B, 1800 hp, BUILT 1973-1976

73/03-73/05	SCL	25	300-324	305,313,WRK/SCR.REST SBD/CSXT 1900-1922
73/11-73/12	SCL	19	325-343	TO SBD/CSXT 1923-1941
73/12	SCL	12	250-261	TO SBD/CSXT 1888-1899
74/01-74/10	NDEM	45	9000-9044	9006,11,13,16,18,21,23,35,41,42,RET.
74/03	TUGX	2	101-102	TEXAS UTILTIES MINING CO. RE# 2301,2302
74/08-74/11	SCL	49	344-392	TO SBD/CSXT 1942-1990
75/05-75/06	MEC	10	400-409	
76/10	PW	1	1801	

BLDR.DATE	RR	QTY.	DELV.NO.	NOTES

MODEL U23B, 2250 hp, BUILT 1968-1977

BLDR.DATE	RR	QTY.	DELV.NO.	NOTES
68/08	DH	8	301-308	RE# 2301-2308, TO MEC 280-287, ALL SCR. 88/02, EXCEPT 285,288.
68/09	DH	6	309-314	RE# 2309-2314, TO MEC 288-293
68/09	DH	1	315	SCRAPPED 1971
68/09	DH	1	316	RE# 2316, TO MEC 294, SOLD TO PERU COPPER IN 86.
69/09	CO	15	2300-2314	2301,2302,2306,2307,2308,2312,2313,2314, SCR.86 BALANCE TO CSXT 3200,3203-3205,3209-3211
69/10	CO	15	2315-2329	ALL SCR. 86, EXCEPT 2318,2321-25,2329 TO CSXT 3218,3221-3225,3229

MODEL U23B
MONON RR.
608, BLT. 70/04
CHICAGO, IL. 70/06

BLDR.DATE	RR	QTY.	DELV.NO.	NOTES
70/03-70/04	MON	8	601-608	TO LN 2700-07, TO CSXT 3230-3237
70/06-70/10	ATSF	32	6300-6331	ALL NOW TRADED OR SCR.
70/12	ATSF	1	6332	REMFG, TO SFB30 7200
70/12-71/02	ATSF	16	6333-6348	ALL T/I TO GE L/88, 6341 RETAINED BY GE AS TEST BED # 26-1
72/05	SOU	5	3900-3904	
72/05-72/06	WP	15	2251-2265	2256 WRK/SCR.79/11, 2259 WRK/SCR.81/09, ALL RETIRED BY 87/09, 2263,2251,2257 TO GE 2000-2002 DEMOS, REBLT. TO B23-S7 IN E/89.
72/08-72/10	PC	50	2700-2749	TO CR SAME#, 2732 SCR, 2739 SCR.85
73/01	MP	7	668-674	RE# 2250-2256, RE# 4500-4506, TO UP 534-550, RET'D TO LESSOR 88/12, THEN ALL BUT 4503,TO CMI 8900's.
73/01-73/04	LN	10	2708-2717	TO SBD 3238-3247, TO CSXT SAME#
73/01-73/04	LN	1	2718	WRK/SCR. 77/11
73/01-73/04	LN	9	2719-2727	TO SBD 3248-3256, TO CSXT SAME#
73/05	MKT	3	350-352	TRADED EMD 84/02, SCR.
73/05	SOU	10	3905-3914	
73/06	MILW	5	4800-4804	RE# 5000-5004(2nd), 5001,5002 SCR.84, ALL NOW RET.

MODEL U23B, cont'd

BLDR.DATE	RR	QTY.	DELV.NO.	NOTES
73/06-73/09	LN	25	2728-2752	TO SBD 3257-3281, TO CSXT SAME#
73/08-73/10	PC	27	2750-2776	TO CR SAME #
74/02-74/04	LN	18	2753-2770	TO SBD 3282-3299,TO CSXT SAME#,2764 RET
74/04	LN	1	2771	WRK/SCR. 80/05
74/04	LN	1	2772	TO SBD 3300, TO CSXT 3300
74/05-74/06	SOU	20	3915-3934	
74/10-74/11	MP	11	2257-2267	RE# 4507-4517 TO UP 541-551
74/12	LN	3	2800-2802	TO SBD 3301-3303, TO CSXT SAME#
74/12	LN	1	2803	WRK/SCR.78/07
74/12	LV	12	501-512	TO CR 2777-2788
74/12-75/02	LN	14	2804-2817	TO SBD 3305-3318, TO CSXT SAME#
75/02	LN	1	2818	RE# 2803 (2nd), TO SBD/CSXT 3304
75/02-75/03	LN	6	2819-2824	TO SBD 3319-3324, TO CSXT SAME#
75/03	MP	3	2268-2270	RE# 4518-4520, ALL RETIRED 87
75/03	MP	1	2271	WRK/SCR 78/10
75/03	MP	2	2272-2273	RE# 4521-4522, TO UP 555-556
75/03-75/06	NDEM	30	9100-9129	9103, 9118 WRK/RET.
75/05	TUGX	1	103	TEXAS UTILITIES MINING CO. RE# 3305
75/05-75/07	SOU	20	3935-3954	3940 WRK/RET 81/09
75/08-75/09	FCP	10	537-546	TO BE RE# NDM 9182-9191
76/06	MP	5	2274-2278	RE# 4523-4527, TO UP 557-561
76/11-77/02	SOU	15	3955-3969	3967 WRK/SCR. 79/06
77/01-77/02	MP	10	2279-2288	RE# 4528-4537, TO UP 562-571
77/05-77/06	CR	10	2789-2798	

MODEL U23B
MISSOURI PACIFIC
2284, BLT. 77/02
VILLA GROVE, IL. 80/06

MODEL U23C, 2250 hp, BUILT 1968-1970

BLDR.DATE	RR	QTY.	DELV.NO.	NOTES
68/03	LSI	2	2300-2301	
69/04	CBQ	9	460-468	TO BN 5200-5208, ALL SCR.86
69/05-69/07	ATSF	20	7500-7519	RETURNED TO LESSOR 84/12, SCR.
69/09	LSI	1	2302	
70/09	LSI	2	2303-2304	
70/10-70/11	PC	19	6700-6718	TO CR SAME#, RE# 6900-6918, 6913 SCR.85

MODEL U30B
WESTERN PACIFIC
3063, ex 763, BLT. 69/04
STOCKTON, CA. 79/06

MODEL U30B, 3000 hp, BUILT 1966-1975

BLDR.DATE	RR	QTY.	DELV.NO.	NOTES
68/01	CBQ	5	150-154	2nd, TO BN 5480-5484, ALL SCR.86
68/01	MILW	5	6005-6009	RE# 5605-5609, ALL RETIRED BY 83
68/09	WP	4	756-759	RE# 3056-3059, ALL RETIRED BY 83
68/11	SLSF	4	832-835	TO BN 5770-5773, ALL RETIRED BY 86
69/04-69/05	WP	10	760-769	RE# 3060-3069, ALL RETIRED BY 83
69/08-69/09	SLSF	8	836-843	TO BN 5774-5781, ALL RETIRED BY 86
70/08-70/10	NW	25	8465-8489	8466,8469-8472,8478,8479,8482,8489 TO NDM 9708-9716 IN M/79, ALL RET.BY L/87. ALL WERE HI-NOSE.
70/11-70/12	NW	10	8490-8499	8491,8492,8494-8498, TO NDM 9717-9723, RET.BY L/87.
70/12-71/05	NW	20	8500-8519	8500-8504,8507,8511,8513,8515,8517,8518 TO NDM 9724-9734 M/79, ALL RET. BY L/87, ALL HI-NOSE.
71/05-71/11	NW	20	8520-8539	8521-8525,8529,8531,8533,8537,8538 TO NDM 9735-9744 ALL NW UNITS RET.BY L/86, NDM's BY L/87.
71/12	CO	10	8200-8209	TO CS, TO CSXT 5328-5337
72/11-72/12	CO	13	8210-8222	CS, TO CSXT 5338-5350
73/04-73/05	SLSF	10	844-853	TO BN 5782-5791, 5786 RET.87/09
74/08-74/09	SLSF	4	854-857	856 WRK/SCR. REST TO BN 5792-5794
74/12	CO	10	8225-8234	CS, TO CSXT 5351-5362
75/03	SLSF	5	858-862	TO BN 5795-5799

BLDR.DATE	RR	QTY.	DELV.NO.	NOTES

MODEL U30C, 3000 hp, BUILT 1967-1976

BLDR.DATE	RR	QTY.	DELV.NO.	NOTES
68/01	DH	6	707-712	TO NDEM SAME # 78/12, ALL RET. BY M/80.
68/01-68/02	CNW	7	930-936	934 SOLD & REBLT TO NJT U34CH 4183, IN 78/10. REST TO NDEM SAME#, ALL NOW RET. EXCEPT 932.
68/02-68/06	SP	30	7900-7929	ALL RET. 7900-7927,7929 T/I GE IN 84
68/03	KAIS	5	1030-1034	KAISER STEEL CO. FONTANA, CA. STORED 86/03
68/03-68/04	MP	6	960-965	RE# 1-6, TO 3300-3305, TO 2965-2970, TO UP 2965-2970,T/I GE 85, 2970 TO ENTERPRISE COAL CO.
68/04-68/06	SOO	10	800-809	SCRAPPED IN 1984
68/05-68/06	CO	9	3304-3312	ALL RET. 83/08, SCR.84
68/06-68/07	CBQ	4	890-893	C&S OWNED, TO BN 5396-5399, SCR.BY 87/03
69/03-69/04	LN	14	1534-1547	1542 SCR. TO SBD 7229-7241, TO CSXT SAME#
69/05-69/06	MP	4	966-969	RE# 7-10,TO 3306-3309,TO 2971-2974,TO UP 2971-2974
69/10	SP	7	7930-7936	ALL T/I TO GE IN 84.
69/10-69/12	FCP	4	401-404	TO BE RE# NDM 7900-7903

MODEL U30C
LOUISVILLE & NASHVILLE
1550, BLT. 69/10
DOLTON, IL. 72/08

BLDR.DATE	RR	QTY.	DELV.NO.	NOTES
69/10-70/03	LN	15	1548-1562	TO SBD 7242-7256, TO CSXT SAME#
70/06	MP	4	970-973	RE# 11-14, TO 3310-3313, TO 2975-2978 TO UP 2975-2978, ALL T/I GE 85
71/03	FCP	4	405-408	405 SCRAPPED, TO BE RE# NDM 7904-7906
71/06	DOT	1	001	U.S.DEPT.TRANSPORTATION, PUEBLO, CO.
71/06-71/07	LN	20	1563-1582	TO SBD 7257-7276, TO CSXT SAME#
71/08-71/09	MP	5	974-978	RE# 15-19, TO 3314-3318, TO 2979-2983 TO UP 2979-2983, ALL T/I GE L/87
72/01	BN	6	5300-5305	RE# 5800-05, MOST RET. L/87, 8502 DONATED
72/01-72/02	BN	14	5306-5319	ALL RET. EXCEPT 5306, 5318. 5308,5311,5313-5315,5317, TO PNC
72/02	MP	5	979-983	RE# 20-24, TO 3319-3323, TO 2984-2988 TO UP 2984-2988,2984,2985,2988, RET.88/05
72/02-72/03	DEEX	6	007-012	012 TO MEC 640, 86/02, RE# 663, 87/01
72/03-72/04	BN	5	5320-5324	5323 TO PNC, 5324 SCR. ALL RET. BY 87/02

MODEL U30C, cont'd

MODEL U30C
LOUISVILLE & NASHVILLE
1499, BLT. 72/08
DOLTON, IL. 72/12

BLDR.DATE	RR	QTY.	DELV.NO.	NOTES
72/02-72/03	DEEX	6	007-012	012 TO MEC 640,86/02, RE# 663, 87/01
72/03-72/04	BN	5	5320-5324	5323, 5324 SCR.ALL RET. BY 87/02
72/04	BN	1	5325	RE# 1776, R/W/B IN 76, RET.BY 87/02
72/04-72/05	BN	9	5326-5334	5327, 5329 SCR. 5328 TO PNC, REST RET. BY 87/02
72/04-72/06	UP	20	2810-2829	2810,2816,2825 RET.BY 85, MOST NOW T/I.
72/06-72/08	LN	30	1470-1499	1499 DELV. IN "XR" SCHEME, WRK/SCR/77 TO SBD 7200-7228, TO CSXT SAME#
72/11-72/12	BN	18	5335-5352	5336 WRK/REBLT,B-UNIT 4500, SCR.86/02
72/12	BN	12	5353-5364	RE# 5900-5911, 5902, 5906, SCR.
73/02-73/05	UP	30	2830-2859	2831,2834,2835,2837,2842,2843,2845,2847, 2851,2853,2854,2856,2857,2858, RET.BY 85.
73/06	MP	5	984-988	RE# 25-29,TO 3324-3328,TO 2989-2993,TO UP 2989-2993
73/06	UP	10	2860-2869	2861,2863,2866-2868 RET.85, 2860,2864 IN 88.
73/07	BN	8	5806-5813	
73/07	BN	7	5912-5918	5913, 5914 SCR.
73/10-73/12	RI	18	4582-4599	RETURNED TO LESSOR, ALL SCR.
73/11-73/12	BN	10	5814-5823	5814 WRK & SCR. L/86
73/11-73/12	BN	10	5919-5928	
74/02	MP	6	3329-3334	SUBLETTERED T&P, RE# 2994-2999, TO UP SAME#, ALL T/I GE, L/87.
74/03-74/04	NW	3	8000-8002	DELV. WITH LO-NOSE
74/03-74/07	UP	35	2870-2904	MANY NOW RET.OR SCR. 2877 SCR. 85
74/04-74/05	BN	10	5824-5833	5830 RET.86, 5832 RET.87/05,REST RET'D LESSOR 89/04, 5825,5828,5830, TO LSI.
74/04-74/05	BN	10	5929-5938	RET'D LESSOR 89/04, 5929,5931,5932,5934,5937 TO LSI.
74/08	MILW	8	5651-5658	ALL STORED, OFF ROSTER
74/08-74/11	BN	30	5365-5394	5366,5368,5389,5393 RET.BY 87/02

MODEL U30C, cont'd

BLDR.DATE	RR	QTY.	DELV.NO.	NOTES
75/04-75/06	UP	15	2905-2919	2912 SCR.87/08,2918 TO WILSON 88/11, 2919 SCR.88/08
75/05	BN	6	5300-5305	(2nd)
75/05	BN	12	5353-5364	(2nd) 5363 WRK/SCR 79/12
75/06	BN	6	5834-5839	
75/06	BN	6	5939-5944	
75/07	DEEX	5	018-022	DETROIT EDISON
76/07-76/10	UP	40	2920-2959	MANY NOW RET.OR SCR. 2956 TO GE REBLT.TO DEMO 3002 C30-S7 E/89.

MODEL U33B, 3300 hp, BUILT 1967-1970

BLDR.DATE	RR	QTY.	DELV.NO.	NOTES
67/12-68/01	SCL	17	1719-1735	1719 WRK.TO RI SLUG 282 IN 78, TO SBD 5600-5615, TO CSXT SAME#, 5600,5602, 5604,5607,5610,5611, SCR.BY 87/02
68/07-68/09	RI	10	290-299	RETURNED TO LESSOR, ALL SCR.
68/09-68/11	PC	26	2890-2915	TO CR SAME#, ALL RET.M/86, 2893,2899,2902 2906,2907,2912, TO IRRC
68/11-68/12	PC	40	2916-2955	TO CR SAME#, 2921,2931,2935 SCR.BEFORE 86, 2916-2920,2922-2925 TO BM 190,193, 194,191,195,196-198,192 IN 84, RET.88/03 192 TO LVAL 903. BALANCE CR, RET.M/86
69/01	RI	5	285-289	RETURNED TO LESSOR, ALL SCR.
69/01	SCL	12	1736-1747	1736 RET. 86/09, TO SBD 5617-5627, TO CSXT SAME#
69/05	RI	10	190-199	RETURNED TO LESSOR, ALL SCR.
70/05-70/06	PC	15	2956-2970	TO CR SAME#, ALL SCR.BY M/86

MODEL U33B
ROCK ISLAND
193, BLT 69/05
FT. WORTH, TX. 80/02
PHOTO: ED SEAY,Jr.

MODEL U33C
ILLINOIS CENTRAL
5053, BLT. 68/04
MARKHAM, IL. 72/03

BLDR.DATE	RR.	QTY.	DELV.NO.	NOTES
MODEL U33C, 3300 hp, BUILT 1968-1975				
68/01-68/02	MILW	4	8000-8003	RE# 5700-5703, 5700 SCR.81, REST RET.83
68/02-68/04	PC	11	6540-6550	TO CR 6845-6855, 6845 TO DH 650, REST SCR
68/04	PC	4	6551-6554	TO CR 6856-6859, 6856 TO DH 651, REST SCR
68/04	PC	2	6555-6556	TO CR 6860-6861, 6860 TO DH 652, 6861 SCR
68/04	PC	2	6557-6558	TO CR 6862-6863, 6862 TO DH 653, 6863 SCR
68/04	PC	1	6559	TO CR 6864, TO DH 654
68/04-68/05	IC	10	5050-5059	5055 WRK/SCR 69/09, REST SCR.84 BY PNC.
68/05-68/06	GN	9	2530-2538	TO BN 5700-5708, ALL SCR. 84
68/07	EL	3	3301-3303	TO DH 751-753, TO CR 6564-6566, RE# 6869-6871 ALL RET BY 86.
68/07	EL	3	3304-3306	TO CR 6567-6569, RE# 6872-6874, ALL RET'D TO LESSOR NW IN 84, T/I GE 85
68/08	PC	1	6560	TO CR 6865, TO DH 655
68/08	PC	3	6561-6563	TO CR 6866-6868, 6866 TO DH 656, REST SCR
69/01-69/04	SP	30	8600-8629	8626 TO ATSF SLUG 144, 8610,8629 RET.85 REST NOW RETIRED.
69/04	GN	6	2539-2544	TO BN 5709-5714, SCR.84
69/04-69/05	SP	15	8630-8644	8644 TO ATSF SLUG 143, 8642 WRK/SCR.69 8638 RET.78/05, REST NOW RETIRED.
69/06-69/08	ATSF	25	8500-8524	RETURNED TO LESSOR 84/12, SCR.
69/07	NP	10	3300-3309	TO BN 5715-5724, 5720 WRK/SCR.79/07, REST SCR.BY PNC IN 84.
69/08	EL	9	3307-3315	TO CR 6570-6578 (3600 hp) RE# 6875-6883 ALL RET. 87/12
69/10	SJGX	2	507-508	S.J.GROVES CONST.TO BN 5764-5765,SCR.86
69/10	SP	2	8645-8646	ALL RETIRED BY LATE 1988
70/02-70/06	SP	41	8647-8687	8686 RET.78/05, REST RET.BY LATE 88.
70/04	SOU	5	3805-3809	ALL RET. 86/03, 3809 TO PEABODY COAL SAME#.
70/09	DH	3	754-756	ALL RET. BY E/88

MODEL U33C, cont'd

MODEL U33C
BURLINGTON NORTHERN
5752, BLT. 71/08
SPOKANE, WA. 76/04

BLDR.DATE	RR.	QTY.	DELV.NO.	NOTES
70/11	DH	3	757-759	757 RET. REST RE# 658,659, RET.E/88
70/12	DH	3	760-762	760 RET. REST RE# 761,762, RET.E/88
71/02	BN	4	5725-5728	ORDERED BY CB&Q, ALL RETIRED BY M/86
71/02-71/03	BN	6	5729-5734	ALL RETIRED BY M/86
71/07-71/09	BN	29	5735-5763	ALL RET.BY M/86, 5752 TO SQUAW CREEK MINE, CONSOLIDATED COAL CO. 86/02
71/10-71/12	SP	26	8688-8713	8691,8694 RET.BY 1978, REST BY L/88
71/12-72/01	SP	14	8714-8727	8718 WRK. ON NDEM,SOLD,NDM REBLT. RE# 8987 86/02, REST RET. BY L/88.
72/01	SOU	5	3810-3814	ALL T/I TO GE 87/02
72/01-72/02	SP	10	8728-8737	8734 RET.78/08, REST RETIRED BY L/88
72/02-72/05	SP	30	8738-8767	ALL RETIRED BY L/88
73/01-73/02	SP	10	8768-8777	ALL RETIRED BY L/88
73/06-73/07	SP	8	8778-8785	ALL RETIRED BY L/88
74/02-74/04	SP	11	8786-8796	ALL RETIRED BY L/88
74/12-75/01	SP	15	8585-8599	8587 RET.78/09, 8586 RET.80, REST RET. BY L/88

MODEL U34CH, 3430 hp, BUILT 1970-1973

70/10-71/05	EL	23	3351-3373	TO CR SAME#, TO NJT 4151-4173
72/12-73/01	EL	9	3374-3382	TO CR SAME#, TO NJT 4174-4182

MODEL U36B, 3600 hp, BUILT 1970-1976

70/05-70/08	SCL	28	1748-1775	TO SBD SAME#, TO CSXT 5700-5727
70/08	SCL	1	1777	TO SBD 1777, TO CSXT 5729
71/03-71/08	SCL	35	1778-1812	1801 SCR. TO SBD SAME#, TO CSXT 5730-5763
71/05	GECX	2	303-304	GE DEMO's, REBLT. TO U30B, WP770, 771, RE# 3070, 3071, SCR. 80/10

MODEL U36B, cont'd

MODEL U36B
AUTO-TRAIN CORP.
4011, BLT. 74/05
DOLTON, IL. 78/06

BLDR.DATE	RR	QTY.	DELV.NO.	NOTES
71/06	SCL	1	1776	DELV. R/W/B, TO SBD 1776, TO CSXT 5728
71/09-71/12	SCL	22	1813-1834	1814 SCR. TO SBD SAME#, TO CSXT 5764-5784
71/11	AT	5	4000-4004	4001,4004 WRK,SCR. 73/03, REST SCR.BY 85
72/01-72/03	SCL	21	1835-1855	TO SBD SAME#, TO CSXT 5785-5805
72/12	AT	5	4005-4009	SCRAPPED BY E/85
72/12	GECX	2	301-302	DEMO's, REBLT. TO U30B, TO CO 8223,8224 TO CS SAME#, TO CSXT 5351, 5352
74/05	AT	3	4010-4012	SCRAPPED BY E/85
76/09	CR	4	2971-2974	ORIG.ORD.BY AT, 4013-16, BUT NEVER DELV.

MODEL U36C, 3600 hp, BUILT 1971-1975

71/10-71/11	CRR	7	3600-3606	TO SCL 2125-2131, TO SBD/CSXT 7300-7306
72/05-72/06	ATSF	6	8700-8705	REMFG. TO, SFC30, 9500 SERIES
72/06	ATSF	1	8706	WRK & SCR. 81/01
72/06	MILW	4	8500-8503	RE# 5800-5803, 5801 SCR.84/12, REST RET. AND STORED BY SOO LINE
72/06-73/03	ATSF	15	8707-8721	REMFG. TO, SFC30, 9500 SERIES
72/11	EL	13	3316-3328	TO CR 6587-6599, RE# 6884-6896, ALL RET.87/12
73/03	ATSF	1	8722	WRK & SCR. 77/11
73/03-73/04	ATSF	13	8723-8735	REMFG. TO, SFC30, 9500 SERIES
73/07-73/11	NDEM	38	8900-8937	8920 WRK/SCR.74/01, 8932,8936 WRK/RET.
74/01-74/03	NDEM	29	8958-8986	
74/05-74/07	ATSF	27	8736-8762	
74/11	ATSF	1	8763	WRK & SCR. 78/03
74/11-75/02	ATSF	36	8764-8799	REMFG. TO, SFC30, 9500 SERIES
75/01-75/02	NDEM	17	9300-9316	
75/02-75/03	FCP	10	409-418	410 RET. REST TO BE RE# NDM 8988-8996

MODEL U36C
SANTA FE
8775, BLT. 74/12
MOJAVE, CA. 79/06

BLDR.DATE	RR	QTY.	DELV.NO.	NOTES
MODEL U36CG, 3600 hp, BUILT 1974				
74/04-74/05	NDEM	20	8938-8957	8949 WRK/RET.
MODEL U50C, 5000 hp, BUILT 1969-1971				
69/10-71/02	UP	20	5000-5019	ALL SCRAPPED BY 1978
71/05-71/11	UP	20	5020-5039	ALL SCRAPPED BY 1978

MODEL U50C
UNION PACIFIC
5013, BLT. 71/01
OGDEN, UT. 73/05

GMD-GENERAL MOTORS OF CANADA LIMITED, DIESEL DIVISION
LONDON, ONTARIO, CANADA

BLDR.DATE	RR	QTY.	DELV.NO.	NOTES
MODEL F40PH, 3000 hp, BUILT 1978				
78/04-78/05	GOT	6	510-515	
MODEL F40PH-2, 3200 hp, BUILT 1986-1989				
86/11-87/01	VIA	20	6400-6419	
87/07-87/08	VIA	10	6420-6429	
89/04-89/05	VIA	29	6430-6458	

MODEL F40PH-2
VIA RAIL CANADA
6405, BLT. 86/11
VANCOUVER, BC. 87/07
PHOTO: JAMES D. BRADLEY

BLDR.DATE	RR	QTY.	DELV.NO.	NOTES
MODEL F59PH, 3000 hp, BUILT 1988-				
88/10-88/12	GOT	16	520-535	
MODEL GF6C, 6000 hp, BUILT 1983-1984				
83/11-84/07	BCOL	7	6001-6007	ASEA COMPONENTS

MODEL GP38-2
CANADIAN PACIFIC
3025, BLT. 83/03
NORTH PORTAL, SK. 83/10

BLDR.DATE	RR	QTY.	DELV.NO.	NOTES
MODEL GP38-2, 2000 hp, BUILT 1972-1986				
72/11-73/03	CN	60	5500-5559	5500-36 RE# 4700-4736, 5537-5540 RE# 221-224, 5541-5551 RE# 200-220 EVEN NO's ONLY, 5552-5559 RE# 201-215 ODD NO's ONLY
74/11	ONR	4	1800-1803	
76/10	TGSX	2	054-055	TEXAS GULF SULPHER CO. (CANADA)
79/05-79/06	DVR	4	216-219	
81/03	DVR	4	220-223	
81/04	ACR	6	200-205	
82/06	DVR	4	224-227	
82/11-82/12	ONR	4	1804-1807	
83/03	ONR	4	2000-2003	
83/03-83/06	CP	20	3021-3040	
83/07	DVR	1	228	
84/09	ONR	2	1808-1809	
85/10-86/06	CP	95	3041-3135	
MODEL GP38-2W, 2000 hp, BUILT 1973-1974				
73/06	CN	1	5560	
73/10-74/01	CN	50	5561-5610	5601,5604 SCR.

MODEL GP38-2W
CANADIAN NATIONAL
5571, BLT. 73/10
REGINA, SK. 83/10

MODEL GP38AC
CANADIAN PACIFIC
3001, BLT. 70/05
REVELSTOKE, BC. 78/04

MODEL GP38AC, 2000 hp, BUILT 1970-1971

70/05	CP	6	3000-3005
71/02-71/03	CP	15	3006-3020

MODEL GP40-2LW, 3000 hp, BUILT 1974-1976

74/03-74/09	CN	91	9400-9490	9435/SCR. 87/03, 9487 SCR.
74/09-74/11	CN	40	9491-9530	
75/02-75/05	CN	65	9531-9595	
75/07-76/05	CN	72	9596-9667	

BLDR.DATE	RR	QTY.	DELV.NO.	NOTES

MODEL GP40-2W, 3000 hp, BUILT 1973-1975

73/12	GOT	4	9808-9811	RE# 700-703
74/11	GOT	3	9812-9814	RE# 704-706
75/09-75/10	GOT	4	707-710	

MODEL GP60
SANTA FE
4009, BLT. 88/06
PHOENIX, AZ. 88/12
PHOTO: JAMES D. BRADLEY

MODEL GP60, 3800 hp, BUILT 1987-

87/12-88/02	SP	20	9600-9619	
88/05-88/07	ATSF	20	4000-4019	(2nd)
88/09-88/10	SSW	15	9620-9634	
89/06-89/07	ATSF	20	4020-4039	(2nd)

MODEL HBU-4, HUMP BOOSTER UNIT, BUILT 1978-1980

78/10-78/11	CN	19	260-278	HUMP BOOSTER SLUGS
80/03	CN	4	279-282	HUMP BOOSTER SLUGS

MODEL MP15AC, 1500 hp, BUILT 1984

84/08	NATI	4	8403-8406	NATIONAL HARBOURS BOARD (CANADA)

MODEL SD38-2, 2000 hp, BUILT 1975

75/12	NAR	4	401-404	TO CN 5700-5703,RE# 4850-4853

MODEL SD40
CANADIAN NATIONAL
5055, BLT. 68/06
HALIFAX, NS. 74/08

BLDR.DATE	RR	QTY.	DELV.NO.	NOTES
MODEL SD40, 3000 hp, BUILT 1966-1972				
67/11-68/12	CN	68	5008-5075	5011,5018 SCR. 5062 SCR.86/03
68/12-69/01	QNSL	6	200-205	204,205 TO CP 5400,5401, IN 85/01
69/02-69/12	CN	50	5076-5125	5103 SCR. 87/03, 5104 SCR.86/03
69/12-71/04	CN	50	5126-5175	5140,5151 SCR.
71/04-71/11	CN	50	5176-5225	
71/06	QNSL	15	205-220	206-218 TO CP 5403-5414, IN 85/01.
71/10	ACR	3	180-182	
71/11-71/12	CN	15	5226-5240	
72/01	NDEM	10	8576-8585	
MODEL SD40-2, 3000 hp, BUILT 1972-1985				
72/02-72/03	CP	24	5565-5588	(1st) 5583,5584,5586,5588 SCR.
72/03-72/04	QNSL	20	221-240	
72/05-72/07	CP	40	5589-5628	5598 SCR. BY 79
73/03	ONR	5	1730-1734	
73/03-73/04	QNSL	20	241-260	
73/04-73/06	CP	16	5659-5674	
73/08	ACR	3	190-192	
73/08-73/10	ACR	6	183-188	
74/01	ONR	3	1735-1737	
74/01-74/02	CP	10	5806-5815	(RCT)
74/02-74/03	CP	20	5816-5835	(RCT)
74/12	CP	6	5800-5805	(RCT)
74/12	CP	1	5836	(RCT)
74/12-75/02	CP	43	5675-5717	(1st) 5693 SCR.
75/05	QNSL	4	261-264	

MODEL SD40-2, cont'd

MODEL SD40-2
CANADIAN PACIFIC
5842, BLT. 77/11
KAMLOOPS, BC. 79/08

BLDR.DATE	RR	QTY.	DELV.NO.	NOTES
75/09-75/11	CP	40	5718-5757	
76/01-76/02	CP	20	5758-5777	
77/10-78/02	CP	23	5837-5859	
78/02	CP	1	5778	
78/02-78/07	CP	11	5779-5789	OWNED BY ONTARIO HYDRO
78/07	CP	5	5860-5864	OWNED BY ONTARIO HYDRO
78/11-78/12	CP	10	5790-5799	
78/12-79/01	CP	15	5900-5914	
79/08-79/09	BN	39	7167-7205	
79/08-79/09	BN	16	8074-8089	
79/10-79/11	CP	35	5915-5949	
80/05-80/07	BN	30	7206-7235	7221 WRK/REBLT TO SD40-2B 7500
80/09	BCOL	12	751-762	751-756 (RCT), 755 WRK/SCR.
80/10-81/03	CP	75	5950-6024	6008 WRK/RET. 86/05
81/03	CP	1	5560	(2nd) BUILT WITH WRK. COMPONENTS
82/12-83/08	CP	30	6025-6054	
83/09	CP	1	5584	(2nd) BUILT WITH WRK. COMPONENTS
83/09	CP	1	5693	(2nd) BUILT WITH WRK. COMPONENTS
84/09-84/10	CP	15	5865-5879	(RCT)
84/11-85/01	CP	15	6055-6069	
85/01	CP	1	5583	(2nd) BUILT WITH WRK. COMPONENTS
85/07	BCOL	5	763-767	767 (RCT), 760 WRK/SCR.86

MODEL SD40-2W, 3000 hp, BUILT 1975-1980

75/05-75/06	CN	21	5241-5261	5253 SCR.
75/06-75/07	CN	17	5262-5278	
76/01	CN	15	5279-5293	

MODEL SD40-2W, cont'd

MODEL SD40-2W
CANADIAN NATIONAL
5277, BLT. 75/07
KAMLOOPS, BC. 78/04

BLDR.DATE	RR	QTY.	DELV.NO.	NOTES
78/07-78/10	CN	20	5294-5313	5299-5313 OWNED BY ONTARIO HYDRO
79/12	CN	10	5314-5323	
80/04-80/05	CN	30	5324-5353	
80/12	CN	10	5354-5363	

MODEL SD40-2F, 3600 hp, BUILT 1988

88/10-88/12	CP	25	9000-9024	

MODEL SD50F, 3500 hp, BUILT 1985-1988

85/04-85/08	CN	25	5400-5424	
85/08-86/02	CN	15	5425-5439	
87/02-87/07	CN	20	5440-5459	

MODEL SD60, 3800 hp, BUILT 1988-

88/11-88/12	SOU	25	6651-6675	DELIVERED NS
89/03-89/04	SOO	21	6021-6041	

MODEL SD60F, 3800 hp, BUILT 1985

85/08-85/10	CN	4	9900-9903	PROTOTYPE TEST UNITS, TO BE RE# 5500-5503
89/02-89/03	CN	20	5504-5523	

MODEL SD60M
UNION PACIFIC
6088, BLT. 89/01
FT.WORTH, TX. 89/02

BLDR.DATE	RR	QTY.	DELV.NO.	NOTES
MODEL SD60M, 3800 hp, BUILT 1988-				
89/01-89/02	UP	25	6085-6109	FIRST UNITS BUILD FOR A MAJOR U.S. RAILROAD WITH CANADIAN STYLE WIDE CAB.
89/04-89/06	UP	50	6110-6159	
89/07-89/08	UP	56	6160-6215	
MODEL SW1200MG, 1200 hp, BUILT 1968-1971				
68/03	IRON	1	431506	IRON ORE CO. OF CANADA, CAROL LAKE, PQ.
71/10	IRON	3	431507-431509	IRON ORE CO. OF CANADA, CAROL LAKE, PQ.
MODEL SW900M, 900 hp, BUILT 1969				
69/03	BCH	1	911	
MODEL YBU-4, YARD BOOSTER SLUG, BUILT 1980				
80/07	CN	12	451-462	YARD SLUGS

MLW-MONTREAL LOCOMOTIVE WORKS
MONTREAL, QUEBEC, CANADA

MODEL C630
CANADIAN NATIONAL
2025, BLT. 68/02
WINDSOR, ON. 87/09

BLDR.DATE	RR.	QTY.	DELV.NO.	NOTES
MODEL C630, 3000 hp, BUILT 1965-1969				
67/12-68/06	CN	42	2002-2043	
68/07-68/10	CP	8	4500-4507	4506 WRK/SCR.
69/07	PGE	4	701-704	TO BCOL SAME #
MODEL DL535E, 1200 hp, BUILT 1969-1982				
69/05	WPY	7	101-107	102,105 OFF ROSTER
71/12	WPY	3	108-110	
82/07	WPY	4	111-114	(WIDECAB) NEVER SHIPPED, WPY SHUTDOWN POSSIABLE SALE TO OVERSEAS BUYER L/88
MODEL LRC, 2700 hp, BUILT 1973				
73/08	MLW	1	JV1	DEMONSTRATOR, RETIRED
MODEL M420B, 2000 hp, BUILT 1975				
75/06-75/07	BCOL	8	681-688	(RCR)
MODEL M420R(W), 2000 hp, BUILT 1974-1975				
74/02	PW	2	2001-2002	HAVE CANADIAN STYLE WIDE CAB
75/05	PW	3	2003-2005	HAVE CANADIAN STYLE WIDE CAB

MODEL M420TR
FERROCARRIL del PACIFICO
529, BLT. 75/08
HOMEWOOD,IL.NEW I/T, 75/09

BLDR.DATE	RR	QTY.	DELV.NO.	NOTES
MODEL M420TR, 2000 hp, BUILT 1972-1975				
72/04	RS	2	26-27	
75/07-75/09	FCP	15	522-536	526,527,528 WRK/SCR. 82, REST TO BE RE# NDM 7600-7611
MODEL M420W, 2000 hp, BUILT 1973-1977				
73/05-73/10	CN	30	2500-2529	2511,2526 SCR.RE# 3500-3529 IN 86
73/09-73/10	BCOL	8	640-647	
74/03-74/07	CN	30	2530-2559	2535,2552 SCR.RE# 3530-3559 IN 86
76/10-77/02	CN	20	2560-2579	RE# 3560-3579 IN 86
MODEL M424W, 2400 hp, BUILT 1980-1981				
80/07-81/05	NDEM	53	9500-9552	
80/07-81/07	FCP	16	560-575	560,563,566,568, RET. REST TO BE RE# NDM 9556-9567
81/08	FUS	3	525-527	TO BE RE# NDM 9553-9555
MODEL M630, 3000 hp, BUILT 1969-1972				
69/09-70/02	CP	8	4550-4557	4552 SCR.
69/10-70/03	CP	4	4570-4573	
69/10-70/03	CP	8	4574-4581	RE# 4562-4569 IN 1971
69/11-70/01	CP	5	4508-4512	
70/01	CP	4	4513-4516	RE# 4558-4561 IN 1971
70/12	PGE	5	705-709	TO BCOL SAME #
71/12	PGE	7	710-716	TO BCOL SAME #, 711 SCR.
72/06-72/08	NDEM	20	8600-8619	
72/12	PGE	6	717-722	TO BCOL SAME #

BLDR.DATE	RR	QTY.	DELV.NO.	NOTES

MODEL M630W, 3000 hp, BUILT 1973

BLDR.DATE	RR	QTY.	DELV.NO.	NOTES
73/10-73/11	BCOL	8	723-730	

MODEL M636, 3600 hp, BUILT 1969-1975

BLDR.DATE	RR	QTY.	DELV.NO.	NOTES
69/11-70/12	CP	44	4700-4743	
70/04-70/09	CN	20	2300-2319	2300-2304,2311,2312,2318, TO QCMX 41-48.
71/01-71/03	CN	20	2320-2339	2321 TO QCMX (QUEBEC CARTIER MINING) # 49.
72/01-72/02	QCMX	3	71-73	QUEBEC CARTIER MINING, 72 WRK/SCR. 72/05
72/06	FCP	8	651-658	654 RET. 82, REST TO BE RE# NDM 8000-8006
73/10	QCMX	3	74-76	QUEBEC CARTIER MINING, (CANADA)
73/11-73/12	FCP	8	659-666	660 RET. REST TO BE RE# NDM 8007-8013
75/03-75/04	QCMX	5	81-85	QUEBEC CARTIER MINING, (CANADA)

MODEL M630
CANADIAN NATIONAL
2339, BLT. 71/03
WINDSOR, ON. 87/09

MODEL M640, 4000 hp, BUILT 1971

BLDR.DATE	RR	QTY.	DELV.NO.	NOTES
71/02	CP	1	4744	4000 hp, ONLY ONE BUILT

MODEL RS18, 1800 hp, BUILT 1956-1968

BLDR.DATE	RR	QTY.	DELV.NO.	NOTES
68/04-68/08	INCO	3	208-2,3,4	INTERNATIONAL NICKEL CO OF CANADA, 208-4 LAST MLW RS18 BUILT
68/06	QITX	1	6	QUEBEC IRON & TITANIUM, (CANADA), ALLARD LAKE MINES

INDEX OF RAILROAD OR COMPANY REPORTING MARKS

* NOT AN OFFICIAL AAR REPORTING MARK

EXPLANATION OF ABBREVIATIONS

1ST	1ST USE OF THIS NUMBER
2ND	2ND USE OF THIS NUMBER
CAT	CATERPILLAR CO.
CBRY	COPPER BASIN RAILWAY,INC.
CCX	CHROME CRANKSHAFT CO.
CMI	CENTRAL MICHIGAN RR
CMNW	CHICAGO, MISSOURI & WESTERN RAILWAY CO.
CRL	CHICAGO RAIL LINK
DELV	DELIVERED
DSRC	DAKOTA SOUTHERN RAILWAY CO.
E/	EARLY
EPC	ENTERPRISE COAL CO.
ETR	ESSEX TERMINAL RAILWAY CO.
EUKA	EUREKA SOUTHERN RAILROAD CO.INC.
GEN	GENERATOR
HL	HELM LEASING CO.
I/T	IN TRANSIT
KITS	GE LOCOMOTIVES SHIPPED IN KIT FORM FOR ASSEMBLY OVERSEAS
L/	LATE
LVAL	LACKAWANNA VALLEY RAILROAD
M-K	MORRISON KNUDSEN CO.
M/	MID
MARC	MARYLAND AREA RAIL COMMUTER SERVICE, A DIVISION OF MDOT
MKC	McKEESPORT CONNECTING RAILROAD CO.
MNCR	METRO-NORTH COMMUTER RAILROAD CO.
MOD	MODEL
MRL	MONTANA RAILLINK,INC.
NHL	NATIONAL HELM LEASING
NHN	NEW HAMPSHIRE NORTHCOAST CORP.
NRE	NATIONAL RAILWAY EQUIPMENT LEASING
ONT	ONTARIO
ORD	ORDERED
ORIG	ORIGINALLY
PNC	PRECISION NATIONAL CORP.
PTD	PAINTED
QUE	QUEBEC
R/W/B	RED,WHITE,BLUE, BI-CENTENNIAL COLOR SCHEME
RCR	HAS RADIO CONTROL RECEIVER
RCT	HAS RADIO CONTROL TRANSMITTER
RE#	RENUMBERED TO
RE-ENG	ENGINE REPLACED WITH
REMFG	LOCOMOTIVE COMPLETELY REBUILT
RET	RETIRED FROM ROSTER, DISPOSITION UNKNOWN
RET'D	RETURNED
S/#	SAME NUMBER
SCR	SCRAPPED
ST	SPRINGFIELD TERMINAL RAILWAY CO.
SUBLTR	SUB-LETTERED FOR ANOTHER OWNER
W/	WITH
WC	WISCONSON CENTRAL LIMITED
WRK	WRECKED

INDEX BY LOCOMOTIVE TYPE

MODEL	BUILDER	PRODUCTION	TOTAL 1968-89	PAGE
GA18	EMD	1968	1	99
GF6C	GMD	1983-1984	7	167
GM6C	EMD	1975	1	99
GM10B	EMD	1976	1	99
GP15-1	EMD	1976-1982	310	99
GP15-1(AC)	EMD	1982	30	99
GP15T(AC)	EMD	1982-1983	28	100
GP38	EMD	1966-1971	528	100
GP38-2	EMD	1972-1985	1954	101
GP38-2	GMD	1972-1986	210	168
GP38-2W	GMD	1973-1974	51	168
GP38AC	EMD	1970-1971	258	106
GP38AC	GMD	1970-1971	21	169
GP39	EMD	1969-1970	23	107
GP39-2	EMD	1974-1984	240	107
GP39X	EMD	1980	6	108
GP40	EMD	1965-1971	654	108
GP40-2	EMD	1972-1986	863	110
GP40-2LW	GMD	1974-1976	268	169
GP40-2W	GMD	1973-1975	11	170
GP40P	EMD	1968	13	113
GP40P-2	EMD	1974	3	113
GP40X	EMD	1977-1978	23	113
GP49	EMD	1983-1985	9	114
GP50	EMD	1980-1985	278	114
GP59	EMD	1985	3	114
GP60	EMD	1985	3	114
GP60	GMD	1987-	75	170
HBU-4	GMD	1978-1980	23	170
HR412W	BBD	1982	11	94
HR616W	BBD	1982	20	94
LRC	MLW	1973	1	175
LRC(B)	BBD	1981-1984	33	94
M420B	MLW	1975	8	175
M420R(W)	MLW	1974-1975	5	175
M420TR	MLW	1972-1975	17	176
M420W	MLW	1973-1977	88	176
M424W	MLW	1980-1981	72	176
M630	MLW	1969-1972	67	176
M630W	MLW	1973	8	177
M636	MLW	1969-1975	111	177
M640	MLW	1971	1	177
MATE-4	GE	1971-1972	25	153
MP15AC	EMD	1975-1983	242	115
MP15AC	GMD	1984	4	170
MP15DC	EMD	1974-1983	354	116

MODEL	BUILDER	PRODUCTION	TOTAL 1968-89	PAGE
MP15T	EMD	1984-1985	43	119
P30CH	GE	1975-1976	25	153
RS18	MLW	1956-1968	4	177
SD38	EMD	1967-1970	47	119
SD38-2	EMD	1972-1979	79	119
SD38-2	GMD	1975	4	170
SD38AC	EMD	1971	17	120
SD39	EMD	1968-1970	54	120
SD40	EMD	1966-1972	492	121
SD40	GMD	1966-1972	267	171
SD40-2	EMD	1972-1986	3193	122
SD40-2	GMD	1972-1985	622	171
SD40-2W	GMD	1975-1980	123	172
SD40A	EMD	1969-1970	18	128
SD40-2F	GMD	1988-	25	173
SD40T-2	EMD	1974-1980	312	129
SD40X	EMD	1979	4	129
SD45	EMD	1965-1971	743	129
SD45-2	EMD	1972-1975	134	132
SD45T-2	EMD	1972-1975	247	133
SD45X	EMD	1970-1971	7	134
SD50	EMD	1980-1986	427	134
SD50F	GMD	1985-1988	60	173
SD60	EMD	1984-	394	135
SD60	GMD	1988-	46	173
SD60F	GMD	1985-	24	173
SD60M	GMD	1988-	131	174
SDL39	EMD	1969-1972	10	135
SDP40	EMD	1966-1970	14	135
SDP40F	EMD	1973-1974	150	136
SDP45	EMD	1967-1970	34	137
SL65	GE	1976-	3	154
SL75	GE	1978-	2	154
SL85	GE	1975-	18	154
SL87	GE	1975	1	155
SL100	GE	1977	2	155
SL110	GE	1974-	44	155
SL115	GE	1976-	17	155
SL120	GE	1977	1	156
SL125	GE	1976-	6	156
SL130	GE	1976	2	156
SL136	GE	1978	2	156
SL144	GE	1975-	12	156
SPV2000	BUDD	1980-1981	24	94
SW1000	EMD	1966-1972	87	137
SW1001	EMD	1968-1986	175	138
SW1200MG	GMD	1968-1971	4	174
SW1500	EMD	1966-1974	693	140
SW1504	EMD	1973	60	143
SW900M	GMD	1969	1	174
T6	ALCO	1958-1969	5	93

MODEL	BUILDER	PRODUCTION	TOTAL 1968-89	PAGE
U18B	GE	1973-1976	163	156
U23B	GE	1968-1977	465	157
U23C	GE	1968-1970	53	159
U30B	GE	1966-1975	163	159
U30C	GE	1967-1976	582	160
U33B	GE	1967-1970	135	162
U33C	GE	1968-1975	375	163
U34CH	GE	1970-1973	32	164
U36B	GE	1970-1976	129	164
U36C	GE	1971-1975	218	165
U36CG	GE	1974	20	166
U50C	GE	1969-1971	40	166
YBU-4	GMD	1980	12	174

ABOUT THE AUTHOR

James T. Bradley, 46, has been a railfan since at least age 5, when his father would take him to a RI commuter stop in Chicago and watch the evening rush hour. Jim has been photographing trains since 1955. At present, is single, has one son, who's photos also appear in this book.

Jim has worked for many railroads since his first rail job for the RI as a towerman. Next was the IC, then ATSF, GTW, C&EI, MKT, and UP. He worked as towerman, switchman, fireman, operator, engineer, and yard clerk. Of all these positions, he says, being an engineer has been, and will always be the most rewarding.

Also, while in the military, Jim was assigned to the Army's 714th Railway Operating Battalion, where he ran steam and diesel, and spent a year running a GE 70T in France.

Other interests include, bowling, pool, model railroading, photography and travel.

Jim has been a contributor in the railfan press for many years, his slide shows have always been a big hit at different rail oriented conventions and shows. This is his first effort at writing and publishing.